UFO
THE GOVERNMENT FILES

PETER BROOKESMITH

BROWN
BOOKS

Brown Packaging Books Ltd
Bradley's Close
74/77 White Lion Street
London N1 9PF

British Library Cataloguing-in-Publication Data
A catalogue entry for this title is available from the British Library

ISBN 1-897884-18-4

Printed in Italy by Vincenzo Bona - Torino

The publishers would like to thank the following sources for the illustrations used in
this book. Every effort has been made to trace the copyright holders where known.

Center for UFO Studies (CUFOS): 6, 11, 21, 24, 26, 32, 34, 40, 43, 44, 47, 49 (tr),
    52, 57, 60, 61, 67 (both), 72, 78, 85, 90, 111, 114, 122, 127, 143, 166
Fortean Picture Library: 8, 17, 30, 49 (br), 54, 56, 58, 62, 63, 65, 70, 73, 74, 75, 92,
    103, 126, 128, 136, 138, 148, 149, 150, 152, 153, 155, 170
Doug Cooper: 145 (both)
Hulton Getty Collection: 10, 28, 119
Images Colour Library/Charles Walker Collection: 12/13, 18, 106, 164
The Kobal Collection: 123, 125
Los Angeles Times: 29
Vincente-Juan Ballester Olmos: 130, 131
Private Collection: 120, 121
Tom Theophanous/Errol Bruce-Knapp: 99, 101
TRH Pictures: 83, 87, 95
United States National Archives: 14, 16 (both), 19, 22, 23, 27, 37, 39, 46 (both), 76,
    77, 79, 80/81, 84, 96, 98, 102, 109 (both), 110 (both), 140, 146, 154, 156, 157,
    159, 161, 163, 167, 168, 169

CONTENTS

A COSMIC WATERGATE?

BELIEF, DISBELIEF, IMAGINATION AND THE UFO ENIGMA

FOR MORE than half a century governments have taken an active interest in unidentified flying objects, or UFOs, of all kinds. World War II demonstrated the overwhelming importance of air power in warfare, and since then no nation has been able to ignore strangers in its skies. Most UFOs, whether detected by military radar or reported by people in the street, turn into IFOs – identified flying objects. What appear, often to experienced observers, to be 'flying saucers' turn out to be aircraft, balloons, stars, planets, artificial satellites, rocket debris, and many other things besides. Even the Moon has been mistaken for a flying saucer occasionally.

It is the UFOs that remain unidentified which intrigue ufologists and

UFOs photographed from an airliner as it approached Teheran in May 1978. The airport radar allegedly had an unidentified object '10 times the size of a jumbo jet' on its screen at the time. The US Defense Attache in Iran forwarded the report to the State Department, but no follow-up investigation is on record.

puzzle the public. They may represent as little as five per cent of UFO reports, but they have also exercised governments, intelligence agencies and military experts. It is the reaction of such authorities to the mysterious element in UFO reports, and the speculations of ufologists, that this book chronicles and explores.

In doing so, it concentrates largely on the American experience of UFOs, and on what the US government has told people to believe about what they have seen or encountered. It focuses too on what the US defense, intelligence and security establishments have said to themselves and to one another about UFOs, and what they really knew about them. And it compares these public and private official reactions with what ufologists have concluded about the UFO enigma.

There are good reasons for concentrating on the American experience with UFOs. Americans tend to insist on exercising their constitutional rights. And because Americans are fortunate enough to have a Freedom of Information Act, the world probably knows more about the US govern-

ment's entanglement with UFOs than it does about the involvement of all other governments combined. As a result, the world pays attention to the attitude of American citizens to the UFO enigma and to their government's approach to it.

This has been especially true during the 1990s, as the overwhelmingly American alien-abduction syndrome and the seemingly endless – certainly frustrating – wrangling over the events near Roswell, New Mexico, in 1947 have pushed most other issues off the floor in ufological debates. Events and encounters from the USA are reported around the world, while, with a few well-known exceptions, those in other countries travel less easily, regardless of their intrinsic interest. Unlike most other countries, the USA has an interested public large enough to support professional ufologists, a vocal and articulate body of skeptics, and media outlets willing to give both debunkers and the most outrageous cranks access to a huge audience. For better or worse, global ufology is driven from the USA.

For all that, a certain pattern can be detected in virtually all governments'

approach to UFOs. To begin with, there is the necessarily hard-nosed military outlook. On the job, the military use the words 'unidentified flying object' to mean just what they say and nothing more. If a UFO appears in their airspace, they treat it as terrestrial, possibly armed, and hostile, until it is identified as harmless or turned away (as used to happen daily over NATO and Soviet borders) or, as a last resort, destroyed.

In light of this, it has always seemed mysterious to many ufologists that military spokesmen the world over insist publicly that UFOs represent no threat to their nation's security. But one has to bear in mind that in this context the military are no longer employing the term in the neutral sense that it has in aviation jargon. What the military front office means by 'UFO' on such occasions is something like: 'An anomalous object (which you might describe as a "flying saucer") or some other aerial entity that we could not readily identify as an aircraft – friendly or otherwise – or as some other man-made object or natural phenomenon; an object that for the time being eludes explanation – and which has evaded our most advanced interceptors.'

Since that kind of UFO has never reliably been reported to harm civilians, or demolish military installations or military aircraft, the conclusion that 'flying saucers have no defense significance' makes perfect sense. UFOs may be weird, and they may be deeply embarrassing to air forces the world over, but at least they don't belong to the Other Side.

Belief and disbelief

Not surprisingly, reactions to the military line of argument vary. Hard-line skeptics tend to buy it and then, depending on the case, go on to expound that stars, planets, lighthouses, balloons, radar 'angels' or

On 3 July 1960 Captain Hugo Niorri of the Argentine Air Force saw this conical UFO on Route 36 between Cordoba and Yacanto, Argentina. He said it appeared to be gray and metallic, and rotated silently on its axis. It flew south before disappearing among low clouds. Computer analysis by Ground Saucer Watch found the object to be a genuine unknown.

malfunctions, human artefacts or natural phenomena – hoaxes, delusions, or mirages, for instance – are responsible for UFO experiences. Hard-line believers, convinced that extra-terrestrials are infesting the skies with ultra-hi-tech craft powered by something like magnetogravitic inter-dimensional hyperdrives, will have none of this. The hard-line believers then split, very roughly, into two camps – those who broadly subscribe to the notion of a 'Cosmic Watergate', and a still more radical fringe.

The Cosmic Watergaters say the official military line is just hot air. They believe governments probably have proof that UFOs and their occupants are extra-terrestrial, and even have the remains of aliens and their craft retrieved and hidden away somewhere after they have crashed. The facts are covered up because governments won't trust the people with the truth. The radical fringe goes further. They reason that the authorities are indeed telling the truth when they deny that UFOs are a security threat — because they're in cahoots with the aliens. Contact has been made, and ETs are secretly cooperating with Earth governments. A few truly far-out, and largely unsavory, characters even maintain that the US government has entered into some kind of devilish pact with aliens.

Both camps have hollered 'Cover-up!' with great gusto for several decades. They still do, even though under the Freedom of Information Act (FOIA) some 30,000 UFO-related government documents have now been brought — although, admittedly, some have been dragged — into the public domain.

Between the poles of the skeptics and the believers lies an ocean of moderate ufologists. Many moderates doubt that UFOs are alien craft but would not deny that the UFO phenomenon contains a genuine enigma — perhaps many enigmas — at its heart. There are also about as many middle-of-the-road 'answers' to the UFO riddle as there are fish in the sea. To consider them justly and comprehensively would be the subject of another, and very different, book than this. But the moderate line on the alleged government cover-up can probably be summed up both fairly and briefly.

It goes something like this. In some cases governments have not told the truth about UFOs, because they weren't UFOs to the government. (Astronomer J. Allen Hynek's first

question about a UFO was always: 'Unidentified to whom?') Those mysterious objects were secret military hardware, possibly flying in places no one wants to admit such things have been. Sometimes accidents involving weapons, illegal acts such as firing missiles over State lines or jettisoning fuel over urban areas, or just traditional military incompetence, may result in what looks like an anomalous event to the uninformed observer. And the military would far rather have people blame such things on flying saucers than on them.

More often, the argument goes, the characteristically condescending tone of official pronouncements has indeed been a cover-up — for embarrassed ignorance. The authorities don't know what lies behind certain UFO events, especially those that edge into the surreal and paranormal, but would lose face by admitting it. So they are driven to dismiss such experiences with desperately 'rational' explanations, ranging from 'spots before the eyes' to 'fireflies', and that old stand-by, 'hallucinations'.

Freedom of information

If there was ever an argument for open government and for paring official secrets down to the bone it is the UFO phenomenon. UFOs as we understand them today — as mysterious, globular or diskoid, often luminous objects — began to plague the USA in 1942. But they did not come blazing into public awareness until Kenneth Arnold's famous sighting of 1947. However, before the 1974 Freedom of Information Act, Americans had no sure way to discover anything solid about the internal discussions and secret decisions about UFOs that were taking place inside the military and the intelligence agencies. All they could do was read between the lines of what was being put about by ufologists. What some of

them had to say was at best imaginative, and at worst pure fiction.

Three decades of rumor and unfounded, remorselessly unscientific speculation allowed all manner of beliefs about UFOs to evolve and flourish in the USA before the FOIA became law. Some of these notions were mildly eccentric, some hilarious, some revealed a variety of blind faiths. A few were sane and a very few were mad, bad and depressingly influential. During that period (as the now-released documents show) the military and security establishments certainly lied, if only by omission, about the extent of their interest in UFOs. And they wriggled uncomfortably in the face of overwhelming evidence that people were seeing inexplicably strange things in the sky, and sometimes in their own backyards.

Every single one of those bizarre experiences may have had a mundane explanation, as official spokesmen ritually insisted. But officialdom seemed unable to recognize that people were reporting events that to them were at least disconcerting, sometimes frightening, and always indecipherable. The authorized explanations for these extremely perplexing experiences seemed to be often inept, and official attitudes have often appeared unjustifiably dismissive. At the same time, most comprehensive official evaluations of the whole phenomenon were kept secret, although rumors about them leaked out from time to time.

Small wonder then that improbable beliefs about UFOs became legion, and that it seemed more and more credible to some that officialdom knew more than it was letting on. Even skeptic Dr Edward Condon, whose analysis of the phenomenon has often been vilified by ufologists, recognized the drawbacks of the official approach. In his USAF-funded report, published in 1969 (see Chapter Three), Condon noted wryly that maintaining secrecy:

Richard M. Nixon announces his resignation as US President on 9 August 1974. Nixon faced impeachment for approving a burglary at the Watergate Building in Washington DC. The scandal spawned a family of nicknames for alleged cover-ups: Irangate, Whitewatergate, and the 'Cosmic Watergate' that, ufologists say, hides contact between aliens and Earth.

UFO phenomenon from the day the words 'flying saucer' entered the language, it would have made the UFO riddle vastly less muddled and confusing for everyone than it is today. That would be true whether UFOs really were all misperceived stars, which they plainly are not, or every one of them an intergalactic dodgem car, which they are not either.

Then and now

In the aftermath of Word War II the American establishment was extremely apprehensive about enemies, without and within. Especially within. They were always identified with Communism. This was, after all, the period of tension between the Soviet Union and the West that led to the 1948 Berlin Airlift in Europe, and in the USA to the madness of the McCarthy years. If few people were more obsessively anti-Communist than the FBI's J. Edgar Hoover, the same kind of nervousness was evident inside US Army security. One of the earliest FBI files of the UFO era, dated 30 July 1947, shows how jumpy the authorities were:

The Bureau, at the request of the Army Air Forces Intelligence, has agreed to cooperate in the investigation of flying discs …The Army Air Forces Intelligence has also indicated some concern that the reported sightings might have been made by subversive individuals for the purpose of creating a mass hysteria.

Having been encouraged for good reason in World War II and caused to flourish by the Cold War, the culture of secrecy has never really died away in the corridors of American power. One immediate external threat – or perceived threat – succeeded another, from Korea to the Cuban missile crisis. And when, deeply wounded in soul and body, the USA withdrew from its futile war in Vietnam, the old enemy, the Soviet empire, was still there as powerful as ever.

opened the way for intensification of the 'aura of mystery' which was already impairing confidence in the Department of Defense. Official secretiveness also fostered systematic sensationalized exploitation of the idea that a government conspiracy existed to conceal the truth …Where secrecy is known to exist one can never be absolutely sure that he knows the complete truth. [1]

By the time government documents on UFOs were released, the belief in a major 'UFO cover-up' had become entrenched. Many papers could be – and were – interpreted to 'prove'

almost any thesis. They certainly demonstrated that a cover-up of sorts had been in place all along. All the American security agencies – the CIA, the NSA, the DIA, the FBI, and the rest – had solidly denied any interest in UFOs for decades. The USAF had closed its investigative office, Project Blue Book, in 1969, and ever since had maintained that it no longer logged UFO reports or took any interest in the phenomenon. The documents showed that every one of these official bodies had tons of UFO-related paperwork on file, stretching back to the 1940s. The long-chanted refrain that government knew more than it was telling inevitably became louder. Today, indeed, it's often taken for granted. Many ufologists refer to 'the cover-up' in the routine tone that a mechanic reserves for talk of hubcaps.

Yet – as Condon was aware – that chorus need never have been so loud, so widespread or so distracting. Had the civil and defense establishments dealt honestly and openly with the

An apparent UFO photographed near Belotic, Yugoslavia, during 1973. According to CUFOS files, the hat-shaped object remains unexplained.

It is, of course, the business of the secret world to be secret. Yet the incessant pressure over the previous decades must have driven the natural penchant for privacy in the armed forces and security services alike into the red zone – until that seemed a normal level of caution to maintain.

Such an exaggerated sense of confidentiality had a secondary effect. That was to allow the intelligence services in particular to do almost anything in the name of national security. The CIA's notorious MKULTRA experiments with psychotropic drugs (undertaken from the late 1940s until they were exposed in the mid-1970s) were conducted on US citizens without their consent, and sometimes without their knowledge. They are reckoned by many to have been but the tip of an iceberg of scandalous abuse. The US Army and Navy also indulged in similar research.[2]

Such ingrained arrogance does not die overnight. It doubtless helped to make the CIA and other intelligence agencies unduly shifty (certainly less than truthful) in their dealings with both the UFO phenomenon and those members of the public who were equally intrigued by it. Some maintain that it persists today, and contributes to the obstructionism that greets many requests for UFO-related papers under the FOIA.

The checks and balances built into the US Constitution are admired by people the world over and, for the most part, assiduously ignored by their governments. But in an age of instant communications, traumas in American public life send waves around the world. And these are doubly powerful. They shake the core belief that, if not

perfect, American institutions are fundamentally decent, honest, open, and responsible. And they prompt others – such as the subjects of the British monarchy – to cogitate on the scope for abuse permitted by their own far less accessible forms of government: 'If that can happen there, what horrors might have happened here?'

Suspicious minds

Once again, the American experience becomes central to global attitudes. Deep in the American psyche, and urbanely expressed in the US Constitution, is a vigorous yet cordial distrust of government. That has become a hostile suspicion in many quarters in the USA, including a large part of American ufology. The strident cries of 'Cover-up!' and 'Conspiracy!' can be seen as echoes of a wider and deeper American unease with public life, and the world, at large.

American ufology today is in unprecedented disarray. At one extreme, tales from the far reaches of ufological paranoia forge a nightmare vision of a government that will lie, bamboozle, cheat and even murder to maintain the Great Secret of alien

contact. Once-classified documents certainly show that, despite their denials, the US military and intelligence establishments have always collected data on UFOs, and conducted debunking programs. There was once even a proposal to enlist the aid of Walt Disney in such a scheme. Yet the government files can also be interpreted to show that the whole edifice of belief in 'flying saucers' is built on several kinds of misinterpretation, hoax and misperception.

So what do the government files really reveal about the official fascination with UFOs? Is there really a vast cover-up – what Stanton Friedman insists is a 'cosmic Watergate'? Are the skeptics right to defend the innocence of government, the military, and the intelligence agencies? And, ultimately, what do ufologists' claims tell us – a little about official secrets, or a lot about ufology?

In seeking the answers to these questions we should be prepared to meet paradox, contradiction, dissimulation, and disorder. It is not just UFOs that are elusive, seductive shapeshifters. As we shall see, they can taint and perturb, illuminate and confuse all who come in contact with them.

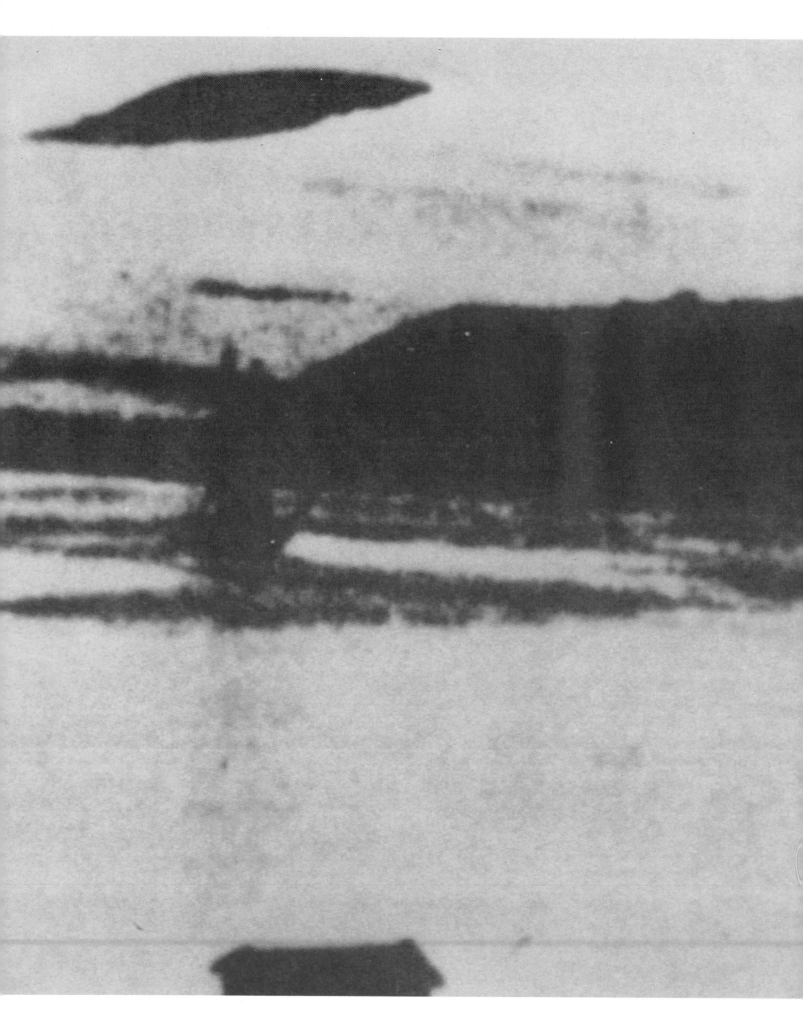

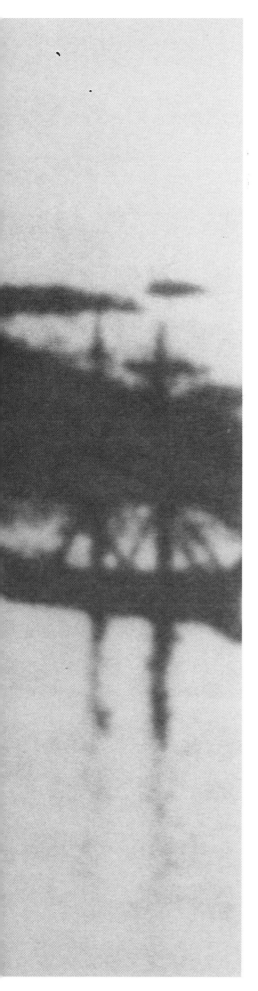

This picture, sometimes said to be the oldest UFO photograph in existence, was taken across the clipper anchorage at Drobak, southern Norway, on 27 July 1907.

Chapter One

NEED TO KNOW

THE YEARS OF FRUSTRATION

1942–1950

WE START WITH more than a bang – we begin with 1430 of them, fired from anti-aircraft guns at just after 3.00 a.m. on 25 February 1942, when a fleet of very unusual 'aircraft' staged a bizarre raid on Los Angeles. No planes were shot down that night. If one observer's calculation is correct, that their speeds were approaching 18,000mph (29,000km/h), this is hardly surprising (see Case #1).

It may seem idiosyncratic to begin this exploration of government UFO files with this event. The age of the UFO is always reckoned to have started in 1947 – on 24 June, in the middle of the afternoon, when news of businessman and private pilot Kenneth Arnold's sighting of nine crescent-shaped craft introduced the world to the idea of 'flying saucers'. And within days government offices were buzzing with the problem of what the mysterious craft were, as dozens of reports of similar sightings flooded in to newsrooms, Air Force bases, and police station houses.

Within days, too, New Mexico rancher 'Mac' Brazel was catapulted briefly into the headlines as reports of his finding wreckage of a downed flying disk echoed round the world, and were then very rapidly scotched by the US Army Air Force. Many now believe that event – since dubbed the Roswell Incident – was correctly reported the first time round, and that an enormous effort has been made ever since to cover up what Brazel really found. The high summer of 1947 was undoubtedly of peak significance in UFO history.

But the UFO phenomenon did not begin in 1947, and nor did the authorities first become interested in UFOs that summer. Objects resembling rockets filled the skies of Sweden in 1946, and led to a full-scale investigation by the military; they also appeared at the other end of Europe, in Greece, and set off a high-powered enquiry there that was, according to a later account, shelved after representations by the Pentagon. Still earlier, the Swedish Flying Corps had investigated hundreds of reports of unidentified 'aircraft' that flew at night all over the country during the winter of 1933–34. Similar sightings occurred in the USA and the UK at around the same time.

The first cover-up?

Why, then, begin in 1942? First, because the Los Angeles 'air raid' is the first UFO event to spark a government investigation – and some ufologists have discerned the beginnings of a cover-up in the official reaction to it. Second, the 'raid' was witnessed by thousands of people and, third, it has all the hallmarks of a genuinely anomalous event. This doesn't mean the Los Angeles air raid was, ultimately, unfathomable (it was readily enough explained at the time). But it did appear to be inexplicable to almost everyone who witnessed it, while those who had to account for the expenditure of a vast number of high-explosive shells to no effect were somewhat strained to put a good face on an embarrassing episode.

Next day, Secretary of the Navy Frank Knox announced from Washington that no planes had been over the city, and the barrage had been the product of war nerves and a false alarm. The government line changed within hours, after General George C. Marshall, the Chief of Staff, gave President F.D. Roosevelt his understanding of what had happened. Marshall wrote:

General George Marshall's secret memorandum of 26 February 1942 to US President Franklin D. Roosevelt describes the most violent reaction on record to a UFO sighting.

The following is the information we have from GHQ at this moment regarding the air alarm over Los Angeles of yesterday morning:

From details available at this hour:

1. Unidentified planes, other than American Army or Navy planes, were probably over Los Angeles, and were fired on by elements of the 37th CA Brigade (AA) between 3.12 and 4.15 a.m. These units expended 1430 rounds of ammunition.

2. As many as fifteen planes may have been involved, flying at various speeds from what is officially reported as being 'very slow' to as much as 200 mph and at elevations from 9000 to 18,000 feet.

3. No bombs were dropped.

4. No casualties among our troops.

5. No planes were shot down.

6. No American Army or Navy planes were in action.

Investigation continuing.

It seems reasonable to conclude that if unidentified airplanes were involved they may have been from commercial sources, operated by enemy agents for purposes of spreading alarm, disclosing locations of anti-aircraft positions, and slowing production through blackout.

Such conclusion is supported by varying speed of operation and the fact that no bombs were dropped.

Case #1

The Los Angeles Air Raid

LOS ANGELES, CALIFORNIA, USA

25 February 1942

Two days before the Los Angeles Air Raid – which took place less than three months after the USA entered World War II – two events occurred simultaneously that could certainly lend weight to the skeptical assessment that 'war jitters' in the area lay behind the barrage of fire that rent the night skies on 25 February 1942. Witness reports however would suggest that something both real and strange visited Los Angeles that night.

At 7.05 p.m. on 23 February a Japanese submarine surfaced some 2500 yards (2.3km) from Ellwood, just north of Santa Barbara, and shelled fuel storage tanks there for 20 minutes. As the attack took place, President F.D. Roosevelt was making a nationwide broadcast warning that nowhere in the USA was safe from enemy action. Fear of Japanese invasion was real at that stage of the war, and continued; an enemy assault on the Aleutian islands in June 1942 led to the heroic construction, in record time, of the Alaska Highway as a supply route for the defense of the northernmost US territory from serious attack.

The LA raid was heralded when lights and flares seen near defense plants led to a four-hour alert from 7.18 p.m. Then, at 2.15 a.m., radar picked up an unidentified target 120 miles (194 km) out to sea. At 2.25 a.m. on 25 February air raid sirens sounded over Los Angeles. The city blacked out, and at 3.16 anti-aircraft artillery (AAA) batteries began firing at 'unidentified aircraft' coming in over the ocean, as searchlight beams pursued them through the sky.

There seemed to be at least two types of craft taking part. Witnesses saw fast-moving, high-flying small objects, red or silver in color, that arrived in formation and then appeared to dodge their way through the AAA salvos at a speeds of up to 5 miles per second (18,000 mph/29,000 km/h). The object tracked on radar seemed luminous to ground observers, and at one point remained stationary for some time. It moved inland and was caught in searchlights over Culver City, where it was photographed and proved impervious to AAA fire. It then moved at a stately 60 mph (75 km/h) to the coast at Santa Monica and then south toward Long Beach, before being lost to sight. Anti-aircraft fire continued until 4.14 a.m. against the smaller UFOs. In the words of witness Paul T. Collins, these were consistently 'appearing from nowhere and then zigzagging from side to side. Some disappeared, not diminishing in brilliance or fading away gradually but just vanishing instantaneously into the night.' Others would 'mix and play tag with about 30 to 40 others moving so fast they couldn't be counted accurately.' Another witness recalled a formation of 'six to nine luminous, white dots in formation' that 'moved painfully slowly – you might call it leisurely – as if it were oblivious to the whole stampede it had created'.

The entire episode lasted for 58 minutes, and consumed 1430 12.8-lb shells in all. The blackout was eventually lifted at 7.21 a.m. No bombs were dropped on Los Angeles, and no aircraft were downed, but buildings were destroyed by shell debris, and three people died of heart attacks brought on by panic.

No proof that this last surmise was accurate has ever been forthcoming, and no papers describing the supposedly 'continuing' investigation have surfaced yet, either. Some ufologists find this suspicious, and further wonder if even in this memo Marshall was concealing something. Could it be the knowledge that the 'aircraft' were not of this Earth? They point out that the official estimates of the UFOs' speeds are hugely at variance with those of witnesses, and that the objects' maneuvers were reportedly quite unlike those that would be expected of conventional aircraft.

They back their case that the military knew these were unusual targets with a further point: in the period between the first alert and the opening of the anti-aircraft barrage, fighters of the 4th Interceptor Command stationed nearby were not sent to engage the intruders.

UNCLASSIFIED

14

Extract of Letter from AFCRL, dated 15 September 1950, Subject: Status of Project Twinkle

TO: Commanding General
Air Materiel Command
Attn: MCREEP-4 Major J. W. Kodis
Wright-Patterson Air Force Base, Dayton, Ohio

"If no fire balls are observed in the next six month period, it is recommended that the project be discontinued. In a phenomenon as sporadic as the fire balls appear to be, it is felt that at least one year is required in order to establish whether their occurrence is or is not a seasonal phenomenon.

4. There is considerable doubt in the minds of some of the project personnel that this is a natural phenomenon. As long as a reasonable doubt exists, it is not wise to discontinue entirely the observations. Dr. Whipple s suggestion that these may be moon reflections on small clouds cannot be discounted. That fire balls have been observed in the past cannot be discounted due to the reliability of several witnesses. It may be considered significant that fire balls have ceased abruptly as soon as a systematic watch was set up. At present it does not appear likely that the next six months of observations will yield any more information than the first six months, but it is felt that even negative information may be significant.

5. It is requested that a six month extension of the Land Air contract be negotiated. It is also requested that the spectrographic equipment abandoned by Holloman Air Force Base due to lack of personnel be turned over to Land Air for operation in the next six month period. At the conclusion of the six month extension, an evaluation of the observations will be accomplished by this Directorate and recommendations as to the future conduct of this project will be forwarded to your command."

UNCLASSIFIED

(UNCLASSIFIED) Project TWINKLE

Directorate of Intelligence
Attention: Colonel John G. Ericksen, Chief
Technical Capabilities Branch
Research Division, Directorate of Research and
Development, Office, DCS/Development

19 Feb 1952
1
Lt Col Clayton/djh/52297
AFDRD-RE

1. Attached is a copy of a letter from the Air Research and Development Command requesting declassification of Project TWINKLE, a project which was carried out by AMC and ARDC for investigation of unusual light phenomena in the general area of Holloman Air Force Base and Vaughn, New Mexico.

2. The Scientific Advisory Board Secretariat has suggested that this project not be declassified for a variety of reasons, chief among which is that no scientific explanation for any of the "fireballs" and other phenomena was revealed by the report and that some reputable scientists still believe that the observed phenomena are man-made.

3. In view of the great interest of the Directorate of Intelligence in such phenomena and the related manifestations, evaluation of the final report of Project TWINKLE with a view to its declassification is requested.

2 Incls
1. cy ltr fr ARDC
   to Hq 14 Jan 52
2. cy of Proj TWINKLE
   Final Report

ALBERT E. LOMBARD, JR.
Chief, Research Division
Directorate of Research and Development
Office, Deputy Chief of Staff, Development

JOHN H. CLAYTON
Lt Colonel, USAF

Two USAF memos discuss Project Twinkle, set up early in 1950 to investigate green fireballs seen in New Mexico from late 1948 until 1951. Dr Lincoln La Paz, an expert on meteors, headed the project and became convinced the fireballs were not natural phenomena.

More dark significance is attached to the fact that for years the Department of Defense denied having any record of the event until obliged to disgorge General Marshall's memo by the FOIA. Even at the time, the Long Beach *Independent* noted: 'There is a mysterious reticence about the whole affair and it appears some form of censorship is trying to halt discussion of the matter.'[1]

A military mystery

From the military point of view, what happened was either a ghastly bungle (if there were no planes) or a depressing display of the 37th CA Brigade (AA)'s terrible marksmanship (if planes there were).

If you subscribe to the 'Snafu' theory of history, which states that most things will go wrong if they can, then 'some form of censorship' is less likely than a simple desire to have everyone forget about the whole episode as quickly as possible. After all, there was a real fighting war to get on with, and everyone had to learn as they went along.

It is, at this distance in time, extremely difficult to tell what did cause the 'raid'. Did 'angels' – false echoes – on the primitive radar of the time perhaps coincide with a few meteors and wreak havoc among jittery gun crews and commanders? Was the giant craft that lumbered into position to take flak over Culver City nothing more substantial than a cloud? Or were actual anomalous flying objects responsible?

Whatever really happened, it is worth noting the discrepancy between the witnesses' and the Army's estimates of the speed of the mystery targets. Ufologists have made much of this, but it's not really that startling. It's practically impossible to make an accurate judgement of the speed or altitude of an amorphous light seen against a dark background, and several studies have shown that people consistently overestimate the speed of such objects.[2] And only one witness has actually gone on record with a calculation that some of the 'aircraft' were flying at 'five miles per second'.[3]

Unlike civilian observers, at least the Army had radar and experience on its side in reaching its conclusions. Those who find it remarkable that US fighters did not join the phantom battle do not seem to have asked exactly how well-equipped or trained 4th Interceptor Command was for night combat. Nor do they seem to

One of a tiny handful of photographs believed to show 'foo fighters'. The mystery lights were seen by aircrew on both sides in World War II and in the Korean War. Most ufologists agree that the phenomenon probably had a natural origin.

have asked a more fundamental question – how many sane commanders would risk sending their pilots into a dark sky that was bristling with friendly fire from the ground?

Those are the rational objections to calling the Los Angeles raid a UFO event, or even much of a mystery. It probably represents no more than a classic pattern of government silence in the face of the inexplicable and embarrassing. But it is now part of the doctrine that virtually everything significant about UFOs is hidden by a 'cover-up'. When the 'raid' occurred, the concepts of 'flying saucer' or 'UFO' had yet to be discovered or invented, and thoughts of extra-terrestrial contact were hardly foremost in most Americans' minds. Only later did ufologists discern their own kind of mystery in the incident, and have since supported their conclusions with their own kind of reasoning.

Foo fighters

During World War II, especially after 1943, there were many reports of balls of light, varying in color and in size from several feet to a few inches across, flying in pursuit of warplanes. Because these 'fireballs' never attacked aircraft, Allied pilots assumed they

were enemy inventions – either reconnaissance drones or psychological-warfare weapons. When captured enemy aircrew were interrogated it became clear that both German and Japanese fliers had also been pursued by foo fighters. The same phenomenon was also reported during the Korean War, between 1950 and 1953.

The objects got their nickname, it seems, from a cartoon character named Smokey Stover, whose catch-phrase was 'Where there's foo there's fire' – presumably a play on the French word *feu*, meaning fire. Not all foo fighters spent their time chasing planes. The earliest known report [4] came from two sailors on board a British troop ship, the SS Pulaski, in the Indian Ocean in September 1941. Together with a ship's gunner, the pair watched a 'strange globe glowing with greenish light, about half the size of the full moon as it appears to us' follow the ship for over an hour.

But the vintage, characteristic foo-fighter accounts came from airmen. Two reports show how various, or changeable, the phenomenon could be. On 14 October 1943, B-17s of the US 384th Bomb Group were returning from a major sortie over Schweinfurt, Germany, when they ran into a formation of 'scores' of small,

silvery disks, about 1in (25mm) thick and 3in (75mm) in diameter, flying toward the bombers. One struck the tail of one aircraft, but without effect, reported Major E.R.T. Holmes in a secret memorandum dated 24 October 1943. At the same time, the bomber's right wing 'went directly through a cluster with absolutely no effect on engines or plane surface'. Mysterious black debris accompanied the mysterious miniature disks.

On 10 August 1944, Captain Alvah M. Reida was piloting a B-29 bomber based at Kharagapur, India, on a mission over Palembang, Sumatra, when his right gunner and co-pilot noticed a sphere 'probably 5 or 6ft (1.5 or 1.8m) in diameter, of a very bright and intense red or orange in color' that contantly throbbed, about 12,500ft (3800m) off the starboard wing. It paced the B-29, which was then flying at 210mph (335km/h) at 14,000ft (4250m). Reida jinxed his plane in the sky to try to shake off the object, but it stayed in precisely the same relative position until, after about eight minutes, the foo fighter 'made an abrupt 90-degree turn and accelerated rapidly, disappearing in the overcast'.

A scientific investigation

The extent of official interest in foo fighters could bear further research, for they seem to have been investigated at some point by several distinguished scientists. The minutes of the secret meetings of the Scientific Advisory Panel on Unidentified Flying Objects (convened in January 1953 by the CIA's Office of Scientific Intelligence) note that 'their exact cause or nature was never defined'. The minutes then reveal that the panel's chairman, Dr H.P. Robertson of the California Institute of Technology, and another panel member, Dr Luis W. Alvarez of the University of California, 'had been concerned in the investigation of these phenomena, but David T. Griggs (Professor of Geophysics at the University of California at Los Angeles) is believed to have been the most knowledgeable person on this subject. It was their feeling that these phenomena are not beyond the domain of present knowledge of physical science, however.'[5]

In public, Donald H. Menzel and Ernest H. Taves [6] took up that challenge and suggested that foo fighters were light reflections from tiny ice crystals formed by super-cold air eddying around battle damage on the aircraft. Hence their variable size and color, their characteristic 'clinging' to aircraft despite all attempts to shake them off, their reappearance in Korea, and their preference for warplanes over civil aircraft. While this theory may indeed account for many cases, it doesn't explain those in which foo fighters reportedly arrived from elsewhere and attached themselves to aircraft, or their occasional effects on planes' electromagnetic systems.

Less a foo-fighter, more a 'conventional' UFO: this dark blob, photographed in 1943, appears to be trailing these American light bombers as they fly on a mission over the Japanese Sea.

Project Blue Book's file card on Kenneth Arnold's historic 1947 UFO sighting. Many explanations have been offered for this event, from Arnold's own – 'atmospheric animals' – to 'earthlights'. The original official explanation was endorsed by UFO skeptic Steuart Campbell in 1994 after an exhaustive analysis.

PROJECT 10073 RECORD

1. DATE · TIME GROUP	2. LOCATION
24 Jun 47	Mt. Rainer, Washington
3. SOURCE	10. CONCLUSION
Civilian	Other (MIRAGE)

KENNETH ARNOLD SIGHTING.

4. NUMBER OF OBJECTS	11. BRIEF SUMMARY AND ANALYSIS
Nine	Observer sighted a large circular objects heading west. They appeared as mirror-like reflections which dipped and twisted at a very high rate of speed. Sketches were made.
5. LENGTH OF OBSERVATION	
2½-3 minutes	See Case File
6. TYPE OF OBSERVATION	
Air-Visual	
7. COURSE	
West	
8. PHOTOS	
☒ Yes Sketches ☒ No	
9. PHYSICAL EVIDENCE	
☐ Yes ☒ No	

FORM
FTD SEP 63 0-329 (TDE)   Previous editions of this form may be used.

Many ufologists now believe foo fighters were a form of plasma or ball lightning, but taken all together the phenomena sound much like classic UFOs or flying saucers. The significant point is that, like the Los Angeles air raid and the mystery rockets seen in Scandinavia in 1946, foo fighters were not seen as an aspect of a single phenomenon until hindsight included them in the UFO canon. As the 1953 CIA panel said: 'If the term "flying saucers" had been popular in 1943–1945, these objects would have been so labeled.'

Birth of an era

The Age of the UFO as we know it today opened on 24 June 1947. At about 3.00 p.m. local time that day, Idaho businessman and private pilot Kenneth Arnold spotted nine weird, crescent-shaped disks flashing through the air as he was flying over the Cascade Mountains in Washington State, USA (see Case #2). Accounts of Arnold's experience were flashed around the world by the news media, and triggered a wave of 'flying saucer' reports across the USA. By 4 July, there had been sightings in every state but Georgia and West Virginia; by 16 July, the US Army Air Forces had received over 850 reports.

The Army did not respond systematically to this deluge of information, for the simple reason that it had no mechanism to handle them; and base intelligence officers had no orders to start investigations of their own. What

convinced the military that the sightings had some substance was a series of events at Muroc Field (now Edwards AFB), in the Mojave Desert, California, on 8 July.

At 9.10 a.m. that day, three officers spent 10 minutes watching three silver-colored UFOs heading west. At 9.20 a.m., Major J.C. Wise, who was warming the engine of a Republic XP-84 Thunderjet, spotted another sphere to the north, yellow-white in color and moving in the same direction (against the wind). Assuming it to be the size of an airplane, he estimated its speed to be 200–225mph (320–360km/h) and its altitude to be 10–12,000ft (3000–3600m).

At 11.50 a.m., five technicians, including a colonel and a major, were watching two P-82 and an A-26 aircraft conduct an ejection-seat experiment at 20,000ft (6100m). They saw a 'round object, white aluminum in color, which at first resembled a parachute canopy' come into view. The ejection-seat canopy opened 30 seconds later. The UFO, clearly nearer the ground, descended three times faster than the parachute, rotating or oscillating. The men noted no 'smoke, flame, propeller arcs, engine noise or

other plausible means of propulsion'. The UFO reached ground level, and then rose again.

At 3.50 p.m., a pilot in a P-51 Mustang at 20,000ft (6100m) sighted a wingless and finless 'flat object of a light-reflecting nature' above him 40 miles (65km) south of Muroc. The UFO was too high for the P-51 to close with it. No air base in the area had aircraft in that vicinity. [7]

After this, classified orders to investigate all UFO reports were rapidly issued. Findings were to be forwarded to the Technical Intelligence Division (TID) of the Air Materiel Command at Wright Field. In July two TID officers visited Kenneth Arnold. Their report – listed as Incident 17 in the files and classified CONFIDENTIAL – grudgingly acknowledged his sincerity and credibility with the remark that 'if Mr Arnold could write a report of such a character and did not see the objects he was in the wrong business and should be engaged in writing Buck Rogers fiction.'[8]

Blame the Russians

As the evidence was gathered through July, TID staff naturally speculated on

Case #2

Kenneth Arnold's Seminal Sighting

CASCADE MOUNTAINS, WASHINGTON STATE, USA

24 June 1947

Flying his own Callair plane, on a business trip from Chehalis to Yakima, Washington, Kenneth Arnold was spending an hour or so during his journey searching for a C-46 transport aircraft belonging to the US Marine Corps that had recently crashed near Mount Rainier with 32 men on board.

Arnold was at an altitude of about 9200ft (2800m) above the town of Mineral (about 25 miles (40km) south-west of the peak of Mount Rainier), and was making a 180-degree turn when 'a tremendously bright flash lit up the surfaces of my aircraft.'

At one minute before 3.00 p.m., 'I observed,' he reported drily, 'far to my left and to the north, a formation of very bright objects coming from the vicinity of Mount Baker, flying very close to the mountain tops and traveling at tremendous speed.' Arnold at first thought that he was watching a formation of jets. 'What startled me most at this point was... that I could not find any tails on them.'

Using the clock in his instrument panel, and Mounts Rainier and Adams as markers, and reckoning the formation would pass about 23 miles (35km) in front of him, Arnold calculated that the nine craft were travelling at over 1700mph (2720km/h) – an astonishing speed for the time (it was only later that year that the sound barrier, about 750mph (1200km/h), was first broken by a jet aircraft). What made this phenomenal speed all the more extraordinary was the way the craft were flying.

Arnold said: 'They didn't fly like any aircraft I had seen before... they flew in a definite formation, but erratically... their flight was like speed boats on rough water or similar to the tail of a Chinese kite that I once saw blowing in the wind... they fluttered and sailed, tipping their wings alternately and emitting those very bright blue-white flashes from their surfaces.'

By the time the nine craft flew beyond the southernmost crest of Mount Adams, Arnold had decided to make for Yakima to report what he had seen. Landing there at about 4.00 p.m., Arnold told his story to an airline manager and discussed it with other professional fliers, before taking off once more for Pendleton, Oregon. The news had traveled ahead of him. Among the crowd of people to greet him there was Bill Becquette, from the local newspaper, the *East Oregonian*.

It was at this time that Arnold described the craft he had seen as flying 'like a saucer would if you skipped it across the water'. This phrase was slightly garbled by Becquette, who thus originated the term 'flying saucers'. Then, with other pilots, Arnold cautiously recalculated his estimate of the UFOs' extraordinary speed. But even the most conservative reckoning still put their velocity at over 1350 mph (2160 km/h). From talking to other airmen, Arnold was now convinced that he had seen a flight of guided missiles, 'robotly controled'. He concluded that the government had chosen this way to announce the discovery of 'a new principle of flight'.

The story broke on the Associated Press wire. For three days at Pendleton Arnold was beseiged with enquiries. Finally, exhausted and unable to work – Arnold sold firefighting equipment for a living – he flew the 200 miles (320km) across the state line to his home in Boise, Indiana. Shortly after arriving there, Arnold was telephoned by his friend Dave Johnson, the aviation editor of the *Idaho Statesman*.

Arnold said later: 'The doubt he displayed of the authenticity of my story told me, and I am sure he was in a position to know, that it was not a new military guided missile and that if what I had seen was true it did not belong to the good old USA. It was then that I really began to wonder.'

One of a series of three pictures taken by postman M. Muyldermans near Namur, Belgium, at about 7.30 p.m. on 5 June 1955. There seems to have been no official interest in the pictures, despite the fame that they achieved.

the origin of the mystery disks. No one seemed to doubt their reality.

One faction at TID put forward the argument that they were alien spacecraft or even animals. But by the end of the month the consensus of opinion was that they were most likely advanced Soviet aircraft, possibly developed from German designs captured in World War II.[9]

One civilian was more certain of the truth and, unlike the Army, made no secret of his views. Ray Palmer, editor of *Amazing Stories* magazine, had already published an assertion that extra-terrestrials were visiting Earth. In July 1946, in terms that were to echo down the entire history of attempts to explain the UFO phenomenon, he wrote: 'If you think responsible parties in world governments are ignorant of the fact of space ships visiting the Earth, you just don't think the way we do.' In the October 1947 issue, he wrote of Arnold's sighting: 'A summation of facts proves that these ships were not, nor can be, attributed to any civilization now on the face of the Earth.'

There are plenty of ufologists who would be prepared to say the same thing today. What many of them may not care to dwell on, however, is the plain significance of Palmer's words in 1946 – if they are even aware of them. The idea that extra-terrestrials might be visiting Earth was not new when Arnold's experience made headlines. Even so, it would be several years before the link between flying saucers and extra-terrestrials would become firmly cemented in the public, or the military, mind.

The Air Force officially concluded that Arnold had been witness to a series of mirages. He had emphasized that 'the air was so smooth that day' and that 'the sky and air was [sic] as clear as crystal'. These conditions are associated with temperature inversions and a high refraction index in the atmosphere and are ideal for the creation of mirages.

The wave of sightings that followed during the summer of 1947 left the Air Force with a public-relations problem that it never managed to solve. As the guardian of the nation's skies, the Air Force was clearly responsible for discovering exactly what flying saucers were. But, as noted, it had no central clearing house to compare and assess UFO reports. At the same time, the Air Force had somehow to reconcile the potential security aspects of UFO investigation – what if a massively publicized sighting did turn out to be a Soviet secret weapon? – with satisfying the public clamor for explanations.

The Air Force's handling of this last problem can fairly be called inept.

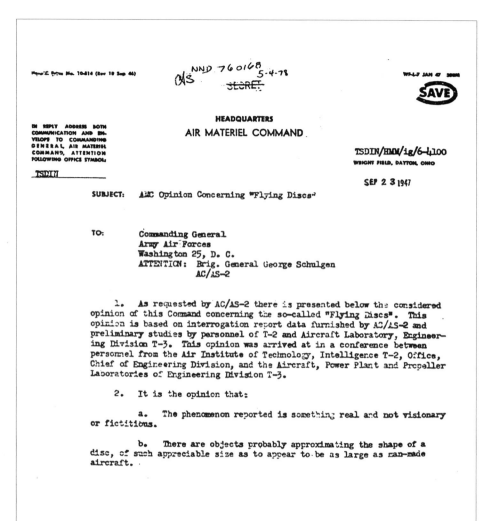

Persistent failures of judgement by the Air Force over the next two decades of UFO-watching created an air of lofty (and unreasonable) official certitude, and made it easier for ufologists with peculiar agendas of their own to make the Air Force line seem less competent, and rather more sinister, than it really was. One of the earliest misjudgements was to allow Arnold to assert, without contradiction, that the USAAF knew what he had seen and had photographs of the objects. This uncorrected misconception planted one of the first seeds of the 'cover-up' theory of UFO history.

'Not visionary or fictitious'

On 23 September 1947 Lt-General Nathan F. Twining, the head of Air Materiel Command (AMC), sent a memorandum to the Commanding

Above and Right: Secret memo of 23 September 1947, detailing Air Materiel Command's opinion of 'flying disks'. At the time, few thought UFOs might be extra-terrestrial, and the military analysts clearly believed the disks were well within the capabilities of Earthly technology.

General Army Air Forces (a style used from force of habit, presumably, as the USAAF had become an independent service, the US Air Force, only five days previously). It was marked for the attention of Brigadier-General George Schulgen, who had asked Twining's command to assess 'the so-called "Flying Discs".'

AMC's opinion was 'based on interrogation report data furnished by AC/AS-2 [i.e. General Schulgen] and preliminary studies by personnel of T-2 and Aircraft Laboratory, Engineering

c. There is a possibility that some of the incidents may be caused by natural phenomena, such as meteors.

d. The reported operating characteristics such as extreme rates of climb, maneuverability (particularly in roll), and action which must be considered evasive when sighted or contacted by friendly aircraft and radar, lend belief to the possibility that some of the objects are controlled either manually, automatically or remotely.

e. The apparent common description of the objects is as follows:-

(1) Metallic or light reflecting surface.

SECRET   U-39552

SECRET.

Basic Ltr fr CG, AMC, WF to CG, AAF, Wash. D. C. subj "AMC Opinion Concerning "Flying Discs".

(2) Absence of trail, except in a few instances when the object apparently was operating under high performance conditions.

(3) Circular or elliptical in shape, flat on bottom and domed on top.

(4) Several reports of well kept formation flights varying from three to nine objects.

(5) Normally no associated sound, except in three instances a substantial rumbling roar was noted.

(6) Level flight speeds normally above 300 knots are estimated.

f. It is possible within the present U. S. knowledge — provided extensive detailed development is undertaken — to construct a piloted aircraft which has the general description of the object in subparagraph (e) above which would be capable of an approximate range of 7000 miles at subsonic speeds.

g. Any developments in this country along the lines indicated would be extremely expensive, time consuming and at the considerable expense of current projects and therefore, if directed, should be set up independently of existing projects.

h. Due consideration must be given the following:-

(1) The possibility that these objects are of domestic origin - the product of some high security project not known to AC/AS-2 or this Command.

(2) The lack of physical evidence in the shape of crash recovered exhibits which would undeniably prove the existence of these objects.

(3) The possibility that some foreign nation has a form of propulsion possibly nuclear, which is outside of our domestic knowledge.

3. It is recommended that:

a. Headquarters, Army Air Forces issue a directive assigning a priority, security classification and Code Name for a detailed study of this matter to include the preparation of complete sets of all available and partinent data which will then be made available to the Army, Navy, Atomic Energy Commission, JRDB, the Air Force Scientific Advisory Group, NACA, and the RAND and NEPA projects for comments and recommendations, with a preliminary report to be forwarded within 15 days of receipt of the data and a detailed report thereafter every 30 days as the investi-

SECRET

-2-   U-39552

SECRET

Basic Ltr fr CG, AMC, WF to CG, AAF, Wash. D.C. subj "AMC Opinion Concerning "Flying Discs"

gation develops. A complete interchange of data should be effected.

4. Awaiting a specific directive AMC will continue the investigation within its current resources in order to more closely define the nature of the phenomenon. Detailed Essential Elements of Information will be formulated immediately for transmittal thru channels.

N. F. TWINING
Lieutenant General, U.S.A.
Commanding

COPY
for
THE NATIONAL ARCHIVES
Record Group No. ____

SECRET

-3-   U-39552

Division T-3. This opinion was arrived at in a conference of personnel from the Air Institute of Technology, Intelligence T-2, Office, Chief of Engineering Division, and the Aircraft, Power Plant and Propeller Laboratories of Engineering Division T-3'. These massed ranks of top technical expertise concluded that:

a. The phenomenon reported is something real and not visionary or fictitious.

b. There are objects probably approximately the shape of a disc, of such appreciable size as to appear to be as large as man-made aircraft.

c. There is the possibility that some of the incidents may be caused by natural phenomena, such as meteors.

d. The reported operating characteristics such as extreme rates of climb, maneuverability (particularly in roll), and action which must be considered evasive when sighted or contacted by friendly aircraft and radar, lend belief to the possibility that some of the objects are controlled either manually, automatically or remotely.

Twining's team considered that it was:

possible within the present U.S. knowledge – provided extensive detailed development is undertaken – to construct a piloted aircraft which has the general description of the [flying disks] above which would be capable of an approximate range of 7000 miles [11,000km] at subsonic speeds.

This may be the source of the often-repeated official claim that UFOs display no significant advance over known science or technology. Twining next asked for the following points to be considered:

(1) The possibility that these objects are of domestic origin – the product of some high security project not known to AC/AS-2 or this command.

(2) The lack of physical evidence in the shape of crash recovered exhibits which would undeniably prove the existence of these objects.

(3) The possibility that some foreign nation has a form of propulsion possibly

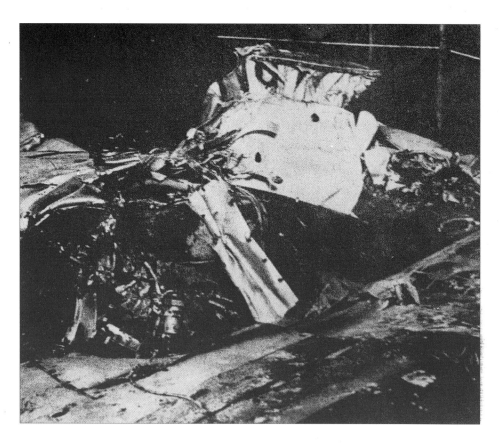

The wreckage of Captain Thomas Mantell's F-51 Mustang fighter. Chasing a UFO, Mantell took his plane to 30,000ft (9150m), more than twice the officially recommended altitude for flying without oxygen, and lost consciousness and control of his aircraft.

nuclear, which is outside of our domestic knowledge.

Twining recommended that:

Headquarters, Army Air Forces issue a directive assigning a priority, security classification and code name for a detailed study of this matter to include the preparation of complete sets of all available and pertinent data which will then be made available to the Army, Navy, Atomic Energy Commission, JRDB, the Air Force Scientific Advisory Group, NACA, and the RAND and NEPA projects for comments and recommendations... A complete interchange of data should be effected.

Meanwhile, AMC would continue investigating UFOs 'within its current resources in order to more closely define the nature of the phenomenon'. There was no hint in Twining's note that the saucers were 'interplanetary'. In noting the complete absence of any material evidence of the disks, the Lt-General's staff even – and with commendable honesty – cast doubt on their own proposition that UFOs were 'something real and not visionary or fictitious'.

Sign of the times

One of AMC's investigations had TID follow up its belief that the saucers were developed from Nazi technology. By the end of the year a review of German wartime research had produced no evidence to support the idea, and it seemed increasingly unlikely that the Soviets would test new technology in US airspace. But two other bits of data had emerged from TID's technical enquiries.

First, if the saucers performed the maneuvers that had been reported of them, then they had to be built from something exotic. No known material would have been able to withstand the velocities or stresses involved. Second, according to the USAF's Aeromedical Laboratory, neither could human flesh. Opinion within TID began to swing toward the extra-terrestrial hypothesis (ETH). On the unproven assumptions that UFO reports were accurate and the objects were real, its proponents reasoned that only a highly advanced otherworldly civilization could have produced such craft. From these flawed foundations was to grow another part of the legend of the UFO cover-up.

On 30 December 1947, General Twining's recommendation of the previous September became reality. Called Project Sign, the full-time UFO research team was to be part of AMC, based at Wright Field (now Wright-Patterson AFB) in Dayton, Ohio. Its security classification was the lowest grade, RESTRICTED, and it had 2A priority (the highest was 1A).

Sign started work on 22 January 1948, and took its job seriously during the 386 days of its existence. So much so that reporters arriving on UFO witnesses' doorsteps frequently found that Air Force investigators had already been and gone.

Such efficiency created the impression that the mystery of the saucers was a top priority with the military. The intensity of Sign's interest seemed to contrast strangely with the stream of prosaic official explanations that the project issued for the vast majority of sightings. Did these gung-ho military sleuths know something the public did not – and if so, how far could their humdrum interpretations be trusted?

The result of Sign's first major investigation, too, had set the stage for this kind of speculation. The death of Air Guard Captain Thomas F. Mantell, Jr, while pursuing a UFO near Godman Field, near Fort Knox, Kentucky, on 7 January 1948 (see Case #3) was almost immediately blamed on the hostility of the saucer. It seems certain that Mantell died because he persisted in the chase, even

Case #3

Captain Thomas Mantell: Martyr to a UFO

GODMAN AFB, near FORT KNOX, KENTUCKY, USA

7 January 1948

The Kentucky Highway Patrol alerted the control tower at Godman Field near Fort Knox that residents at Maysville, Irvington, Owensboro and Madisonville had reported a UFO moving west at an erratic pace. There were also witnesses further south in Nashville, Tennessee, and, much later that day, to the north at Lockbourne AFB, Columbus, Ohio. Numerous witnesses, including the base commander at Godman, observed it from 1.20 p.m. onward. Descriptions agree the object was white, but vary as to shape, from 'like an upside-down ice cream cone' to 'umbrella-shaped'. The sky was clear, but with considerable haze.

At 2.45 p.m., four F-51 Mustangs of the Air National Guard arrived near Godman on a ferrying flight from Marietta, Georgia, to Standiford Field near Louisville, Kentucky, and were asked to investigate. One, low on fuel, flew on to Standiford. The others, led by Captain Thomas Mantell, went after the UFO.

At 15,000ft (4575m), under maximum power, Mantell radioed the control tower that the UFO was 'metallic and tremendous in size', and 'appears to be moving about half my speed'. At an altitude of 22,000ft (6700m), the two remaining wingmen dropped out. One, Lt B.A. Hammond, informed Mantell that they were abandoning the intercept because of lack of oxygen. Mantell responded by saying he was going to 'close in for a better look'. He made no further calls, but continued to climb. By 3.15 p.m. his plane was lost to sight. A search was launched almost immediately. Just after 5.00 p.m. the wreckage of Mantell's F-51 was found, with the port wing, rear fuselage and tail ripped off, on a farm near Franklin, Kentucky. His body was in the aircraft, its cockpit hatch still locked shut. His watch had stopped at 3.18, which was taken as the time of impact.

Crash investigators thought it most likely that Mantell had blacked out at about 25,000ft (7600m), while his F-51 Mustang flew on up to 30,000ft (9150m), lost power, leveled off and then circled before going into a spiraling power dive. The positions of the controls suggested Mantell may have recovered consciousness and tried to break out of the dive. Put under intolerable stress, the plane disintegrated before hitting the ground.

though his plane had no oxygen. It is possible that sheer excitement simply got the better of him, combined with a wild misjudgement of the true height of the UFO.

Sign first, and publicly, explained the UFO as the planet Venus, on the advice of their consultant astronomer, Dr J. Allen Hynek. Venus was in the right place to concur with the witnesses' reports from Godman. But they would have seen the planet only as a pinprick of light in the sky, and it would have been hard to spot in the weather conditions, especially as it was at only half its maximum bright-

ness. Nonetheless, at first, the press and public accepted the Air Force conclusion, and the rumors inspired by the first news reports of the incident – that a 'death ray' had been seen shooting from the UFO, that Mantell's body had vanished from the plane (or had been found riddled with bullets), that the wreckage was radioactive – died away.

In due course, however, the Mantell case would be revived by saucer-believers along with much of this legendary detail. By then, Project Sign's written report (which was classified at the time) had become public.

To the saucerian faithful, it appeared to be gobblydegook when Sign's consultant astronomer Dr J. Allen Hynek suggested that:

It is most unlikely... that so many separated persons [at Maysville, Irvington, Owensboro and Madisonville, Kentucky; Nashville, Tennessee; and Columbus, Ohio] should at that time have chanced on Venus in the daylight sky. It seems therefore much more probable that more than one object was involved: the sightings might have included two or more balloons (or aircraft) or they might have included Venus (in the fatal chase) and balloons. ...The latter explanation seems more likely.

This picture was passed to Dr J. Allen Hynek by the director of the Ondrejov Observatory in Czechoslovakia. No details of the sighting are available, but the picture indicates how the concept of the UFO is widespread throughout the industrialized world.

This conclusion, declassified and released on 30 December 1949, seemed the work of desperate men – not least because only eight months before, on 27 April, Sign had released a report to the press questioning the 'Venus' solution and admitting the case was listed as 'Unidentified'.

Interplanetary aspects

It seems reasonably certain that Mantell was chasing a balloon. In the early 1950s, when Captain Edward Ruppelt re-investigated the case, the US Navy stated it had secretly sent Skyhook balloons over the area. The appearance of these balloons matches descriptions by Mantell and ground witnesses in Kentucky.

By the time the Skyhooks reached there, they were probably 60,000ft (18,300m) high. Skyhooks were huge – up to 600ft (183m) tall and 100ft (30m) across at the top – and undoubtedly they would have appeared to be smaller and nearer to Mantell. His 'UFO' was probably launched from Camp Ripley, Minnesota.[10] Venus may have been the object seen initially at Godman, and was almost certainly the object seen from Columbus, Ohio.

The Sign team had found no balloons in 1948. They drew a blank on weather balloon launches in the area and then, although they were aware of the classified Skyhook project and could have investigated it, they chose not to pursue the idea further. The contradictions in their behavior and their public pronouncements stemmed from the divisions within the project.

Adherents of the ETH at Sign were content to label the sighting an 'Unknown'. Others, more cautiously if not entirely happily, felt that a logical, even if unproven, prosaic solution was better than none. For a while, the public accepted it. Then the speculative, if essentially correct, full report was published in late 1949, contradicting what Sign had said before. Suspicions were aroused again that the Air Force was hiding something – especially as it had no evidence for its convolutedly stated case. But by then, the ETH – although there was no direct evidence for that, either – was well on the way to respectability in the public mind.

Within the Sign team, one more event tipped the scales toward the ETH, and eventually led to Sign's downfall. During the early hours of 24 July 1948, Captain Clarence S. Chiles and First Officer John B. Whitted were piloting a Douglas DC-3 on Eastern Airlines Flight 576 to Atlanta, Georgia. The night was clear, with a bright moon and light, broken cloud above the plane, which was flying at a height of 5000ft (1525m).

At 2.45 a.m., about 20 miles (30km) southwest of Montgomery, Alabama, the pilots caught sight of what they first thought was a jet aircraft coming toward them, just above the DC-3 on the starboard side.

Then, they informed Air Force investigators, they saw the object was wingless, cigar-shaped, with 'no fins or protruding surfaces'. Chiles said that it seemed to be:

powered by some jet or other type of power shooting flame from the rear some 50 feet [15m]. There were two rows of windows, which indicated an upper and lower deck, [and] from inside these windows a very bright light was glowing. Underneath the ship there was a blue glow of light. The fuselage appeared to be about three times the circumference of a B-29 [Superfortress]. The windows were very large and seemed square. They were white

with light which seemed to be caused by some type of combustion.

I estimate that we watched the object at least five seconds and not more than 10 seconds. We heard no noise nor did we feel any turbulence from the object. It seemed to be at about 5500 feet [1675m]. [It] flashed down and we veered to the left and it veered to its left... Then, as if the pilot had seen us and wanted to avoid us, it pulled up with a tremendous burst of flame out of its rear... After it passed, it [zoomed] up into some light broken clouds [at 6000ft/1825m] and was lost from view.

Whitted later said it looked like 'one of those fantastic Flash Gordon rocket ships in the funny papers'. Only one passenger, Clarence L. McKelvie, was awake. He saw 'this strange, eerie streak', which was 'very intense', but he could 'discern nothing in the way of definite shape or form', being 'so

startled I could not get my eyes adjusted to it before it was gone.'[11]

J. Allen Hynek felt 'the object must have been an extraordinary meteor' that created a 'subjective impression of a ship with lighted windows'. Sign's investigator Captain Sneider believed the object was a rocket, and wrote: 'That this development is possibly of foreign origin would seem to be a logical premise.' By 'foreign', Sneider meant 'extra-terrestrial'. Most of his colleagues agreed.

Within a few days, Sign started work on a report addressed to the Air Force top brass. Titled *Estimate of the Situation*, it rehearsed 'saucer' sightings from before Arnold's to the present. All had been reported by reliable witnesses such as pilots and scientists, and all were 'unknowns'. Saucers, Sign concluded, were real, material objects and came from outer space. The report was completed by the end of September and, bound in black and stamped TOP SECRET, sent up the chain of command.

From Sign to Grudge

Estimate of the Situation landed on the desk of USAF Chief of Staff General Hoyt S. Vandenburg early in October. Within days, he rejected its conclusions as unjustified by the evidence presented. The document was declassified a few months later, and all copies were ordered burned.

This was a classic, if understandable, blunder that would return to haunt the Air Force for decades. The destruction order became public knowledge in the mid-1950s, and inevitably fueled a burgeoning belief

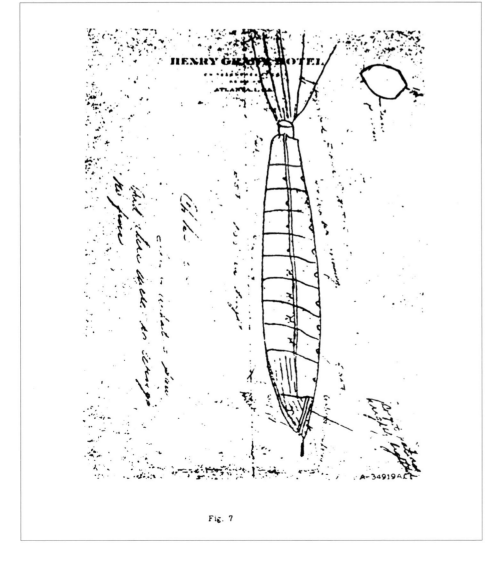

Fig. 7

Captain Clarence Chiles' sketch of the 'rocket' he and his co-pilot claimed came so close to their DC-3 airliner in July 1948 that it rocked the aircraft. The case became a classic in UFO lore.

in a massive government cover-up. A few copies of the document apparently escaped the flames – later UFO investigators for the USAF such as Captain Edward Ruppelt (who first revealed its existence) and Major Dewey Fournet reported seeing them in the 1950s.

The Air Force then managed only to encourage the growth of the *Estimate's* legendary status by denying for years that it had ever existed – even though the USAF had cleared Ruppelt's account for publication. No copy of the report itself has so far surfaced. *Estimate* has nevertheless become a key, albeit invisible, 'exhibit' in the believers' case that at every opportunity officialdom has ruthlessly buried hard evidence that UFOs are extra-terrestrial.

At Sign, the effect of General Vandenburg's summary rejection of the *Estimate* was slow but sure. Over the next few months, adherents of the ETH were quietly reassigned to other work, until the skeptics had finally become the majority.

Some were former believers, their view changed by the collapse of two more initially enticing pieces of data. A singularly aerobatic UFO chased by Air Guard Lieutenant George F. Gorman in an F-51 Mustang over Fargo, North Dakota, on the night of 1 October 1948 was laid to rest as a lighted weather balloon. And a series of green fireballs that swarmed around Kirtland AFB at Albuquerque, New Mexico, during the winter of 1948–49 were deemed to be meteors by a top-level panel of military and civilian scientists at Los Alamos in mid-February 1949.

On 11 February 1949, Sign was interred along with its unacceptable

A dashing, cigar-chewing Air Force Chief of Staff, General Hoyt Vandenberg, then aged 49, arrives in Berlin, Germany, in 1948 to study the airlift of supplies into the besieged city. Vandenberg was not impressed by the belief in alien visitors expressed by staff of Project Sign.

notions, and was renamed 'Project Grudge'. Sign's final report reflected the in-fighting that had gone on at the project over the previous year. While it offered sober discussions of disks as aerodynamic planforms and the feasibility of the wingless 'rocket' seen by Chiles and Whitted, it also used hard science to drive a gaping hole through popular ideas that the saucers were powered by rays, beams, magnetism or anti-gravity devices. On the ETH, it argued carefully:

It is hard to believe that any technically accomplished race would come here, flaunt its ability in mysterious ways and then simply go away. ...The lack of purpose in the various episodes is also puzzling. Only one motive can be assigned; that the space-men are 'feeling out' our defenses without wanting to be belligerent. If so, they must have been satisfied long ago that we can't catch them. It seems fruitless for them to keep trying the same experiment.

Although visits from outer space are believed to be possible, they are believed to be very improbable. In particular, the actions attributed to the 'flying objects' reported during 1947 and 1948 seem inconsistent with the requirements for space travel. [12]

Keyhoe's conversion

Grudge differed from Sign not only in regarding the ETH as too improbable for serious consideration, but also in publishing its reports rather than keeping them secret. In this way, the Air Force hoped to deflate public fascination with UFOs, partly by showing it had nothing to hide and partly by sheer force of logic. The strategy failed dismally, thanks largely to the obsessions of one man.

The first public sign of the new attitude was a long press release that was issued on 27 April 1949, and a pair of coolly skeptical articles, written by Sidney Shalett with Grudge's full co-operation, and published in the *Saturday Evening Post* in the following 10 days. For some, these actions crystalized and clarified their suspicions, or confusions, about the USAF's approach to the saucer mystery. If the USAF was so convinced that UFOs were explicable, why were they so interested in them?

One who homed in on the apparent contradiction was Ken Purdy, the editor of *True* magazine. From New York in May 1949 he telegraphed Donald E. Keyhoe, a freelance hack who was based in Washington, DC, and who was struggling to make a living writing for pulp magazines: HAVE BEEN INVESTIGATING FLYING SAUCER MYSTERY. FIRST TIP HINTED GIGANTIC HOAX TO COVER UP OFFICIAL SECRET ... CAN YOU TAKE OVER WASHINGTON END?

At a meeting in June Keyhoe offered four ideas on what the 'official secret' might be: the saucers were

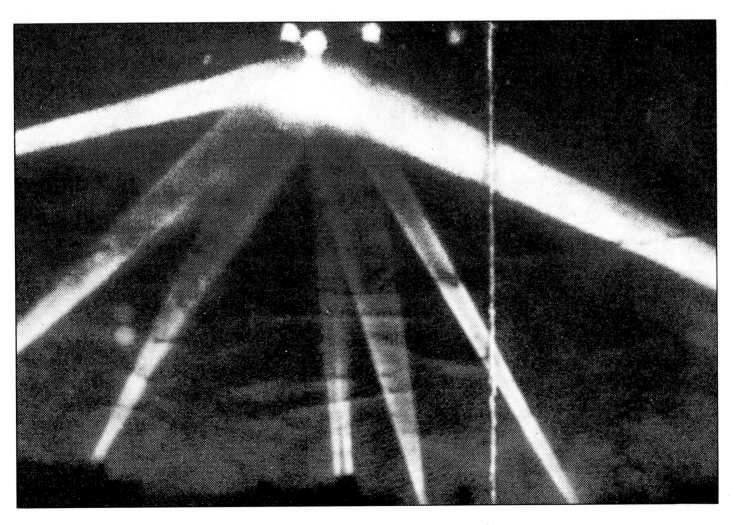

Searchlights converge on a slow-moving target and flak bursts above it during the 'air raid' on Los Angeles that took place during the small hours of 25 February 1942. Hindsight has included the event in the canon of UFO history.

GOLD MEDAL BOOK

THE FLYING SAUCERS ARE REAL

DONALD KEYHOE

According to Donald Keyhoe's ground-breaking book of 1950, flying saucers were not only real, but the US government knew it and refused to trust the American people with the facts.

(a) the saucers were from outer space, and (b) the government wanted to hide the fact. These basic tenets allowed him, like most conspiracy theorists, to have everything both ways, while opinion, scuttlebutt and speculation metamorphosed seamlessly into facts, usually presented through totally recalled dialogue.

The incipient paranoia is clear enough. The essential presumption was that the Air Force is all-powerful. It can plant stories or suppress them at will; therefore the stories that do emerge must do so for a reason.

A grand plan

Keyhoe knew what it was – 'part of an elaborate program to prepare the American people for a dramatic disclosure'. The theme is faithfully repeated by ufologists to this day. Keyhoe believed he was part of the grand plan – that the USAF wanted him to reveal that the saucers were spacecraft. Keyhoe, in his book based on his article for *True's* January 1950 issue, also became the first person in history to state another of ufology's constant refrains: 'The official explanation may be imminent.'

His book, *The Flying Saucers Are Real*, was published in June 1950. Its slightly breathless accounts of visits to the Pentagon and citations of highly placed (but often anonymous) sources covered a woeful ignorance. Keyhoe's account of the Air Force's attempts to grapple with the UFO enigma demonstrated his consummate skill as a popular journalist. But it was brewed from his imagination and his unshakeable faith in interplanetary saucers.

non-existent; they were Soviet missiles; they were US missiles; or they were an official hoax, meant to convince the Soviets that the USA had an extraordinary new weapon system.

Then Purdy suggested the saucer might be interplanetary craft. If they were, Keyhoe thought out loud, 'It could set off a panic that would make that Orson Welles thing [the famous 1938 broadcast of H.G. Wells's *War of the Worlds*] look like a picnic.' The

'panic argument' has been the standard justification for the mutually supportive combination of ETH and alleged cover-up ever since.

The exchange launched Keyhoe on a new career as an ETH promoter and gadfly to the government. Within hours Keyhoe convinced himself of the truth of his own and Purdy's leap of logic. He set about examining the UFO literature anew, interpreting everything in the light of two axioms:

Keyhoe clearly knew, and revealed, nothing of the factions within Project Sign, *Estimate of the Situation*, or the real rationale behind Grudge's new openness. Keyhoe interpreted every UFO incident in the darkest light – most conspicuously, the tragic death of Thomas Mantell which, he strongly implied, was alien-induced.

Keyhoe also introduced many other themes that have, ever since, hovered on the fringes of ufology – saucers as Nazi inventions (but developed by the British), hints of the 'Bermuda Triangle' and Arctic UFO bases. Rumors of crashed saucers full of little green Venusians were, however, dismissed as hoaxes.

Crash go the saucers

Others proved to be less circumspect. Also in 1950, Frank Scully, a columnist on the showbusiness magazine *Variety*, published his best-selling *Behind the Flying Saucers*. The book recounted how a landed saucer had been found on a plateau close to the tiny town of Aztec in New Mexico. The disk was 99ft (90m) in diameter and contained the corpses of 16 aliens, each between 3ft and 3ft 6in (90cm and 105cm) tall. They were 35 to 40 years old, and had perfect teeth.

According to Scully's informants, a 'Texas oilman' named Silas M. Newton and his colleague 'Dr Gee' – the latter a pseudonym for a 'specialist in magnetism' – the bodies were in the custody of the US military, along with two other landed flying disks. 'Dr Gee' was obliged to remain anonymous, as he was one of the scientists called in to examine the saucers, but he was able to reveal that the UFOs were powered by 'magnetic propulsion' and came from Venus. Inside the captured UFOs booklets had been found written in pictorial script. The saucers themselves were made of an extremely light metal whose composition had baffled government chemists

and was so hard it had withstood 'the use of $35,000-worth of diamond drills'.

Scully may have been entirely sincere in his belief in all these details, but he certainly did not check the testimony of Newton and the shadowy 'Dr Gee', or their credentials. His account was first debunked by a journalist, J.P. Khan, in 1952 but when, during the 1980s, a researcher called William Moore delved further into the background to Scully's book he discovered that the true explanation for the story was almost as bizarre as the account itself.[13]

Around 1948 or 1949, a Hollywood actor named Mike Conrad had hit on the idea of making a science-fiction movie about UFOs with a base in Alaska.

To create interest in the project, Conrad claimed that the film would include footage of genuine UFOs, and also hired a promoter to pose as an FBI agent and spread the story to the media that the FBI had custody of this footage. When Scully in due course read this planted rumor in the papers, he apparently decided to go public with a story that Newton and 'Dr Gee' (real name: Leo GeBauer) had been telling him for months. But for the detail about the UFOs coming from Venus and being found near Aztec, NM, it was essentially the same story put about by Conrad. Newton did not know that Conrad's story was a hoax; Scully did not know about Conrad's publicity ploy.

Newton and GeBauer were both convicted confidence tricksters. They were apparently regaling all and sundry throughout the Southwest with versions of the Aztec tale. (Scully related three versions of it.) Their motive was purely commercial. GeBauer had built a 'gizmo' that, he said, was based on technology found in the downed saucer, and it could detect oil and gold deposits. The pair would demonstrate the widget's effica-

cy on land that they just happened to own, and on a good day would part the gullible from their money in return for some worthless real estate.

They succeeded not only in making Scully believe them, but – by a choice irony – in alerting the FBI, whose chief, J. Edgar Hoover, in due course received a memo on the subject. This document, often cited as proof that the US government is holding saucer wreckage and alien corpses, is in fact a commentary on a piece of hearsay.

Tales of duplicity

Scully contributed liberally to the notion of a giant cover-up of UFO reality and of government, especially military, duplicity: 'If the Pentagon tells you flying saucers are here don't believe them. If they say they are a myth don't believe them. Believe me.'

Behind the whole saga was the source from which Newton and GeBauer, and very likely Conrad, had lifted their tall tales: a 'tongue-in-cheek story' published in 1948 by George Bawra, editor of the Aztec, NM, *Independent-Review* about a Venusian saucer that had crashed locally. Scores of papers recycled the story over the next year.

Ahead of this tangle of lies and legends lay the obsession of ufological circles in the 1990s: the crash of a UFO and the discovery of alien bodies somewhere near Roswell, New Mexico, in 1947. [14]

By the end of 1950, a number of indelible themes had entered public discussion and, more importantly, perception of UFOs. By the same time, the USAF had wound down Project Grudge. At the Air Technical Intelligence Center (ATIC – the old TID under a new name), the UFO investigation team had been reduced to a single junior officer. The two sides in the debate over UFO reality could scarcely have been further apart.

Chapter Two

MEN IN BLUE AND GRAY

AN OFFICIAL STRATEGY DEVELOPS

1951–1966

BY THE BEGINNING of the 1950s the American public had been exposed to most of the ideas and beliefs to which mainstream UFO partisans would cling over the next three decades. Although other notions – for instance, that flying disks had crashed in the Southwestern deserts – were also in circulation, they would not really come into their own until the 1980s. But by then ufology had undergone a sea-change so drastic that actual UFOs in the sky had been pushed into second or even third place behind more exotic concerns.

In the early 1950s, people who 'believed in' flying saucers would have agreed, by and large, that:

Aviation industry executive James Pfeiffer photographed this UFO from a restaurant beside the Ipameri River in Brazil, on 8 May 1966. Pfeiffer estimated the object's size as 70ft (23m); computer analysis by Ground Saucer Watch put its size at 60ft (21m). The UFO apparently set down in the woods and emitted a whining sound 'noisy enough to bring the restaurant employees out to watch'.

● Flying saucers were real, material objects that came from outer space – although from where exactly was a matter of debate.
● They had been visiting Earth for decades and probably centuries.
● They exhibited a technology and aerobatic capacity well in advance of anything on Earth.
● The aliens were observing, not meddling with, life on Earth.
● The US government, and probably all major governments, knew that the saucers were extra-terrestrial but were keeping the fact secret to prevent mass panic.

From 1950 until 1969, when the USAF officially pulled out of UFO-watching, various arms and agencies of the US government tried to contend with this interlocking series of beliefs and their development. The official struggle was waged partly in public, partly in secret.

The government was often accused of being deceitful, and it fended off the charge with varying degrees of veracity. On the official side were the Air Force, which remained the public face of the government's interest in UFOs, the CIA and, to a much smaller extent, the FBI.

Donald Keyhoe was instrumental in defining the way the UFO phenomenon was seen in the 1950s and for years afterwards. Throughout the whole period he pestered, cajoled and denounced the Air Force and its efforts to grapple with UFOs, while adding new elements to the UFO myth through his inimitable books and magazine articles.

Although influential, Keyhoe was nevertheless only the agitated tip of a large iceberg. Fixed belief in flying saucers may not have been very widespread, and direct experience of them even less so, but interest was intense.

Throughout these years, the USAF thus found itself constantly reacting to events and opinions, unable to control them and, even more frustrating, seemingly unable to convince anyone that it held the high ground in the argument. This was partly because the Air Force used only the most primitive techniques of persuasion in presenting its case, and sometimes deployed none at all. And it was partly because the USAF was trying to counter deep conviction with rational argument, which (as all skeptics sooner or later discover) is a lost cause.

From New Grudge to Blue Book

To begin with, the Air Force had no argument at all, for in effect Grudge had been closed down since its last report was issued at the end of December 1949. Then there was a flurry of sightings, most of which were confirmed by radar, around the US Army base at Fort Monmouth, New Jersey, over two days in September 1951 (see Case #4).

Seeking explanations, Director of Air Force Intelligence Major-General C.P. Cabell and his staff were appalled to discover that the USAF was employing but a solitary token lieutenant to investigate and solve UFO sightings. Grudge was rapidly reactivated; in charge was Captain Edward J. Ruppelt. He set in motion a system, backed by new regulations, to channel UFO reports directly to ATIC, to standardize investigation forms, and to make a statistical analysis of the data

on file. Dr J. Allen Hynek was appointed chief scientific consultant. Monthly progress reports would be classified, but the project would co-operate with the press. The staff would not speculate on the cause of unidentified sightings.

In a briefing to Major-General John A. Samford (the new head of Air Force intelligence) in December 1951, Ruppelt stated there was no proof 'flying saucers' existed. He presented the reborn Grudge as an intelligence-gathering exercise, designed to discover any items of military significance among the 'unknowns'.

Ruppelt insisted the subjects of the reports be called 'unidentified flying objects' (UFOs), not 'flying saucers'. The phrase had been used before, in Sidney Shallett's *Saturday Evening Post* articles and in some Grudge reports, but Ruppelt's habitual use of the neutral-sounding term helped to give saucer reports a new air of respectability in the public mind.

Ruppelt's new reporting system was in place by March 1952 and Grudge was renamed Project Blue Book. On 3 April a press release announced that the USAF was still studying UFOs, but had reached no conclusions.

Alan R. Smith, aged 14, took this photograph at about 1.45 a.m. on 2 August 1965 from his back yard in Tulsa, Oklahoma. Five other witnesses saw the UFO change color from white to red to blue-green. The USAF Photo Analysis Division analysed the picture for Project Blue Book and agreed it was a material object, less than a mile (1.6km) from the camera, and about 30ft (10m) in diameter. They also observed that it resembled the effect 'obtained by photographing a multi-colored revolving filter flood light'. After computer analysis in 1977 Ground Saucer Watch declared that the picture 'represents an extraordinary flying craft of large dimension'.

Case #4

The Fort Monmouth Sightings

US ARMY SIGNAL CORPS RADAR CENTER, FORT MONMOUTH, NEW JERSEY, USA
10–11 September 1951

At 11.10 a.m. on 10 September a student radar operator picked up a low-altitude target. For three minutes he tried to switch the radar to automatic tracking, but the equipment failed to respond. The student exclaimed: 'It's going too fast for the set! That means it's going faster than a jet!'

At 11.38 a.m., the pilots of a Lockheed T-33 Silver Star jet trainer at 20,000ft (6100m) over Point Pleasant, New Jersey, saw a 'dull silver disk' descending below them. They estimated its altitude at 5000ft (1500m) and its size at 30–50ft (9–15m) in diameter. The T-33 gave chase, whereupon the UFO stopped descending, hovered briefly, then flew away northward and out to sea.

At 3.15 p.m., Fort Monmouth headquarters urgently demanded the radar center track a UFO that had been seen high in the sky to the north. It appeared as a slow-moving silver speck to the naked eye, and the radar plot gave its altitude as 93,000ft (28,350m), well beyond the range of any known aircraft.

The following morning, two radars picked up a target that neither set could track automatically. The UFO climbed almost vertically, leveled out, climbed again, and finally went into a dive. In the afternoon came the final sighting, of a further slow-moving target.

Project Grudge succeeded in discovering the causes of all the sightings, but not before the mini-flap had thoroughly disturbed Air Force intelligence commanders. The first target had been an aircraft. The student operator had failed to set his radar correctly for automatic tracking. Balloons were responsible for both the T-33 sighting and the second radar sighting. It turned out that the call from headquarters had sounded 'frantic' because officers there knew the 'UFO' was a balloon and were anxious to settle a bet on its altitude.

Another balloon caused one of the next day's sightings, while the radar signals were also bouncing off a layer of warm, humid air, hitting the ground and then being reflected back. The resulting track, apart from being false, gave the impression of a target moving at very high speed.

On the face of it, this could only confirm Donald Keyhoe's claims – that the USAF was far too interested in UFOs for its public, skeptical line to be entirely credible. And now the Air Force was saying in so many words that it was keeping an open mind on the subject. Supposedly, it was 'keeping the answer secret,' in Keyhoe's words, 'until the country could be prepared'. [1]

Ruppelt's policy of openness had, in fact, come too late. Whatever it did the USAF could not win against this double-edged conspiracy theory (which, for Keyhoe, also happened to be profitable). If the Air Force persist-ed in keeping its UFO investigations secret and denying the reality of the saucers, it was accused of hiding the Big Secret. If it investigated UFOs swiftly and publicly, and with an open mind, it 'proved' the existence of the saucers and the Air Force 'program' of preparing the country for the truth.

To add to the confusion came a *Life* magazine article published on 7 April 1952, hot on the heels of the Air Force's announcement of its new policy. Titled 'Have we visitors from outer space?', it cited an Air Force general in the Pentagon who 'strongly believed flying saucers were interplan-etary spaceships', along with leading aerospace scientists of like views. It also reviewed 10 'unsolved' cases – several specially declassified for *Life* by the Air Force – and strongly implied that the ETH was the only solution to them. The article was widely read. Besides being 'trailed' by some 350 newspapers across the USA in the week before its publication, it was fol-lowed by further pieces on the saucers in *Life*, *Look* and *Time* magazines, as well as a host of newspaper articles.

This unprecedented press coverage was followed by the biggest sightings flap in UFO history, which culminat-ed in the 'siege' of Washington DC that July (see Case #5).

Case #5

The Siege of Washington

WASHINGTON, DC, USA

19–20 July and 26–27 July 1952

19–20 July: between 11.40 p.m. and 5.00 a.m., two radars covering Washington picked up eight UFOs in restricted air space. The objects were flying at 100–300mph (160–420km/h), and suddenly accelerating to phenomenal velocities. Airline pilots were also reporting strange lights in the sky over the capital, behaving in the same fashion. Jet interceptors, delayed by an earlier investigation of UFOs over New Jersey, arrived at 3.30 a.m.; the UFOs disappeared, then reappeared after the jets departed. At one point, radar controlers following events at Andrews AFB saw a large, blazing orange sphere hovering over the base.

26–27 July: starting at 9.00 p.m., between six and 12 UFOs performed similar maneuvers. At 2.00 a.m., interceptors from Wilmington, Delaware, were scrambled, but again the UFOs disappeared from sight and from radar screens as soon as the jets came within radar range, and reappeared 10 minutes later, when the planes were returning to base. However, at about 3.20 a.m., when a fresh flight of fighters came on the scene, the UFOs remained visible. One pilot, Lt William Patterson, reported himself surrounded by a ring of enormous blue-white lights, which flew off before he was given permission to fire on them.

An investigation by the Civil Aviation Authority's Technical Development and Evaluation Center found the cause of the radar returns was a temperature inversion – hot, humid air above a layer of colder, dryer air. Eddies formed where the two met, creating a 'lens' in the inversion that would deflect a radar signal to the ground and thence back to the antenna. (In one instance the signal was finally bouncing off a steamship in the Potomac River.) Weather records show temperature inversions over the capital on both weekends, such as to create radar returns not at low altitude, but at around 4000ft (1200m).

The investigators also discovered that the radar echoes always moved in the same direction as the wind. As the eddies dissipated, the returns would vanish between sweeps of the radar dish, giving the impression of a UFO accelerating away at enormous speed. On only one occasion did all three of the radar installations around the capital show a blip at the same location. Excitement over the radar returns probably led fliers to identify them with otherwise unremarkable light sources. One airline pilot told Ruppelt that there were so many lights around Washington that it was easy to look in any direction and take one as 'mysterious'.

Over the whole of the 1952 flap, Project Blue Book received 82 UFO reports in April (54 of them between 16 and 30 April), 79 reports in May, 148 reports in June, 536 reports in July, 326 in August, 124 in September and only 61 in October. The total for the year was 1501, of which 303 (20 per cent) were logged as 'unknowns'. Both figures were records in the 22-year history of USAF UFO-watching.

The flap of 1952

The *Life* article probably helped to create a 'feedback loop' that greatly increased the rate of reports. The historian Curtis Peebles suggests what may have happened:

Life *said the Air Force was interested in flying saucers. People would then be more likely to report a sighting. The new regulations meant that reports that might have been ignored or thrown away before were now sent to Blue Book. The open press policy meant that questions were not brushed off as before. This, along with the increased number of reports, resulted in more newspaper articles which caused people to watch the skies.*

In his memoir of his time with Blue Book, Ruppelt asserted that a number of USAF generals who privately endorsed the ETH had unofficially encouraged *Life* writers to promote the 'interplanetary aspect'. The officers ranked 'so high that their personal opinion was almost policy'.[2] As the Air Force had assiduously rejected the ETH until then, and would do so again, it is curious that it should covertly try to boost it.

A secret memo dated 3 January 1952 to the recently appointed head of USAF Intelligence, Major General John A. Samford. The consensus of speculation had reverted to the notion that the saucers might be Soviet craft; the memo is one of many in government files pleading ineffectually for a concerted research effort into UFOs.

Ruppelt believed there was a major split in the Air Force and other government agencies between believers and non-believers, and that it deepened as fresh reports flooded in that summer. No doubt such a split did occur. But in 1993 *Just Cause*, the journal of the UFO pressure group Citizens Against UFO Secrecy (CAUS), suggested there might be another reason for top-level approval of the ETH.[3]

CAUS researchers found numerous gloomy reports in US newspapers of the time about the ineffectuality and poor recruitment of the USAF's Ground Observer Corps (GOC), a volunteer body established to watch the skies for enemy aircraft.

CAUS speculated that the USAF high command may have promoted the ETH through *Life* magazine (and more subtly by giving Ruppelt everything he asked for) in order to promote skywatching – and so draw recruits into the GOC. The Air Force even dropped hints that a 24-hour GOC alert on 14 July 1952 was 'really' to look out for flying saucers.

Two days before, President Harry S Truman personally appealed for volunteers to join GOC. The USAF also made some remarkable admissions at this time, such as that low-flying aircraft were invisible to radar, and that their detection relied on ground observers. CAUS also pointed to 'the lack of timely Air Force response to the wave' and to 'the amount of immediate, behind-the-scenes information coming from the government' at the same time.

DECLASSIFIED PER EXECUTIVE ORDER 12356, Section 3.3, NND 841508
By W G Lewis   NARS, Date Jan 29, 1985.   SECRET
Auth CS, USAF

SECRET

DEPARTMENT OF THE AIR FORCE
HEADQUARTERS UNITED STATES AIR FORCE
WASHINGTON 25, D. C.

2 JAN 1952

AFOIN-A

3 JAN 1952

MEMORANDUM FOR GENERAL SAMFORD

SUBJECT: (SECRET) Contemplated Action to Determine the Nature and Origin of the Phenomena Connected with the Reports of Unusual Flying Objects

1. The continued reports of unusual flying objects requires positive action to determine the nature and origin of this phenomena. The action taken thus far has been designed to track down and evaluate reports from casual observers throughout the country. Thus far, this action has produced results of doubtful value and the inconsistencies inherent in the nature of the reports has given neither positive nor negative proof of the claims.

2. It is logical to relate the reported sightings to the known development of aircraft, jet propulsion, rockets and range extension capabilities in Germany and the U.S.S.R. In this connection, it is to be noted that certain developments by the Germans, particularly the Horton wing, jet propulsion, and refueling, combined with their extensive employment of V-1 and V-2 weapons during World War II, lend credence to the possibility that the flying objects may be of German and Russian origin. The developments mentioned above were completed and operational between 1941 and 1944 and subsequently fell into the hands of the Soviets at the end of the war. There is evidence that the Germans were working on these projects as far back as 1931 to 1938. Therefore, it may be assumed that the Germans had at least a 7 to 10 year lead over the United States in the development of rockets, jet engines, and aircraft of the Horton-wing design. The Air Corps developed refueling experimentally as early as 1928, but did not develop operational capability until 1948.

3. In view of the above facts and the persistent reports of unusual flying objects over parts of the United States, particularly the east and west coast and in the vicinity of the atomic energy production and testing facilities, it is apparent that positive action must be taken to determine the nature of the objects and, if possible, their origin. Since it is known fact that the Soviets did not detonate an atomic bomb prior to 1949, it is believed possible that the Soviets may have developed the German aircraft designs at an accelerated rate in order to have a suitable carrier for the delivery of weapons of mass destruction. In other words, the Soviets may have a carrier without the weapons required while we have relatively superior weapons with relatively inferior carriers available. If the Soviets should get the carrier and the weapon, combined with adequate defensive aircraft, they might surpass us technologically for a sufficient period of time to permit them to execute a decisive air campaign against the United States and her allies. The basic philosophy of the Soviets has been to surpass the western powers technologically and the Germans have given them the opportunity.

4. In view of the facts outlined above, it is considered mandatory that the Air Force take positive action at once to definitely determine the nature and, if possible, the origin of the reported unusual flying objects. The following action is now contemplated:

a. to require ATIC to provide at least three teams to be matched up with an equal number of teams from ADC for the purpose of taking radar scope photographs and visual photographs of the phenomena;

b. to select sites for these teams, based on the concentrations of already reported sightings over the United States; (these areas are, generally, the Seattle area, the Albuquerque area, and the New York-Philadelphia area) and

c. to take the initial steps in this project during early January 1952.

W. M. Garland
Brigadier General, USAF
Assistant for Production
Directorate of Intelligence

1 Incl
Tech. Rept #76-45

Both the Air Force and the GOC undoubtedly benefitted from the 1952 flap. CAUS found that recruitment to both more than doubled in some areas that summer. It also found it possibly significant that the Air Force waited until 29 July before holding a press conference, led by General Samford, to reduce 'the alarmist nature of the coverage' by the media generated by the series of events in Washington.

Enter the CIA

As the agency responsible for all foreign intelligence activity, the CIA had kept a watching brief on saucer reports for years – and with Air Force co-operation, as the surviving paperwork makes clear. For example, a Dr Stone of the Office of Scientific Intelligence (O/SI) surveyed the CIA's UFO files in March 1949. He was not impressed. His memo on the subject begins: 'A rapid perusal of your documents leaves one confused and inclined to supineness.' It ends on an equally weary note:

The 'flying disks' will turn out to be another 'sea serpent.' However, since there is even a remote possibility that they may be interplanetary or foreign aircraft, it is necessary to investigate each sighting.

The 1952 flap changed all that. The documents that were released under the FOIA show that as the flap grew, the CIA gathered UFO reports from overseas radio broadcasts, press reports and intelligence agents in locations as diverse as the Belgian Congo, East Germany, Algeria and Spain. No evaluations were attached to these reports.

But on 29 July, as General Samford was reassuring the press that Blue Book possessed the solution to the flap in hand, Ralph L. Clark, Acting Assistant Director for Scientific Intelligence, wrote to the Deputy Director of Intelligence:

In the past several weeks a number of radar and visual sightings of unidentified aerial objects have been reported. Although this office has maintained a continuing review of such reputed sightings during the past three years, a special study group has been formed to review this subject to date. O/CI [Office of Current Intelligence] will participate in this study with O/SI and a report should be ready about 15 August.

Feverish correspondence

A flurry of memos followed. Two significant points were raised on 1 August by Edward Tauss, acting chief of the Weapons and Equipment Division. Observing that a large percentage of UFO reports were 'clearly "phoney" ' and that the residue of 'unexplainable' reports probably could be resolved 'if complete information were available', he went on:

2. Notwithstanding the foregoing... so long as a series of reports remains 'unexplainable' (interplanetary aspects and alien origin not being thoroughly excluded from consideration), caution requires that intelligence continue coverage of the subject.

3. It is recommended that CIA surveillance of subject matter, in coordination with... ATIC, be continued. It is strongly urged, however, that no indication of CIA interest or concern reach the press or public, in view of their probable alarmist tendencies to accept such interest as 'confirmatory' of the soundness of 'unpublished facts' in the hands of the US government.

CIA agents, even senior ones, are human like anyone else, and Tauss clearly felt it necessary to acknowledge the 'interplanetary aspects' that had lately been bandied about in the press. And he recognized that the CIA should avoid being cornered by the double-edged Keyhoe Hypothesis as the Air Force had been. It's also not impossible to read into this a genuine and responsible desire to keep 'alarmist' tendencies to the minimum, as well as the bureaucrat's habitual passion for being left alone in peace to get on with his job.

Three briefing papers, all classified SECRET, emerged in answer to the Office of Scientific Intelligence's initiative. One, dated 14 August, considered the theories that US secret weapons, Soviet experiments, or 'the man from Mars' lay behind UFO reports, and the Air Force's position that given enough data all saucer sightings could be explained.

The second, dated 15 August, elaborated on the Air Force's explanations for sightings. It dealt with the psychological factors that could help create a seemingly inexplicable experience, astronomical causes of UFO reports, and 'little known natural phenomena', including electromagnetic and electrostatic effects. The paper concluded: 'Here we run out of even "blue yonder" explanations that might be tenable, and, we are still left with numbers of incredible reports from credible observers.' But, it commented: 'No debris or material evidence has ever been recovered following an unexplained sighting.'

The third document revealed the two dangers, as the CIA saw them, of UFOs. Remarking that 'we have found not one report or comment, even satirical, in the Russian press' on UFOs, the writer wondered, in light of 'present American credulity', 'whether or not these sightings could be used [by the Soviets] from a psychological warfare point of view either offensively or defensively'. The other danger was directly related to the 1952 flap:

At any given moment now, there may be a dozen official unidentified sightings plus many unofficial. At the moment of attack, how will we, on an instant basis, distinguish hardware from phantom? ...Until far greater knowledge is achieved of the causes back of the sightings... we will run the increasing risk of false alerts and the even greater danger of tabbing the real as false.

On 24 September, the Assistant Director for Scientific Intelligence Dr H. Marshall Chadwell based a memo on this paper to the CIA's Director,

General Walter Bedell Smith. He wondered if UFO sightings could be controled, predicted or used in psychological warfare by the Soviets (given that 'a fair proportion of our population is mentally conditioned to the acceptance of the incredible'). In short, belief in flying saucers might be manipulated to create a flap, which could confuse the US Air Warning System and camouflage a surprise Soviet attack. Chadwell ended:

I consider this problem to be of such importance that it should be brought to the attention of the National Security Council in order that a community-wide effort towards its solution may be initiated.

The Robertson Panel

After much internal discussion, and even some argument, on 4 December 1952 the CIA proposed to the Intelligence Advisory Committee (IAC) that a scientific panel should review the whole UFO question and assess any possible threat to national security. The IAC, representing the military, the State Department, the Atomic Energy Commission, the CIA and the FBI, agreed.

Chadwell asked Dr H.P. Robertson, an expert in relativity theory and cosmology at the California Institute of Technology, to recruit a suitable group of scientists. Robertson assembled a star team of some of the most eminent of his peers: nuclear physicist Dr Luis Alvarez, astronomer Dr Thornton Page, Dr Samuel A. Goudsmit (who had discovered the 'spin' of electrons), and geophysicist Dr Lloyd V. Berkner. Associate members were the astrophysicist Dr J. Allen Hynek and

rocketry expert Frederick C. Durant. The scientists gathered in Washington DC on the morning of 14 January 1953 and considered evidence until the afternoon of 17 January.

Many ufologists have variously presented the Robertson Panel's deliberations and conclusions as trivial and superficial, a watershed in the

official approach to UFOs, the authority for a cult of secrecy, the beginning of a decades-long campaign of disinformation, proof that the CIA is the keeper of the Grail of saucer secrets, and much more. A large proportion of these imputations stem from the refusal of the CIA to declassify the whole of the Panel's report until 1979.

TAB C

SCIENTIFIC ADVISORY PANEL ON

UNIDENTIFIED FLYING OBJECTS

14 - 17 January 1953

MEMBERS	ORGANIZATION	FIELD OF COMPETENCY
Dr. H. P. Robertson (Chairman)	California Institute of Technology	Physics, weapons systems
Dr. Luis W. Alvarez	University of California	Physics, radar
Dr. Lloyd V. Berkner	Associated Universities, Inc.	Geophysics
Dr. Samuel Goudsmit	Brookhaven National Laboratories	Atomic structure, statistical problems
Dr. Thornton Page	Office of Research Operations, Johns Hopkins University	Astronomy, Astrophysics

ASSOCIATE MEMBERS

Dr. J. Allen Hynek	Ohio State University	Astronomy
Mr. Frederick C. Durant	Arthur D. Little, Inc.	Rockets, guided missiles

INTERVIEWEES

Brig. Gen. William M. Garland	Commanding General, ATIC	Scientific and technical intelligence
Dr. H. Marshall Chadwell	Assistant Director, O/SI, CIA	Scientific and technical intelligence
Mr. Ralph L. Clark	Deputy Assistant Director, O/SI, CIA	Scientific and technical intelligence

INTERVIEWEES (con't)	ORGANIZATION	FIELD OF COMPETENCY
Mr. Philip G. Strong	Chief, Operations Staff, O/SI, CIA	Scientific and technical intelligence
Mr. Stephen T. Possony	Acting Chief, Special Study Group, D/I USAF	Scientific and technical intelligence
Capt. Edward J. Ruppelt, USAF	Chief, Aerial Phenomena Branch, ATIC, USAF	Scientific and technical intelligence
Mr. J. Dewey Fournet, Jr.	The Ethyl Corporation	Astro Eng.
Lt. R. S. Neasham, USN	USN Photo Interpretation Laboratory, Anacostia	Photo interpretation
Mr. Harry Woo	USN Photo Interpretation Laboratory, Anacostia	Photo interpretation

Few of these charges are supported by what the panel did and said. It reviewed 75 sighting reports from 1951-52 that Blue Book considered the best documented of the period, 89 summaries of various categories of sighting ('Formations, Blinking Lights, Hovering, etc.'), a report of sightings at Holloman AFB, New Mexico, and a report from Project Twinkle; heard of progress at Blue Book and Project Stork (the statistical analysis of sightings commissioned from the Battelle Institute, later to be published as Blue Book's *Special Report #14*); watched movies of UFOs taken at Tremonton, Utah, in 1952 and Great Falls, Montana, in 1950 and another of flying seagulls; heard an intelligence assessment of Soviet interest in American UFO sightings; and pondered sundry official forms, regulations, analyses of radar effectiveness, foreign intelligence reports and 'copies of popular published works dealing with the subject'. The material was presented by ATIC commander

Brigadier General William M. Garland, Captain Ruppelt of Blue Book, Captain Dewey Fournet, formerly of Blue Book, two members of the US Navy's Photo Interpretation Laboratory, and three CIA O/SI members, including Dr Chadwell.

Strange conclusions?

In discussing cases, the distinguished scientists drew general conclusions that might have been calculated to outrage saucer believers. For example:

The Panel Members were impressed (as have been others, including O/SI personnel) in [sic] the lack of sound data in the great majority of case histories... After review and discussion of [six] cases (and about 15 others, in less detail), the Panel concluded that reasonable explanations could be suggested for most sightings and 'by deduction and scientific method it could be induced (given additional data) that other cases could be explained in a similar manner.'

This is all a long way from a conspiracy to create a massive cover-up;

A classic cigar-shaped UFO allegedly seen by Joe Ferriere near Woonsocket, Rhode Island, USA. The witness claimed that a dome-shaped object, which he also photographed, emerged from the craft. It is striking not least for its capacity to absorb light.

Dewey Fournet's conclusion that many of the phenomena could 'only' be explained as extra-terrestrial was rejected because 'the cases cited by him... were raw, unevaluated reports'.

Some frustration with the scarcity of completely unambiguous evidence became manifest throughout the proceedings. The minutes record: 'The absence of any "hardware" resulting from an unexplained UFO sighting lends a "will-o'-the-wisp" nature to the ATIC problem.'

Individual anomalies often collapsed simply because of the erudition, expertise and experience of the panel members. At one point Drs Berkner and Alvarez took time to

Report of the Scientific Advisory Panel on Unidentified Flying Objects

MEMORANDUM FOR: ASSISTANT DIRECTOR FOR SCIENTIFIC INTELLIGENCE,

CENTRAL INTELLIGENCE AGENCY

17 January 1953

1. Pursuant to the request of the Assistant Director for Scientific Intelligence, the undersigned Panel of Scientific Consultants has met to evaluate any possible threat to national security posed by Unidentified Flying Objects ("Flying Saucers"), and to make recommendations thereon. The Panel has received the evidence as presented by cognizant intelligence agencies, primarily the Air Technical Intelligence Center, and has reviewed the best documented incidents.

2. As a result of its considerations, the Panel concludes:

   (a) That the evidence presented on Unidentified Flying Objects shows no indication that these phenomena constitute a direct physical threat to national security.

   We firmly believe that there is no residuum of cases which indicates phenomena which are attributable to foreign artifacts capable of hostile acts, and that there is no evidence that the phenomena indicate a need for the revision of current scientific concepts.

3. The Panel further concludes:

   (a) That the continued emphasis on the reporting of these phenomena does, in these parlous times, result in a threat to the orderly functioning of the protective organs of the body politic.

   We cite as examples the clogging of channels of communication by irrelevant reports, the danger of being led by continued false alarms to ignore real indications of hostile action, and the cultivation of a morbid national psychology in which skillful hostile propaganda could induce hysterical behavior and harmful distrust of duly constituted authority.

4. In order most effectively to strengthen the national facilities for the timely recognition and the appropriate handling of true indications of hostile action, and to minimize the concomitant dangers alluded to above, the Panel recommends:

   (a) That the national security agencies take immediate steps to strip the Unidentified Flying Objects of the special status they have been given and the aura of mystery they have unfortunately acquired;

   (b) That the national security agencies institute policies on intelligence, training, and public education designed to prepare the material defenses and the morale of the country to recognize most promptly and to react most effectively to true indications of hostile intent or action.

   We suggest that these aims may be achieved by an integrated program designed to reassure the public of the total lack of evidence of inimical forces behind the phenomena, to train personnel to recognize and reject false indications quickly and effectively, and to strengthen regular channels for the evaluation of and prompt reaction to true indications of hostile measures.

H.P. Robertson	Chairman
Lloyd V. Berkner	Associated Universities, Inc.
S.A. Goudsmit	Brookhaven National Laboratories
Luis W. Alvarez	University of California
Thornton Page	Johns Hopkins University

Case #6

The Levelland Encounters

LEVELLAND, TEXAS, USA

2 November 1957

UFOs were seen within a radius of 20 miles (30km) around Levelland, Canadian and Midland in Texas, and at Clovis, New Mexico, within a space of two and a half hours. In the USSR that night, the Soviets launched Sputnik 2.

At Levelland the night was dark, overcast and drizzly, with the cloud ceiling at 400ft (120m). Just before 11.00 p.m., and just after a heavy thunderstorm had hit the town, Levelland police took a report from farmhand and part-time barber Pedro Saucedo who, together with his friend Joe Salaz, had observed a torpedo-shaped UFO, approximately 200ft (60m) in length and 6ft (2m) wide. At first they thought that it was part of the lightning. The UFO was blue, and it had yellow-and-white flames coming from the back. When it moved toward the witnesses' truck, the lights and motor died, and the pair jumped out. They felt a blast of heat as it rushed overhead at about 300ft (90m) from the ground. The truck's lights then came on again. Saucedo estimated the UFO's speed at 600–800mph (950–1300km/h).

Around midnight, 19-year-old Texas Tech student Jim Wheeler's car was affected about 4 miles (6km) east of town. The engine, lights and radio failed. Wheeler got out of his car to check it, saw an oval-shaped object, and got back in his car. As he described it to the Air Force, 'the size of the object was that of a baseball at arm's length. He estimated the object was 75 to 100ft [23 to 30m] at its longest dimension. [It] was white in color, with a greenish tint, possibly caused by the tinted windshield of [the] car.' Wheeler continued to watch the UFO for four or five minutes. It then rose straight up into the sky and flew out of sight.

At 12.45 a.m., a glowing red UFO had much the same effect on a truck driven by Ronald Martin. At about 1.30 a.m., Sheriff Weir Clem saw brilliant red oval lights flash across the road ahead of him. Numerous other witnesses reported similar events that night, involving UFOs on the highway and electro-magnetic effects on their vehicles.

More than one ufologist has suggested that the Levelland flap was engineered by clandestine government agencies to distract attention from the Sputnik launch and the Soviet space program, which was then markedly more successful than the comparable US effort.

Blue Book had a more prosaic explanation. The witnesses' accounts varied so much that it seemed unlikely they were describing the same thing. Saucedo's report 'could not be relied upon'. When questioned, he seemed to have 'no concept of direction and was conflicting in his answers'. Apart from Wheeler, all the witnesses said they saw streaks of light. Blue Book concluded that in the weather conditions (which were strangely missing from press accounts of the events) the most likely causes were electrical phenomena such as ball lightning. The engine failures were put down to 'wet electrical circuits'.

propose different design improvements in radar sets to eliminate misleading or false echoes. A typical case, from Los Alamos, involved 'a series of observations... from August 1950 to January 1951, when cosmic ray coincidence counters behaved queerly.'

Looking at the relevant circuit diagrams and records, 'Dr Alvarez was quickly able to point out that the recorded data were undoubtedly due to instrumental effects that would have been recognized as such by more experienced observers.'

In short, the panel was unimpressed by the evidence – although it was the best ATIC could supply. The still-famous Tremonton movie, on which (as ufologists love to repeat) the US Navy Photo Interpretation Laboratory had lavished 1000 man-hours, was given short shrift. The scientists raised no less than 11 objections to the Navy analysts' conclusion that the objects depicted were large, 'self-luminous' and fast-moving, and they suggested some simple experiments to establish their most likely identity. (The films viewed by the Robertson panel are dealt with in detail in Chapter Three.)

And the panel made two crucial points, one practical and one iron-clad in scientific principles, in their subsequent discussion:

It was felt there will always be sightings, for which complete data is [sic] lacking, that can only be explained with disproportionate effort and a long time delay, if at all. [An] educational or training program should have as a major purpose the elimination of popular feeling that every sighting, no matter how poor the data, must be explained in detail. Attention should be directed to the requirement among scientists that a new phenomena [sic], to be accepted, must be completely and convincingly documented. In other words, the burden of proof is on the sighter, not the explainer.

Conspiracy-hunting ufologists have made much of the debunking 'education' program recommended by Robertson and his colleagues. The first point to be made is that it was never put into action. Only the Air Force responded; shortly afterward it reverted to a rather surly and condescending tone when discussing UFOs in public. The second is that the specific suggestions show that the panel's members certainly did not lack humor, for all their serious scientific bent. Don Marquis, creator of Mehitabel the Mystery Cat and her protégé Archie the verse-writing cockroach, and Leo Rosten, author of the Hymie Kaplan stories (and originator of the saying, à propos W.C. Fields, that 'a man who hates dogs and children can't be all bad') were mentioned as potential collaborators, along with Walt Disney and Arthur Godfrey.

Wayward analysis

One can't help feeling that conspiracy addicts who insist that the Robertson panel rejected perfectly good evidence for UFOs, and proposed debunking in order to hide some hideous greater secret guarded by the CIA, either have not read the minutes of the panel's meetings or are wilfully misrepresenting them. The only reasonable conclusion that can be drawn from the previously SECRET documents is that the Robertson panel agreed with the CIA that a fascination with UFOs could be exploited by an enemy, and that a flood of UFO reports could possibly distract military attention from an actual attack.

'Debunking' should take the form of greater openness and education – not a cover-up. The reasons for the CIA's subsequent 'sanitising' of the documents to remove all signs of Agency involvement in the Robertson panel and all mention of jamming the air defense system were equally straightforward.

First, the CIA was perfectly well aware of what Keyhoe and his ilk were saying and did not want to help cultivate 'a morbid national psychology' or feed any 'aura of mystery' by being seen to be involved. Second, it would have been madness to hand the Soviets the brilliant idea that they could manipulate UFO-mania to their own, possibly devastating, advantage.

Technological progress and a slow recognition of political realities made the US military and security agencies less preoccupied, in time, with the idea of a surprise Soviet nuclear attack. Their concern was so intense in 1953 partly because the generals were still fighting the previous war. The trauma of Pearl Harbor was only a dozen years in the past.

The aftermath

The Robertson panel predicted that the number of UFO reports would rise in 1953; in fact, they declined. Blue Book recorded 509 sightings for the year, with 42 (7.8 per cent) logged as 'unknowns'. In August, Ruppelt, a

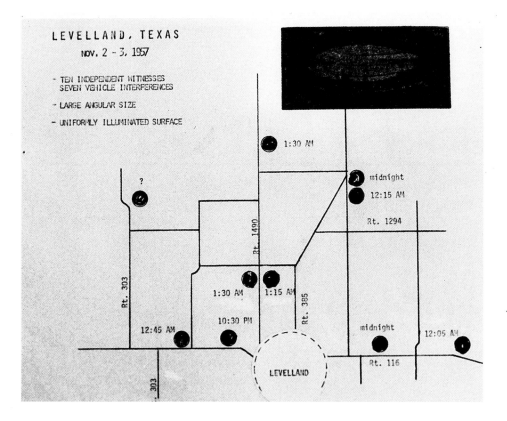

LEVELLAND, TEXAS
NOV. 2 - 3, 1957

- TEN INDEPENDENT WITNESSES
  SEVEN VEHICLE INTERFERENCES
- LARGE ANGULAR SIZE
- UNIFORMLY ILLUMINATED SURFACE

A map of Levelland, Texas, from CUFOS files shows the range of locations from which UFOs were reported on 2 November 1957. Most witnesses reported streaks of light, which USAF investigators attributed to lightning.

reserve officer, was released from active duty as the Korean war came to an end, and the Air Force handed responsibility for Blue Book to an enlisted man. At the CIA, interest in UFOs became so subdued that only a part-time analyst and file clerk stood vigil over the data. In the civilian world, however, speculation about saucers was thriving.

Keyhoe's tales

Leading the pack again was the irrepressible Donald Keyhoe. In *Flying Saucers from Outer Space*, 1953, Keyhoe continued to invent details of life in the Air Force and rewrite UFO history, particularly in his interpretation of the Washington 'siege'.

He now maintained that there were three contending groups within the Pentagon: the believers, who were convinced by the evidence; the 'silence group', who were believers too but feared mass panic if the truth were told; and 'hardheaded nonbelievers', who had not even read the evidence. On no evidence at all Keyhoe also asserted that the Robertson panel – of which he had picked up only rumors – had concluded that the saucers were 'interplanetary'. The book was to sell half a million copies.

The Air Force responded, as far as it could, by following the policy set by Robertson – reducing the number of reports by stressing the low proportion of 'unknowns'. On 5 May 1955, it

published the results of Project Stork as Blue Book's *Special Report #14*, a hefty 106 pages of text together with a further 147 pages of tables. In essence, its findings were consistent with every other study the government had initiated (and, indeed, was to authorize in the future):

It can never be absolutely proven that flying saucers do not exist... Scientifically evaluated and arranged, the data as a whole did not show any marked patterns or trends...

A... combination of factors, principally the reported maneuvers of the objects and the unavailability of supplemental data such as aircraft flight plans or balloon-launching records, resulted in the failure to identify as KNOWNS most of the reports of objects classified as UNKNOWNS...

It is emphasized that there was a complete lack of any valid evidence consisting of physical matter in any case of a reported unidentified aerial object...

It is considered to be highly improbable that any of the reports of unidentified flying objects examined in this study represent observations of technological developments outside the range of present-day scientific knowledge.

Keyhoe's third book, *The Flying Saucer Conspiracy*, was published during the same year, and it too stuck to his well-worn furrow – lots of dialogue about government censorship of UFO 'facts' – and featured an early version of the 'unexplained' disappearance of Flight 19, one of the staples of the now long-discredited Bermuda Triangle legend. One of his wilder ideas was that a series of mysterious pittings of windscreens in Canton, Ohio, were a retaliation by inhabitants of the Moon against experiments with artificial meteors.

Plumber and chicken farmer Joe Simonton shows one of the buckwheat cakes that he claimed were given him by alien visitors to his yard on 18 April 1961.

Case #7

The Case of the Alien Pancakes

EAGLE RIVER, WISCONSIN, USA

18 April 1961

Joe Simonton, a 60-year-old plumber (he objected when the press called him a 'chicken farmer') lived alone in a shack on the outskirts of Eagle River. He was about to wash up his breakfast dishes at about 11.00 a.m. when he heard a noise like 'knobby tires on a wet pavement'. Through the window he saw a silver object coming down into his yard. It was 'brighter than any chrome I had ever seen', about 12ft (3.5m) high and 30ft (9m) in diameter, shaped like two inverted bowls with exhaust pipes around its rim. Simonton went out and approached the craft as it settled, hovering just above the ground. A hatch opened, and inside he saw three clean-shaven men, each about 5ft (1.5m) tall, 'very nice looking fellows... each one very well built', who looked 'of Italian descent'. They were wearing black suits with turtleneck tops and knitted helmets.

One handed Simonton a two-handled jug, indicating he needed something to drink. Simonton went inside, filled the jug with water, and returned to the craft, where another man was now frying food on a flameless grill. Simonton noticed that the interior of the ship was 'the color of wrought iron, a sort of dull black', and contained several instrument panels. He indicated he would like to have some food in return for his water, and was given four pancakes, each about 3in (75mm) across. One occupant then closed the hatch, and the ship rose gently to 20ft (6m) from the ground. It then sped away south with a blast that bent some nearby pine trees, but without 'any sign of fire, smoke, vapor or odor that I could see or smell'. The whole encounter had lasted no longer than five minutes.

Simonton reported the event to a friend who was a county judge and member of NICAP, and who sent NICAP and the USAF a pancake each to analyze. Simonton tried a third cookie himself, and said it tasted 'like cardboard'. The analyses showed the pancakes were made from hydrogenated oil shortening, starch, wheat bran, soybean hulls and buckwheat hulls. The US Department of Health, Education and Welfare's Food and Drug Laboratory considered the pancake was 'of terrestrial origin'. Unusually, the recipe lacked salt. Dr Jacques Vallée has since pointed out that salt-free food is fairy fare, and that traditionally fairies particularly like buckwheat cakes. Vallée implies that 'fairies' and 'aliens' are aspects of the same phenomenon.

The USAF sent Major Robert Friend and Dr J. Allen Hynek to investigate. They concluded that Simonton had been eating pancakes for breakfast and had undergone a 'waking dream' so vivid that he was unable to tell it from reality. Sheriff Schroeder of Eagle River, who had known Simonton for 14 years, said he 'obviously believed the truth of what he was saying' about his unique encounter.

Keyhoe also made much of Joint Army-Navy-Air Force Publication 146, issued in December 1953. Known as JANAP-146, it set out instructions for reporting 'vital intelligence... which may indicate a possible attack', i.e. sightings of unidentified aircraft, missiles, submarines, ships, 'ground parties' and, of course, UFOs. Such reports were to be kept secret on penalty of up to 10 years in jail or a $10,000 fine.

Keyhoe ignored the common-sense and obvious intelligence value of this approach. He treated the order as if it referred exclusively to UFOs, and vilified it as part of a tentacular 'blackout' of the 'truth' about the saucers, and the men in the Moon, by his chimerical 'silence group'. [4]

In January 1957 the battle between Keyhoe and the USAF entered a new phase when Keyhoe, in a palace coup, took over an ailing UFO club in Washington DC, called the National Investigations Committee on Aerial Phenomena (NICAP).

To judge from his writings Keyhoe never lacked ego, and perhaps even had delusions of grandeur; at any rate

DEPARTMENT OF
HEALTH, EDUCATION, AND WELFARE
FOOD AND DRUG ADMINISTRATION
WASHINGTON 25, D. C.
June 8, 1961

Colonel Philip C. Evans
Aerospace Technical Intelligence Center
United States Air Force
Wright-Patterson Air Force Base
Ohio   Attn: AFCIN-4E

Dear Colonel Evans:

We have completed our examination of the material
submitted with your letter of May 5. Microscopic analysis
shows the presence of fat, starch, buckwheat hulls, wheat
bran, and soybean hulls. The material appears to be a
portion of an ordinary pancake made predominantly of
buckwheat. Bacteriological examination and measurement of
radioactivity gave results which are consistent with the
view that the article is an ordinary pancake of terrestrial
origin.

Remainder of the cake is being returned, herewith.

Sincerely yours,

M. L. Yakowitz
Assistant to the Director
Division of Administrative Review
Bureau of Enforcement

Enclosure
Pkg (remnants of cake)

Left: The HEW's straight-faced report on the Simonton pancake finds nothing extra-terrestrial about them.
Below: Project Blue Book's official record card of the Simonton event – with the witness's name unfortunately misspelled.

given a tour of their saucer near Kearney, Nebraska.

In the midst of the flurry of reports the Air Force released a review of its UFO studies over the previous 10 years, which rehearsed the usual litany of denials that the 'unknowns' were hostile, extra-terrestrial, beyond current scientific knowledge, a security threat, and repeated that 'there was no physical or material evidence; not even a minute fragment of a so-called flying saucer was ever found.' The public was not impressed.

They were probably even less impressed when Blue Book released its assessments of the major sightings on 15 November. Curtis Peebles' account reveals how the USAF shot itself in the foot by being so laconic:

The Levelland account was only 60 words long. (The Air Intelligence Information Report was nineteen pages long.) There were none of the details in the original case files and none of the reasons behind the Air Force's conclusions – just a flat statement

he now turned NICAP into a national platform for his views. To give the organization unassailable respectability, he enticed a small galaxy of retired admirals, generals and academic luminaries to sit on NICAP's board of governors (the posts were a sinecure). He bombarded the press with publicity, and watched membership grow.

Keyhoe's aim was now to persuade Congress to hold hearings on UFOs and thus force the 'truth' out into the open. The energy Keyhoe devoted to this task over the next dozen years suggests that he did indeed believe his own imaginings.

Early November 1957 saw another flap reach its climax, of which the Levelland, Texas, case has entered the UFO canon as a classic (see Case #6); other key sightings were at White Sands and Orogrande, New Mexico, and from the USS Sebago, which was

at sea 200 miles (320km) south of New Orleans. The hullabaloo was then further confounded by a certain Reinhold Schmidt, who claimed to have met a group of aliens (who were speaking in High German) and been

Joe Symington	PROJECT 10073 RECORD CARD			
1. DATE 18 Apr 61	**2. LOCATION** Eagle River, Wisconsin		**12. CONCLUSIONS** ☐ Was Balloon ☐ Probably Balloon ☐ Possibly Balloon	
3. DATE-TIME GROUP Local __1100__ GMT __18/1800Z Apr 61__	**4. TYPE OF OBSERVATION** ☒ Ground-Visual ☐ Ground-Radar ☐ Air-Visual ☐ Air-Intercept Radar		☐ Was Aircraft ☐ Probably Aircraft ☐ Possibly Aircraft	
5. PHOTOS Physical Specimen ☒ Yes (Pancake) ☐ No	**6. SOURCE** Civilian		☐ Was Astronomical ☐ Probably Astronomical ☐ Possibly Astronomical	
7. LENGTH OF OBSERVATION 5 minutes	**8. NUMBER OF OBJECTS** One	**9. COURSE** Object landed.	☐ Other __Hallucination__ ☐ Insufficient Data for Evaluation ☐ Unknown	
10. BRIEF SUMMARY OF SIGHTING Object shaped like 2 soup bowls together, as a round saucer configuration. Aprox 30 ft in diameter and 12 ft. thick at center tapering to 1 ft at rim. Brighter than chrome. Exhaust pipes 6" - 8" in diameter spaced 1 ft apart around rim. Landed and encounter with space people ensued. Object caused severe air turbulance when departing. Sounded like snow tires on pavement at high speed only louder. Jet like sound. Landed outside observers window.			**11. COMMENTS** Case received wide publicity through news media and saucer fans. Investigated by Air Force at scene and in the opinion of the investigators the witness was found to be a balanced person of good mental health and that he actually believes that the sequence of events really happened. However the inconsistancies coupled with lack of supporting evidence tend to indicate that the witness suffered an hallucination followed with delusion.	

ATIC FORM 329 (REV 26 SEP 52)

as to the cause. The two-page press release also contained a major error – the order of the White Sands sightings was reversed...[5]

Such a terse and, essentially, uninformative response smacked of arrogance and impatience. It created the impression that officials would rustle up any rational-sounding cause to dispose of a UFO experience. To many, that meant the Air Force was explaining away the reports – which in turn implied that something real lay behind them. NICAP accused Blue Book of ridiculing the witnesses. On this occasion, one can see why.

More air force blunders

The Air Force made its next public-relations gaffe on 22 January 1958, when Keyhoe faced an Air Force spokesman and arch-skeptic Dr Donald Menzel on CBS TV. Keyhoe wanted to state his erroneous version of the Robertson panel's conclusions; the Air Force objected forcefully. When, live on the air, Keyhoe departed from his agreed script, the producers faded his mike. Viewers were left with the impression that the Air Force had had him silenced.

Next came the turn of the CIA. While lobbying Congress, NICAP learned through political contacts that the CIA had convened the Robertson panel, and asked for a copy of its report. In April 1958, the CIA released an admittedly 'sanitised' version, omitting details of its own role in the meeting and its fears of Soviet manipulation of a UFO scare.

Thus, stripping UFOs of their 'aura of mystery' appeared to make no sense whatsoever. As NICAP commented in the June 1958 issue of its *UFO Investigator*: 'It seems obvious from the CIA evasion that important facts about this long hidden study are being kept from the public.'

NICAP was right, but about the wrong thing. Their convictions may have been strengthened when, after

some hopeful signs, that year the Senate Subcommittee on Government Operations together with the House Subcommittee on Atmospheric Phenomena decided against hearings, the latter on Blue Book's advice. Nonetheless, with the best of intentions, the USAF and the CIA had blundered into reinforcing the very ideas they had hoped to demolish. Perhaps because of these mistakes, the USAF ordered another study into the operations of Blue Book.

The beginning of the end

Blue Book, or at least being 'in charge' of UFOs, was an embarrassment to the Air Force, but its discomfort was partly of its own making. Blue Book had to field enquiries from press and public as well as investigate reports. At the same time its resources were being quietly reduced. First 4602 Air Intelligence Service Squadron (AISS), which had provided Blue Book with its field investigators, was disbanded in July 1957; the work was passed to 1006

AISS, but its funding was cut.

It was less a matter of cover-up than pressure on the part of the project's tiny staff that led to cursory assessments of reports and their sometimes arbitrary assignment as 'identified'. The public relations problem – USAF credibility – worsened, but still remained unresolved.

In October 1958 there was a recommendation to increase Blue Book's staff to 18 or 20. Civilian investigators were doing a faster, more effective job than the Air Force, while Keyhoe was castigated as a 'political adventurer' at the heart of the public-relations problem. No action was taken. A year later another review confronted the issue barefaced:

The program... has resulted in unfavorable publicity for the Air Force... specifically the Aerospace Technical Intelligence Center [ATIC's new title]. The Air Force needs to eliminate this costly, and to date unproductive program. Complete elimination is

A curious molar-shaped UFO that was photographed at Oak Ridge.

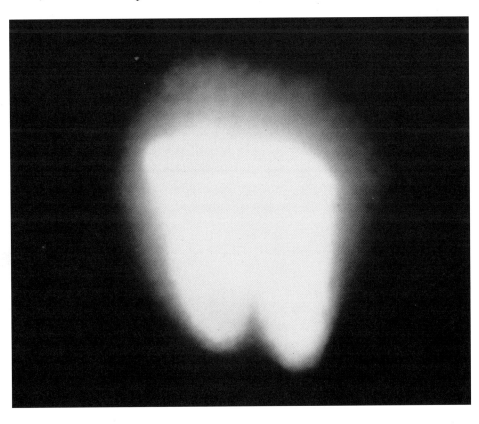

Case # 8

The Landing at Socorro

SOCORRO, NEW MEXICO, USA

24 April 1964

At about 5.45 p.m. Lonnie Zamora, on patrol in the Socorro Two State Police cruiser, gave chase to a speeding black Chevrolet. The pursuit took him south out of town. Then Zamora heard a brief roar and saw flame in the sky to his right. There was a shack containing dynamite in the vicinity, and he thought it had blown up. Zamora abandoned his chase and swung his Pontiac off the highway onto a dirt road that led over a ridge and past the shack. The blue and orange, smokeless, long and narrow flame was now descending toward the ground. Zamora drove slowly down the other side of the ridge. The noise had stopped and the flame had vanished.

He suddenly noticed 'a shiny type object to [the] south' 300–600ft (90–180m) away, below him in a gully. 'It looked,' Zamora told FBI agent J. Arthur Byrnes Jr later the same day, 'like a car turned upside down... standing on [its] radiator or trunk.' Next to the object were 'two people in white coveralls... One of these persons seemed to turn and look straight at my car and seemed startled – seemed to quickly jump somewhat.' They seemed 'normal in shape – but possibly they were small adults or large kids.' Zamora radioed Sgt Sam Chavez in Socorro, and approached on foot to within 100ft (30m) of the object. He now saw it was oval and smooth, with no windows or doors, on girder-like legs. He noted red insignia on its side, about 30in (75cm) wide. Then the roar began again, low frequency at first, rising rapidly and getting 'very loud'. The object emitted flame and kicked up dust. There was no sign of the 'persons' he had seen before.

Zamora thought the thing might explode, and ran back beyond his car to the top of the ridge. The roar stopped, and he looked back to see the UFO 'going away from me in a south-west direction... possibly 10 to 15ft [3 to 4.5m] above the ground, and it cleared the dynamite shack by about 3ft [1m].' The UFO, now traveling very fast but no longer emitting either noise or flame, rose up and sped away. It 'just cleared' a mountain in the distance and disappeared. Sgt Chavez, Zamora, FBI Agent Byrne (in Socorro on another case) and Deputy Sheriff James Lucky investigated the spot where the UFO had landed, and where the brush was still smoking. In the ground, in an asymmetrical diamond pattern they found four burn marks, and four V-shaped depressions, 1–2in (25–50mm) deep and roughly 18in (50cm) long. These corresponded to the 'legs' Zamora had seen on the craft. Five other, smaller marks nearby were labeled 'footprints'.

The case had an intriguing postscript. At about 3.00 a.m. on 26 April Orlando Gallego saw a UFO, identical to that reported by Zamora, land over 200 miles (300km) north of Socorro at La Madera, New Mexico. Gallego and his family denied all knowledge of the Socorro sighting or of Zamora. Police reportedly found evidence of burning around the site, and four dents in the ground.

---

desirable, but it should certainly be disassociated with [sic] the intelligence community where it is extremely dangerous to prestige.

ATIC tried to interest other commands in the project. Not even the Office of Public Information wanted anything to do with it. The problem rumbled on; in 1961 Blue Book came under the USAF's Foreign Technology Division as part of a general reorgani-zation. Yet another scrutiny by Colonel E.H. Wynn in April 1962 proposed closing the project and farming out responsibility for reports to individual bases. Still nothing was done. Ironically, it would be a major wave of sightings that pushed the USAF into a major reassessment of the UFO phenomenon, and decided the fate of Blue Book.

The saucers return

The great wave of the mid-1960s can be said to have opened with the curious events at Socorro, New Mexico, on 24 April 1964 (see Case #8)[6]. When Dr Hynek and two Air Force officers arrived on 28 April to investigate the matter, they discovered that Jim and Coral Lorenzen of the

Right: *A contemporary press report of Lonnie Zamora's 1964 sighting at Socorro, New Mexico. Note that Zamora at first denied seeing 'any sign of life around the object'.*

Below: *Jim and Coral Lorenzen, founders of the Aerial Phenomena Research Organization, which came to specialize in cases involving UFO occupants and abductions.*

Aerial Phenomena Research Organization (APRO) – the great rival of NICAP for the soul of ufology in the 1960s – had already interviewed the principal witnesses.

At Hynek's instigation, the USAF checked – to no avail – if an aerospace company had been privately testing a craft like the one that the chief witness, State trooper Lonnie Zamora, apparently saw. At first the USAF thought a lunar exploration module (LEM), then being developed, was responsible. But no LEM resembles what Zamora beheld, nor was one tested in the Socorro region until over a year later.

The USAF did not, however, follow up Hynek's request to trace a car driver, who had told the manager of a gas station on US Highway 85 that he had seen some kind of aircraft just south of town, in trouble and landing – and with a police car approaching it.

Publicity stunt?

Skeptics have imputed motives for a hoax to Socorro's mayor, who owned the landing site and may have been keen to attract tourists there, and have suggested that Zamora saw a plasma and imagined the rest. However, one of the most telling pieces of evidence against the reality of Zamora's story came from Felix Phillips and his wife, who were in their house, some 1000ft (300m) from the landing site.

'I WAS SCARED'
Flying Saucer Spotted By 'Reliable Witness'

By CHARLES RICHARDS
United Press International

SOCORRO, N.M. (UPI)—It's a good place for a flying saucer. Right on the edge of White Sands missile range on the wide open New Mexico desert, just 30 miles northwest of the site of the world's first atomic blast.

Socorro policeman Lonnie Zamora says he saw it, and police and military men seem inclined to believe him.

Zamora is a "very reliable witness," Army Capt. Richard T. Yolder, uprange commander of White Sands' Stallion Range, said. Holder, whose headquarters is near this central New Mexico town, was called in by local police after Zamora reported seeing the object Friday.

Deputy Sheriff James Luckie said he believes "it's something out of the ordinary, something very few have ever seen."

Ran Away

"I was scared," Zamora said. He said his experience taught him one thing: If it happens again, he will still run away like he did Friday, but he will not tell a soul about what he saw.

Zamora said he spotted an egg-shaped object on the desert about a mile south of Socorro. He denied seeing any signs of life around the object and said the machine rose and flew slowly away until it faded from sight.

He said he spotted what appeared to be a pair of white coveralls near the saucer, but could not tell if anything or anyone was in them. The object, about the height of a car but larger, appeared to be made of a shiny, aluminum-like substance, Zamora said. It flew away after he got within about 100 yards, he said.

Officers Investigate

Two investigating officers were at the scene Sunday from Kirtland Air Force Base in Albuquerque. Maj. William Connor and Sgt. David Moody used a Geiger counter to check the area, where the only evidence of an unusual visitor was a

'I TELL YA I SAW IT'--Socorro, N.M., policeman Lonnie Zamora (left) Sunday tells how he spotted an egg-shaped flying object Friday near Socorro. He said the unusual machine rose off the ground and flew slowly away as he watched. With him is Lt. David Moody, assistant UFO (unidentified flying objects) investigator of Kirtland Air Force Base in Alburqueque. Zamora is described as a "reliable witness."-- UPI TELEPHOTO.

Alabama Catholics Told To Desegregate Schools

By United Press International

Roman Catholics in Alabama today greeted with quiet acceptance the news that all handful of Negroes attending Catholic schools in the state would be desegregated next September.

Archbishop Thomas J. Toolen Sunday signaled the most sweeping integration yet of Alabama schools by announcing

the plan which would affect approximately 25,000 students.

Alabama currently has only a handful of Negroes attending integrated classes.

The order, which also affects even north Florida counties in the diocese, was contained in a pastoral letter read to each congregation Sunday at services.

Another southern racial customs Sunday sparked a walk out of the New York delegation to the Adjutants General Association convention meeting New Orleans.

A Negro member of the New York delegation, Col. Otho van Exel, was refused hotel accommodations at the all-white facility where his associates were registered. The delegation acting on orders of New York Gov. Nelson Rockefeller, pulled out of convention because of the discrimination.

Other racial developments

Union Brass Urges

George and the G-men

ADAMSKI'S CLOSE ENCOUNTERS WITH THE FBI

In May 1952, the Special Agent in Charge (SAC) of the San Diego office of the FBI wrote a confidential memo to FBI Director J. Edgar Hoover. The subject was one George Adamski who, apart from talking a lot about flying saucers, had passed some mildly favorable remarks about Russia and some uncivil ones about the USA. The FBI, ever on the watch for left-wing malcontents, checked Adamski out. On 12 January 1953 agents from the FBI and the Air Force Office of Special Investigations (AFOSI) interviewed him. At the end of the month they closed the case; they seem to have regarded Adamski as no more than a harmless nut.

George Adamski ran a four-seat burger stand in Palomar Gardens, on the southern slope of Mt Palomar, California. He described himself as a 'philosopher and teacher'; his acolytes called him 'Professor'. Adamski was convinced that the other planets of our Solar System were inhabited. On 9 October 1946, he saw what he believed to be confirmation – 'a gigantic space craft... hovering high above the mountain ridge to the south of Mount Palomar'.

Adamski began giving lectures on UFOs and extra-terrestrials and from his audiences heard rumors that flying saucers had been landing in 'various desert areas not a great drive from Mount Palomar'. In his 1953 book *Flying Saucers Have Landed*, Adamski claimed that on Thursday 20 November 1952 he himself had met a visitor from another world in the desert.

Communicating with a mixture of hand signals and telepathy, the alien said he was from the planet Venus. The Venusians were on Earth because they were concerned about radiation from atomic explosions: too many of these would destroy Earth. The saucer had not brought the Venusian directly to Earth, but had been launched from within the atmosphere by a giant 'mother ship', which Adamski had seen earlier. The craft was powered by 'magnetism'.

Asked if he believed in God, the spaceman replied yes, but observed that Venusians lived according to the laws of the Creator and not the laws of materialism as Earth people did. People from the other planets in the Solar System – all were inhabited – and from other systems too were visiting Earth. Some of their craft had crashed on Earth, shot down by 'men of this world'.

None of this exercised the FBI very much, but they were distinctly upset when a Riverside newspaper reported on 13 March 1953 that Adamski had claimed 'all his material had been cleared with the FBI and Air Force Intelligence'. Four days later FBI and AFOSI agents descended on Adamski at his home, 'severely admonished' him, watched while he mailed a letter to the paper 'correcting' its report, and extracted from him a signed statement that he would not make the claim again. The three agents witnessed the statement with their own signatures.

On 17 December, FBI and AFOSI agents were back on Adamski's doorstep, and this time 'read him the Riot Act'. He had again claimed his material had been cleared with the FBI and the USAF. This time he had concocted a document to prove it – and it brazenly sported the signatures of the G-men from his undertaking not to mention the FBI! Adamski was threatened with arrest. After this, Adamski turned the tables yet again, by implying that the FBI had tried to silence him – an obvious ploy to align himself with Donald Keyhoe's conspiracy theory. Keyhoe, who could be right about some things, had always tagged Adamski a fraud.

Adamski admitted as much himself, and he had previous experience in sailing close to the legal wind. During the Prohibition era he founded a monastery, called the Royal Order of Tibet, in Laguna Beach near Los Angeles. Naturally, this unimpeachably respectable establishment had a special dispensation to make wine for its religious rituals. 'I made enough wine for all of Southern California!' Adamski was later reported to say. 'I was making a fortune. If it hadn't been for Franklin Roosevelt ending Prohibition I wouldn't have had to get into this saucer crap.'

Right: *FBI report of George Adamski's claim that his speeches on flying saucers had been 'cleared' by the FBI and the USAF. Adamski had lifted the names of the agents on his phoney 'clearance' from a document he had earlier signed promising not to make such claims.*

Below: *Adamski receives a 'cease and desist' order from FBI and AFOSI agents. He then used the occasion as 'proof' that the government was trying to silence him.*

They saw and heard nothing.

NICAP, which had always rejected reports of UFO occupants, endorsed Zamora's account. APRO regarded the event as 'an intelligence operation' by the ufonauts. Blue Book finally classified the sighting as an 'unknown'. Hynek believed that 'a real physical event' had occurred. Zamora 'certainly must have seen something,' he said.

UFO frenzy

Saucer – or UFO – reports increased dramatically after the Zamora sighting. Blue Book recorded 562 sightings, 19 (3.4 per cent) of them 'unknowns' in 1964, and 887 in 1965, of which 16 (1.8 per cent) were unidentified. After a particularly intense flap across the Midwest in August 1965, many newspapers mocked the Air Force's skepticism – and suggested it knew something about the reality of flying saucers.

In 1966 the totals would rise to 1112 with 32 (2.9 per cent) 'unknowns'. Among the 'identifieds' was a pair of incidents that were to transform the Air Force's involvement with UFOs for good. In the wake of that alteration, public perceptions of UFOs and government interest in the phenomenon would flounder for the best part of a decade – and then harden into something altogether darker than anything Donald Keyhoe could have imagined.

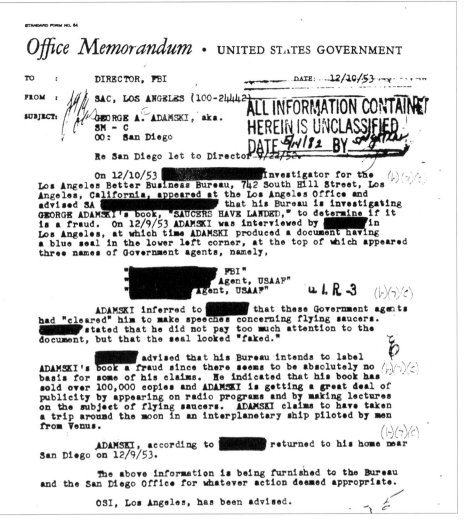

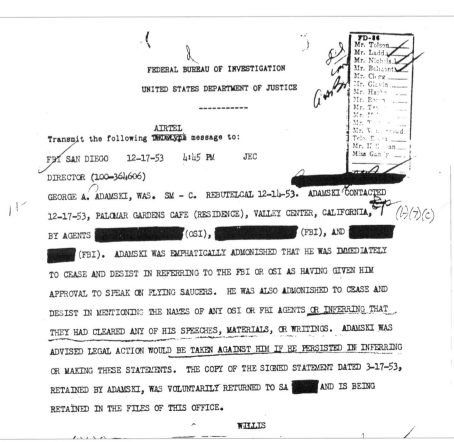

Chapter Three

MEN IN WHITE

THE CONDON INVESTIGATION
1966–1969

THE FALL OF BLUE BOOK in 1969 can be seen as a huge cataract, rather than a mere watershed, in the river of UFO history. A little upstream from the cloud of spray and broken white water that ufology was to become in the 1970s lies a broad, deep and treacherous stretch of water that represents the Condon committee's research and report.

Beyond that, two fast-running streams join the main current and cause a visible turbulence. One flowed from the Air Force; the other from the press, politicians and public. Each led by different routes to the establishment of the Condon committee. And both tributaries have the same source – Blue Book's scientific consultant, the astronomer Dr J. Allen Hynek.

From the mid-1950s, while the Air Force fretted over what to do with Blue Book, Hynek periodically tried to galvanize his employers into putting decent resources into UFO research. He had been more than dissatisfied with the way the Batelle Institute had interpreted the figures of 'unknowns' in *Special Report #14*, and believed that the phenomenon might yet yield 'scientific paydirt' if it were to be comprehensively examined.

This didn't happen. As he put it: 'Blue Book files are replete with cases labeled "Insufficient Information", whereas in many cases the proper label should have been "Insufficient Follow-up".'[1] Indeed, he felt, no case had been so exhaustively investigated that its bones were picked truly clean. And no amount of tactful goading had led to any improvement in Blue Book's procedures.

To add to that perennial professional dissatisfaction came something more personal. The Socorro case in 1964 had opened a door in his mind, leading him to question his previous blanket skepticism to occupant reports – close encounters of the third kind, as

he was to dub them. To my knowledge, Hynek could never bring himself to buy the extra-terrestrial hypothesis (I discussed this with him many times); and this was one reason why, for years, the Socorro case both puzzled and bothered him. In 1965 the whole UFO phenomenon was beginning to perplex him in a way it had not before.

A serious move

With these things on his mind, Hynek must have been delighted when Lt Col J.F. Spaulding of the USAF's Office of Information wrote to him on 13 August 1965 to raise 'the question of exploring with the National Academy of Sciences the possibility of their looking into the UFO problem'. Hynek swiftly replied that it was his 'considered opinion' that a civilian panel of scientists should be requested 'to examine the UFO problem critically for the express purpose of determining whether a major problem really exists.'[2]

Spaulding raised the same question with the Air Force's Chief Scientist

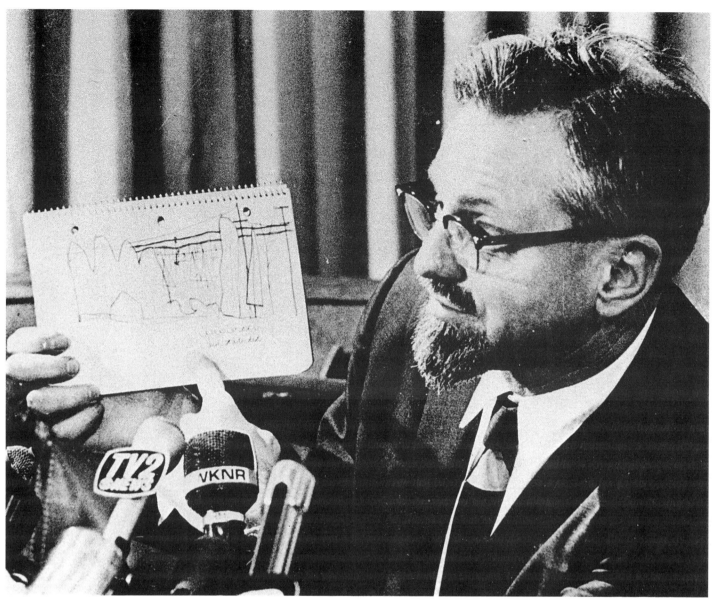

Dr J. Allen Hynek presents the media with his historic 'swamp gas' explanation for some of the UFO sightings in Michigan in March 1966.

and the Secretary of the Air Force. On 28 September, his boss, Major-General E.B. LeBailley, asked the Air Force Scientific Advisory Board to set up a 'working scientific panel' which would review Blue Book's 'resources, methods and findings.' The resulting Ad Hoc Committee, which was chaired by the optical physicist Dr Brian O'Brien, consisted of two psychologists, two electrical engineers, and an astronomer, and it met in February 1966.

Its report, which was issued in March 1966 and was classified SECRET, acknowledged the validity of the traditional Air Force arguments about UFOs, but it also recognized the meagerness of the staff alotted to Blue Book and the poor quality of much of the data in its files. Blue Book should be strengthened 'to provide opportunity for scientific investigation of selected sightings in more detail and depth than has been possible to date.'

Of the detailed recommendations, the key one was that the Air Force should contract with a number of universities to investigate 'perhaps 100 sightings a year' in depth; 'such a program might bring to light new facts of scientific value'.[3]

Cross-state confusion

What the Foreign Technology Division might have made of this initiative by the Office of Information we will never know. On 14 March, before press or public knew anything of the O'Brien report, the Michigan flap began (see Case #9). The sightings made headlines nationwide; Hynek was despatched to find a solution on 21 March. Once he had arrived in Ann Arbor, the Air Force told him to hold a news conference with his explanation on 25 March.

Two UFOs had been seen in swamps, and Hynek decided on 'a "possible" explanation I could offer to reporters' – that the Hillsdale and Dexter sightings were caused by

Case #9

Swamp Gas

HILLSDALE and DEXTER, MICHIGAN, USA
20 and 21 MARCH 1966

Spring 1966 saw a rash of UFO reports in Michigan, involving about 200 witnesses. Dr J. Allen Hynek was sent to investigate the sightings in response to public demands that the Air Force 'do something'.

Just before dawn on 14 March, according to reports made by numerous citizens and several police officers, UFOs streaked across the skies of three counties around Ann Arbor. A deputy sheriff said: 'These objects could move at fantastic speeds, make very sharp turns, dive and climb and hover with great maneuverability.' There was another display in the area three days later.

On 20 March, at 7.30 p.m., 47-year-old truck driver Frank Mannor went outside his house at Dexter, 12 miles (19km) from Ann Arbor, to hush his barking dogs. 'When I turned back I saw this meteor,' he recounted. 'It stopped and settled to the ground, then rose again. It was about half a mile away. I called my wife and my kids out, and we watched it for 15 minutes.'

Mannor and his son Ronnie then walked to within 1500ft (450m) of the UFO. 'It was sort of shaped like a pyramid, with a blue-green light on the right-hand side and on the left a white light. I didn't see no antenna or porthole. ...The white light turned to a blood red as we got close to it, and Ron said, "Look at that horrible thing." ' The 'thing' then vanished. The UFO had landed in a swamp. More than 50 other people in the neighborhood, some of them policemen, reported seeing it there.

The following day, a further 50 witnesses (12 of them police officers) saw a UFO near Ann Arbor like the one the Mannors had reported. In the evening, no less than 87 co-eds at Hillsdale College, 65 miles (100km) south-west of Ann Arbor, spent four hours watching a glowing, football-shaped UFO for over four hours as it maneuvered near the campus, looped around an airport beacon, and finally disappeared over a nearby swamp. They said the UFO 'swayed, wobbled and glowed' as it flew, and at one point headed straight for a dormitory window, then suddenly halted.

Civil defense director William Van Horn, with an assistant dean of Hillsdale College also witnessed the events. Van Horn had the UFO in sight through binoculars and was certain it was some kind of craft. It vanished as police arrived to investigate, then reappeared when they had left.

Near Dexter the next day, two police officers and three other witnesses saw a large glowing object rise from a swamp on a farm. It hovered for a while at an estimated altitude of 1000ft (300m) then departed. One witness described it as 'a domed disk' showing lights, with a 'quilted' surface and antennae below. The location suggested to Hynek his 'possible explanation' that the sightings were simply distortions of burning marsh gas.

The sightings had been trumpeted all over the media from coast to coast; around Ann Arbor, Hynek said, it had been impossible to investigate properly because emotions were running so high. One evening during his visit he was in a police cruiser when a UFO report came over the radio. Several police vehicles converged on an intersection, and officers leaped out pointing and shouting excitedly at the mystery object. Hynek, the professional astronomer, recognized it as the star Arcturus. The episode, he said, was a 'sobering demonstration' to him.

Dr Edward Uhler Condon, director of the University of Colorado's study of UFOs for the USAF. Condon's skills as a diplomat were sadly lacking in his management of the project, but his integrity as a scientist was beyond doubt.

They were echoed by Hynek, and the idea of an independent scientific review was supported time and again by House Committee members. As soon as the hearing was over, Brown ordered the USAF Chief of Staff to act on the O'Brien report. Thus had Hynek, by two complementary routes, secured the promise of his longed-for, in-depth, impartial investigation. No doubt he would rather have helped achieve it by force of argument alone.

A difficult task for the Air Force

The Air Force did not find it easy to persuade an academic institution that it should take on such a study, which was now limited to one establishment. Those approached during the summer of 1966 were leery of the subject, feeling their scientific reputations could suffer simply by being associated with it. Eventually, the University of Colorado at Boulder agreed to take the work. The contract both protected and demanded the university's scientific integrity:

The work will be conducted under conditions of strictest objectivity by investigators who, as carefully as can be determined, have no predilections or preconceived positions on the UFO question. This is essential if the public, the Congress, the Executive and the scientific community are to have confidence in the study.

The Air Force announced the agreement on 7 October 1966. The project director – whose reluctance too had to be overcome – was to be Dr Edward U. Condon. The project

burning marsh gas. He duly announced this conclusion, with heavy qualifications, ending: 'I am not making a blanket statement... I emphasize that I cannot prove in a Court of Law that this is the full explanation of these sightings.'

The press reports gave the impression he had said exactly the opposite. The media 'wanted little green men,' Hynek commented. 'I watched with horror as one reporter scanned the [press release], found the phrase "swamp gas", underlined it, and rushed for a telephone.' Press cartoonists lampooned him, and Michigan was briefly dubbed 'the Swamp Gas

State'. Even the staid *New Yorker* 'marveled' at the 'stupendous inadequacy' of the solution that Hynek had appeared to offer.[4]

A wave of public outrage at the 'insult' to the witnesses led the Michigan representatives Weston E. Vivian and the House minority leader Gerald Ford to call for a 'full-blown' congressional investigation into UFOs. The House Armed Services Committee responded with a closed session that took place on 5 April 1966. During the hearing, Secretary of the Air Force Harold D. Brown revealed the recommendations of O'Brien's Ad Hoc Committee.

would be co-ordinated by Assistant Dean Robert Low.

In many ways Professor Condon was an ideal choice for the task. His scientific credentials were beyond reproach: he had contributed to the development of radar and the atomic bomb, and he had written the standard textbook on atomic spectra. During the early 1950s his recommendation that the Atomic Energy Commission ought to be be put under civilian control had been accepted.

For this, he apparently inspired the enmity of Richard Nixon, was attacked by the House Un-American Activities Committee, and had his security clearances revoked. Surviving this onslaught, in 1958 he accused the US government of misrepresenting the effects of nuclear fallout. Condon was no yes-man, and had no need to prove his integrity.

He also had a well-developed sense of the ridiculous. As the project evolved, he was particularly entertained by stories of contactees such as George Adamski and his imitators. Then as now, jests about any aspect of their weighty subject rarely amused the UFO fraternity.

Among believers, Condon's reputation for objectivity rapidly evaporated as word spread of his irreverence with regard to the subject under consideration – which extended to practical jokes. One prank led to a reception committee representing the governor of Utah, complete with brass band, waiting several hours at the Bonneville Salt Flats racetrack for a telepathically predicted UFO landing.

On 31 July 1969, schoolgirls Patti Barr and Kathy Mahr were preparing for bed at a farm near Garrison, Iowa, and saw a large red object rise from a nearby soy bean field. Next day, the beans were wilting in the place the girls saw the object. The photograph shows where the plants died.

The Low memorandum

Contrary to the agreement with the Air Force, several members of Condon's team were already predisposed to accept the ETH. Chief among them were psychologist Dr David Saunders, who also believed implicitly in Keyhoe's cover-up theory (he thought it more plausible than the ETH), electrical engineer Dr Norman E. Levine, and Mary Lou Armstrong, the project's administrative secretary. They were also close to Donald Keyhoe, who broadly supported the study and provided it with case material from NICAP regional investigators.

Within a year the believers were openly at loggerheads with Condon, who had aggravated them with various public revelations of his growing skepticism. When on 27 September 1967 the *Rocky Mountain News* reported that he was 'disenchanted' with UFOs and was unimpressed by NICAP's contributions to the study, Keyhoe withdrew NICAP's support.

At this point the atmospheric physicist Dr James McDonald, who was another disciple of Keyhoe, became central to the way the Condon investigation would be perceived in the future. McDonald had hoped to join the project but was not invited to do so.

To compensate, and some would say to meddle, he had maintained excellent contacts with the ETHers on its staff. As a result, he had been made privy to an internal memo, written in August 1966 by Robert Low, and discovered by accident in his files in July 1967.

In McDonald's and Saunders' eyes, it appeared to compromise the integrity of the whole enterprise. McDonald has been characterized as 'an angry, aggressive, driven, manipulative and ambitious individual.'[5]

This view is not often echoed in the ufological literature, but one can see how such a picture could be drawn from his subsequent behavior toward Condon, imperfect as he too may have been.

Orange County traffic investigator Rex Heflin took this and three more photographs of an apparent UFO on 3 August 1965 near the Santa Ana Freeway in California. The Condon Report spends an exhaustive 18 pages on the case, and concludes the pictures have 'little probative value'. Later computer analysis showed they were not all taken at the same time, and confirmed a USAF opinion that the UFO was a model suspended on a string.

McDonald learned of the crisis between Condon and his staff from Saunders, and on 31 January 1968 he wrote a seven-page letter to Low, complaining about all aspects of the project. In the course of his harangue, he quoted Low's memo back to him. This document merits a certain amount of consideration.

In August 1966, musing on whether the University of Colorado would be well-advised to take on the UFO study, Low had first outlined the opinion of those academics and administrators who were against doing so:

In order to undertake such a project one has to approach it objectively. That is, one has to admit the possibility that such things as UFOs exist. It is not respectable to give serious consideration to such a possibility. Believers, in other words, remain outcasts. ...The simple act of admitting these possibilities just as possibilities puts us beyond the pale, and we would lose more in prestige in the scientific community than we could possibly gain... [One colleague] compares the situation to [psychologist Dr J.B.] *Rhine and the ESP study at Duke* [University, N. Carolina].

Low then presented the opinions of colleagues who were in favor of taking on the project, and finally gave his own view – in a passage that has become legendary in UFO circles:

The analogy with ESP, Rhine and Duke is only partially valid. The Duke study was done by believers who, after they had finished, convinced almost no one. Our study would be conducted almost exclusively by nonbelievers who, although they couldn't possibly prove a negative result, could and probably would add an impressive body of evidence that there is no reality to the observations.

The trick would be, I think, to describe the project so that, to the public, it would appear a totally objective study but, to the scientific community, would present the image of a group of nonbelievers trying their best to be objective but having an almost zero expectation of finding a saucer.

Psychology in action

Low suggested that the study should emphasize the psychological aspects of UFO reports, instead of concentrating on 'the old question of the physical reality of the saucers'; that approach might at least produce some worthwhile scholarly papers.

'It is premature to have much of an opinion,' he admitted at the time. But the university had the potential to 'carry the job off to [its] benefit' if it received 'the proper people involved' and it could successfully project 'the image that we want to present to the scientific community'.

It is worth saying that Low's memo was concerned solely with the light in which scientists and academics would view the university if it accepted the Air Force contract. Over and over he uses terms like 'image' and 'present'. It was not about the way the project

Case #10

The Trent Photographs

McMINNVILLE, OREGON, USA

11 May 1950

UFO sightings occurred frequently in the McMinnville area. Mr and Mrs Paul Trent had previously observed a number of them from their small farm, which stood near the Salmon River Highway about 10 miles (15km) south-west of town. Ufologists are usually wary of photographic evidence from 'repeater' witnesses.

Mrs Trent said she was outside feeding her rabbits at about 7.45 p.m. and saw a very bright, 'almost silvery' object silently 'sort of gliding' toward the farm. She called to her husband, who was inside the house. He didn't answer, so she ran in to get him, and to fetch a camera. She took two shots before the UFO rapidly accelerated away to the north-west. (In another account, Mrs Trent said they were both outside when the UFO appeared, and her husband took the pictures.)

Surprisingly enough, the Trents waited until the film was finished before having it processed, at first showed the pictures only to friends, and took little care of the negatives. A local banker learned of the pictures and alerted the local newspaper. The *McMinnville Telephone Register* printed them on 8 June 1950. The Trents later claimed that they were visited by two 'FBI men' some weeks afterward, but the FBI has denied any involvement or interest in the case.

Astronomer William Hartmann analyzed the shots for the Condon committee and calculated by photometry that the 'craft' was about about 0.8 miles (1.3km) from the camera in the first shot. He concluded they were probably genuine. Robert Sheaffer's later analysis found that the pictures were taken in the early morning, not the evening, and minutes rather than seconds apart. Lens smudges would account for the UFO's apparent brightness. Sheaffer speculated that the UFO was a model suspended on a string from an overhead power line that is clearly visible in the original pictures. Hartmann accepted his argument.

In the 1970s, Dr Bruce Maccabee repeated both sets of tests and concluded there was no time lag between the shots, while the object was over 0.6 miles (1km) distant, with a diameter of approximately 100ft (30m). Ground Saucer Watch digitally 'interrogated' the original negatives, found no trace of any string from which a model might have been suspended, and calculated that the object was 65–100ft (20–30m) in diameter. GSW agreed, however, that the photos were taken in the morning.

would actually be run. The word 'trick', placed in this context, is clearly used in the sense of technique, manner or mode (of presentation) – in other words, to mean 'the way round the "image" problem'.

It was not employed to imply some sort of elaborate deception, sham, deceit, shenanigan or fraud. But that was the sense that would be inferred by Saunders and his cronies on the project, and by McDonald, and by succeeding generations of wiseacre ufologists ever since.

Political football

Within days Condon fired both Saunders and Levine for leaking the memo. It was not a secret that could be kept for long. On 14 May, John G. Fuller published an article in *Look* magazine that fumed about 'Condon's and Low's prejudice' and how the project was 'being gravely mishandled', and that also quoted Low's memo in evidence.

Fuller had been fed most of his information (including the memo) from McDonald, and he had followed it up with a visit to Boulder. Both Condon and Low offered 'no comment' to questions about the unease among their team members.[6]

The accusation that Condon was wasting taxpayers' dollars naturally brought some politicians into the fray. One, Representative J. Edward Roush, had already been primed by McDonald, and he agonized to the House that the country was 'poorer – $500,000 later – not richer in information about UFOs.'

Through his contact with Roush, McDonald was able to lobby other politicians and staff members; and by June Roush was prepared to sponsor a symposium on UFOs before the House Committee on Space and Aeronautics, on which he sat. McDonald, using Roush's facilities, invited the speakers.

All but Dr Donald Menzel – who demanded to be heard after learning the names of the rest – and Dr Carl Sagan were chosen for their pro-UFO views. The testimony shows that the majority believed the saucers were real, nuts-and-bolts craft from outer space, although few – not even McDonald – were bold enough to say so outright.[7]

McDonald intended the symposium, held on 29 July, to lead to full-scale Committee hearings. They never happened. Politicians had far too many other things to think about in 1968. In Vietnam, the year had begun

with a military defeat, but media victory, for the Viet Cong's Tet Offensive. In April, Martin Luther King's assassination led to riots in 168 American cities. In June, Robert Kennedy was shot dead. On campuses nationwide, there were anti-war, anti-government, virtually anti-parent demonstrations, some tantamount to riots. Reflecting the riven, inward-looking state of the USA, the Air Force recorded only 375 UFO sightings in 1968, the lowest since 1951.

It is difficult to tell whether McDonald's campaign to discredit the Condon study arose from disappointment or spite that he was not invited to join it (or even to lead it), or if it was simply the product of his obsessive belief in UFO reality and the ETH; which in turn led to his misunderstanding of the Low memo. Whatever his motives, McDonald largely succeeded in raising several doubts about Condon's probity. The

long-term effects of his machinations were manifold.

The Condon myth

James McDonald managed to create an indelible impression (soon reinforced by David Saunders' book, *UFOs? Yes!*, published in December 1968) that the Low memorandum had dictated the attitude and outcome of the Condon study.

In fact, as Condon wrote in his report, the memo was never more than a rumination on 'the University of Colorado and its standing in the university world. ...It had nothing to do with [Low's] personal outlook on the UFO question'. Condon himself had never heard of it, until McDonald quoted it to Low.

But its assessment, and the factionalism that divided Condon's staff, make clear that the USAF's demand for 'strictest objectivity by investiga-

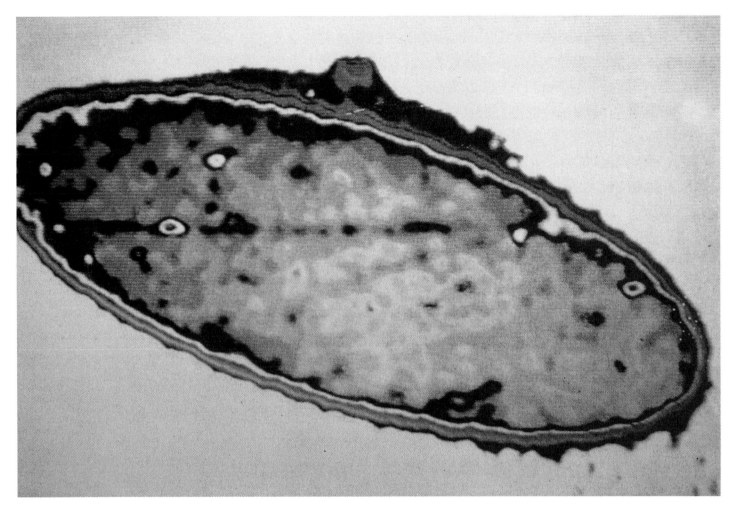

Left: *One of the 'classic' photographs taken by either Mr or Mrs Paul Trent in May 1950. The uncropped picture clearly shows a power line from which a model could conceivably have been hung, but computer analysis showed no evidence of a string or wire attached to the object.*

Above: *A computer-enhanced version of the other Trent photograph. The color-coding technique makes details of light and shade in the picture easier to read, and here shows the object has a flat bottom.*

tors who... have no predilections or preconceived positions on the UFO question' was, in reality, impossible to fulfill. Some kind of tension was bound to plague such a project, because there could hardly have existed a soul in the land who did not have an opinion – or predilection – of some kind about the existence of flying saucers.

As Low was aware, most members of the scientific community in 1966 looked askance at UFOs, and even more so at UFO beliefs – just as they do today. Condon was above all a scientist, and he intuitively understood that the ultimate expression of faith in the interplanetary nature of flying saucers lay at the contactee or 'crackpot' end of the UFO phenomenon.

To him, a single thread ran from ET saucers to contactees. On the other hand, McDonald (like Keyhoe) thought contactees could, and should, be detached from 'real' UFOs. As he wrote to Low, he thought 'crackpots constitute part of the noise that can be filtered out easily and effectively' from the rest of the phenomenon.

Unfortunately, McDonald's argument won't survive scrutiny. The contactee delusion (hoaxers aside) is only the psychopathic version of the hiatus in logic that produces the ETH. It does not follow from an inexplica-ble sighting of an unidentified entity in the sky that the object perceived is from outer space, is technologically advanced, and/or is under intelligent control. All these 'conclusions' are really presumptions, and are logically and scientifically indefensible. A truly scientific approach would say: First catch your object; then we can investigate its qualities. Until then, all we can say from the evidence is that a UFO is just – an unidentified flying object.

No hard evidence

No object was ever forthcoming; only reports of objects. Time and again the reports – some of elaborate and intricate devices – turned out to describe misperceived natural phenomena and other usual suspects, transmogrified into something wondrous by the mind of the witness (see Case #15). It was (it still is) entirely reasonable to judge that if 95 per cent of sightings were

explicable, as they were, then the remaining five per cent probably represented more of the same. This is the same principle by which scientists judge the result of a scientific experiment to be valid as long as 95 per cent (or more) of the data is consistent.

In light of this, we might note here that Allen Hynek's treatment of the statistics in *Special Report #14* was somewhat cavalier. Hynek claimed the report's conclusions were invalid, because 22 per cent of the reported 2199 sightings analyzed were 'unknowns'.[8] In cold fact, only 213 reports were classed as 'excellent', and of these only 71 cases – a paltry 3.23 per cent of all the reports – remained unidentified. It is tendentious to make hay out of the proportion of 'unknowns' within the 'excellent' category without looking at the larger picture. Even the 435 poorest reports yielded 363 identifications.

Nevertheless, in the atmosphere of the mid-1960s, some sympathy for the ETH among project members was inevitable, however flawed, just as a 'hard' scientist like Condon was bound to be predisposed against it. Had different individuals been involved, this tension might not have grown into the unbridgeable rift it did. Condon certainly could have deployed both his sense of humor and his scientific gifts more diplomatically and more constructively, to persuade rather than to confront or mock (or more often, simply ignore) the beliefs abroad among his team.

The canard encouraged by McDonald that Condon, the University of Colorado, and according

In two frames from the Great Falls 16mm movie taken in April 1952, the twin UFOs are just visible. Even the Condon committee was not entirely sure the 'UFOs' were merely aircraft, as a number of skeptics have concluded.

Case #11

Mariana's Movie

GREAT FALLS, MONTANA, USA

15 April 1952

Nick Mariana, the general manager of the Great Falls 'Selectrics' baseball team, and his 19-year-old secretary, Virginia Raunig, were inspecting the field in the empty Legion Ball Park at about 11.25 a.m. A bright flash caught Mariana's eye, and he observed two bright silvery objects 'like two new dimes', apparently rotating, flying over the town at an estimated speed of 200–400mph (320–640km/h). He quickly ran to his car to fetch his 16mm movie camera and filmed the UFOs for 16 seconds. Raunig also saw them. Mariana thought they were about 50ft (15m) wide and about 150ft (45m) apart.

Mariana showed the film to local community groups; a member of one wrote to Blue Book, and investigators interviewed Mariana in October 1950. Blue Book's conclusion after viewing the film was that the UFOs were a pair of F-94 fighters that landed at Malmstrom AFB only minutes after the sighting. Mariana maintained both he and Rautig had seen jets in the sky after the UFOs had flown away.

In 1952, Blue Book borrowed the film again. When it was returned, Mariana said, 30 frames distinctly showing the rotation of the UFOs had been clipped from the film. The Air Force denied taking more than a single frame, which was damaged. The 1953 Robertson panel examined the film and accepted that it showed aircraft.

William Hartmann analyzed the film for the Condon study, and added a new element of mystery to Mariana's movie: he found it showed that the UFOs had a constant eliptical shape. He acknowledged there were 'several independent arguments' against the theory that the movie showed aircraft.

to some the USAF too, colluded to produce a 'negative' report has clung to the Colorado project like an unhappy specter. Naturally, it has fed the belief that the USAF – or, the emerging champion villain, the hapless CIA – has always hidden crucial data. McDonald complained openly that the project paid too little attention to 'obfuscatory' cases – that is, ones that (to him) hinted at a 'cover-up'. Condon himself said he could find no evidence of a conspiracy to silence (of course, all such avowals only prove the opposite to diehard conspiracy buffs). Most obviously, however, the number of 'unknowns' in the cases cited in the report gives the lie to the legend of a premeditated plot to shuffle awkward data under the carpet. According to

one count, only 52 per cent of the cases discussed are 'definitely' explained, a statistic that in turn has drawn the fire of skeptics.

Condon and reality

I have spent so much time on the troubles that beset the Condon committee because the legends about it have long obscured the reality, and are recited still as inexorable wisdom in countless UFO books. Saunders, and McDonald especially, seem to have been driven and blinded by their faith

A popular, unabridged edition of the Condon Report, which runs to close on 1000 pages.

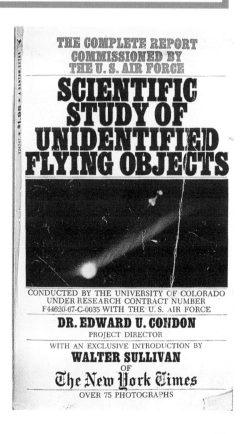

Case #12

Newhouse and the Navy

TREMONTON, UTAH, USA

2 July 1952

At 11.10 a.m. about 7 miles (11km) north of Tremonton, Navy Chief Warrant Officer and expert aerial photographer Delbert C. Newhouse, driving with his wife and two children, saw 12 'gun-metal colored' objects, each 'like two pie cans, one inverted on top of the other' flying west in changing formation. He stopped the car and shot 40ft (12m) of 16mm color film of the UFOs. They seemed huge and very high, but Newhouse could not accurately guess their size, speed, distance or altitude. He did say 'if they had been the size of B-29s they would have been at 10,000ft [3000m] altitude'. Newhouse submitted the film to Blue Book about five weeks later.

Blue Book interviewed Newhouse several times and worked on the film for several months. The USAF photography lab at Wright-Patterson AFB could not identify the objects on the film but thought they were not 'airplanes or balloons, and we don't think they are birds.'

The USAF then passed the footage to the US Navy Photographic Interpretation Laboratory (PIL), who spent about 1000 man-hours analyzing it frame by frame. They too failed to identify the objects, but believed they were internally lighted, not reflections, 'because there was no blinking while passing through 60 degrees of arc'. They calculated that if the UFOs were 10 miles (16km) from the camera, their speed would be 7560mph (12,000km/h); if 2.5 miles (4km) away, their speed would be 1890mph (3000km/h).

In January 1953, the Robertson Panel viewed the film, and another of seagulls in flight. They acknowledged PIL's enthusiasm and dedication, but objected to their conclusions on 10 grounds: (1) A semi-spherical object can readily produce a reflection of sunlight without 'blinking' through 60° of arc. (2) Although no data was available on the 'albedo' of birds or polyethylene balloons in bright sunlight, the apparent motions, sizes and brightnesses of the objects were considered strongly to suggest birds, particularly after the Panel viewed a short film showing high reflectivity of seagulls in bright sunlight. (3) PIL description of the objects as 'circular, bluish-white' in color would be expected in cases of specular reflections of sunlight from convex surfaces where the brilliance of the reflection would obscure other portions of the object. (4) There was no valid reason to attempt to relate the objects in this sighting to those seen at Great Falls. (5) The intensity change in the Tremonton lights was too great for acceptance of the PIL hypothesis that the apparent motion and changing intensity of the lights indicated extremely high speed in small orbital paths. (6) The investigators had apparently not had guidance from those familiar with UFO reports and explanations. (7) Analysis of the light intensity of the objects had been made from duplicate rather than original film. The original had a much lighter background and the objects thus appeared much less bright. (8) The method of measurement of light intensity appeared faulty because of unsuitable equipment and questionable assumptions in making averages of readings. (9) No data had been obtained on the sensitivity of Kodachrome film to light of various intensities using the same camera type at the same lens openings. (10) Hand 'jitter' series in the early part of the film were not removed from the plots of the later part of the film.

The Panel decided the objects were most likely to be birds.

After having re-examined the film for the Condon study, and watching some flocks of birds at Tremonton, William K. Hartmann concurred, remarking: 'There is no conclusive or probative evidence that the case involves extraordinary aircraft.'

After making a computer-assisted analysis in 1976, on the other hand, Ground Saucer Watch concluded the objects were disks that were about 50ft (15m) across, and 5–7miles (8–11km) distant.

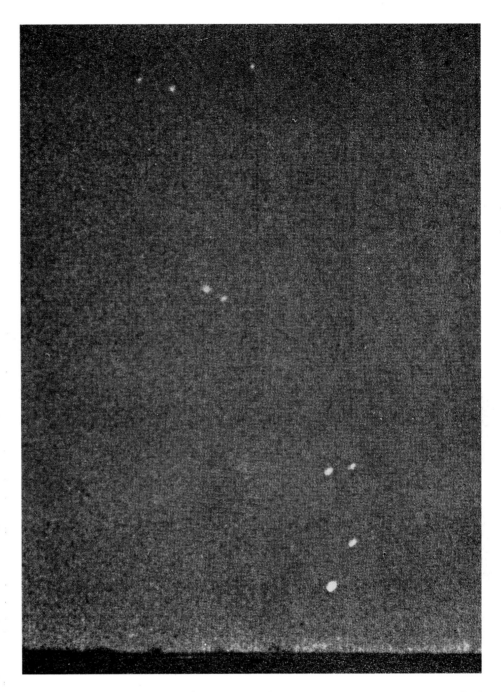

A frame from Delbert C. Newhouse's much-disputed movie of UFOs filmed on 2 July 1952 near Tremonton, Utah.

in the ETH. They reacted unscrupulously to what was a sterile dispute over those beliefs, with the baseless accusation that Condon and Low had abandoned objectivity, betrayed the principles of science, and were sabotaging the work of the Colorado study. That Condon and Low did nothing of the kind is evident to anyone who bothers to read their report. Admittedly, this is no light task.

Scientific approval

The *Final Report of the Scientific Study of Unidentified Objects* as presented to the USAF occupied three bound volumes and 1465 pages. Before delivery it was read and endorsed by the National Academy of Science. (McDonald had attempted to find out the names of the review panel so that he could lobby them, but was rebuffed.) Two paperback editions were published, both stretching to nearly 1000 pages.

One of the ritual lamentations of the ufologists down the ages has been that Condon's assessment of the UFO phenomenon, which led the report off under the title 'Conclusions and Recommendations', bore little or no relation to the overwhelming evidence of a real mystery that appeared in the following pages. I have even said this myself, publicly, in print. I now think my opinion was based on a misperception, from scanning the text instead of reading it with due attention. Condon wrote:

The emphasis of this study has been on attempting to learn from UFO reports anything that could be considered as adding to scientific knowledge. Our general conclusion is that nothing has come from the study of UFOs in the past 21 years that has added to scientific knowledge. Careful consideration of the record as it is available to us leads us to conclude that further extensive study of UFOs probably cannot be justified in the expectation that science will be advanced thereby.

The key words in that passage are 'science' and 'scientific'. Condon proceeded to write, in characteristically urbane and articulate style, an essay on the workings of what the philosopher Michael Polanyi was to call 'the republic of science'[9] – the regulation of scientific discovery by scientists. He drew the logical, and liberal, conclusion: that if scientists thought the report's findings were wrong, and had ideas for more accurate studies, 'such ideas should be supported... each individual case ought to be carefully considered on its own merits.'

Condon did not say – perhaps because to him it was so obvious that he was no longer aware of the point – that UFO sightings are not, in fact, amenable to the scientific method: they cannot be repeatedly tested in a laboratory. Only in relatively rare instances (see Case #15) can the reports be tested against a known reality. As he said further on, it was his team's task to investigate 'curious

Case #13

Venom in the Night

BENTWATERS and LAKENHEATH AFBs, near IPSWICH, SUFFOLK, ENGLAND

13 August 1956

The Royal Air Force bases at Bentwaters and Lakenheath in eastern England were both leased to the USAF. Any unknown aircraft coming from the east over the North Sea was reckoned to be potentially hostile. On the night of 13–14 August several UFOs flying at fantastic speeds were picked up by several military radars simultaneously, from 9.30 on. The final intrusion was the most dramatic.

At 10.55 p.m. ground radar at Bentwaters picked up a target coming in from the sea at 2000–4000mph (3200–6400 km/h). The UFO flew directly over the base and disappeared from the screen 30 miles (50km) to the west. At the same time a control tower operator saw a bright light streak over the airfield, and the pilot of a USAF C-47 (Dakota) 4000ft (1200m) above the base saw a fuzzy light flash between the plane and the ground. The UFO appeared on radar at Lakenheath, performing weird aerobatics. The base alerted the RAF, who scrambled a Venom NF2a fighter from RAF Waterbeach. The Venom pilot soon made visual and radar contact, and reported his guns were locked-on to the target. The UFO then seemed to flip over and come up behind the fighter, which unsuccessfully tried to shake it off. A second Venom joined the first, but found nothing. Two Lockheed T-33s returning to Bentwaters joined the hunt for 45 minutes, but also found nothing. The UFO was last seen on radar heading north at a steady 600mph (1000km/h).

The Condon committee called this 'the most puzzling and unusual case in the radar-visual files', and concluded: 'the apparently rational, intelligent behavior of the UFO suggests a mechanical device of unknown origin as the most probable explanation'.

Donald Menzel and Ernest Taves, in *The UFO Enigma* (1977) begged to differ. They noted that only one of five aircraft involved made visual or radar contact with the UFO. The Venom normally operated with a pilot and a radar operator, but on this occasion 'the pilot was alone, doubling as his own radar man – an extremely difficult, if not impossible, task'. The APS-57 radar in the aircraft did not have 'gunlock' capability. The ground radar, scanning once every 15 seconds, could not have shown the target actually circle behind the Venom, but only disappearing from the screen and reappearing behind the aircraft. Menzel and Tavez suggested the radar signal bounced off the Venom, then to the ground, and back to the antenna. The second blip was in fact a 'ghost' of the fighter, which would explain why it kept pace with it. (The pilot could see nothing in the air behind him.)

The sighting occurred during the Perseid meteor shower, which would explain the visual sightings; some of the ground radar sightings were quite possibly generated by instabilities in the equipment itself. 'Experienced radar designers, engineers, and operators, confronted with the radar data of the Bentwaters–Lakenheath case, are, to say the least, unimpressed,' wrote Menzel and Taves.

entities distinguished by lack of knowledge of what they are, rather than in terms of what they are known to be'. This was a reversal, in principle, of the starting point accepted by almost every endeavor to increase knowledge known to the history of the scientific disciplines. Nonetheless, the quality, depth and integrity of the

analyses conducted, from modern UFO experiences and UFOs in history, through plasma physics and the 'natural philosophy' of flying saucers, surpasses anything that the ufological community had produced at that time, and most of what it has had to offer since. But that was all far too subtle for passionate ufologists.

Counter-attack and endgame

Their objection to Condon's conclusion was based on the sighting reports – or rather, on the final assessments of the reports. As noted, more than half the cases the Condon study considered, in detail or in passing, could be called 'unexplained'. A more conservative estimate would put 'unknowns' in the Condon Report at about one in three cases. This was far higher than the Blue Book rate (which between 1947 and 1969 averaged 5.5 per cent and, if one removed the anomalous figures for 1952, sank to 3.58 per cent), and far higher too than civilian investigators' groups regularly achieved – and they were believers.

The ufological outrage at Condon is usually inspired by the flawed supposition that what is not explicable in the reports is extra-terrestrial. As I've tried to explain, this does not follow. It was at least a tactical error by Condon not to anticipate the believers' reaction. It would have made his report stronger if his team had examined (as O'Brien had suggested) 100 well-documented cases. If these had been 'best cases' as advised by NICAP, APRO and Blue Book, he would have deflected yet more criticism.

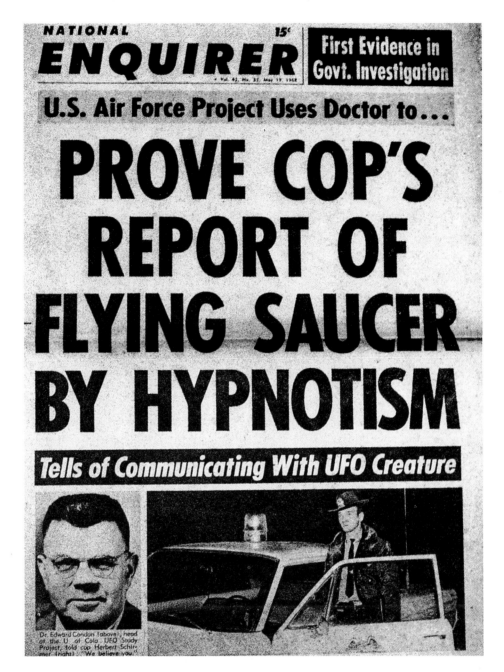

NATIONAL **ENQUIRER** 15¢

First Evidence in Govt. Investigation

U.S. Air Force Project Uses Doctor to...

PROVE COP'S REPORT OF FLYING SAUCER BY HYPNOTISM

Tells of Communicating With UFO Creature

Dr. Edward Condon (above), head of the U. of Colo. UFO Study Project, told cop Herbert Schirmer (right): "We believe you."

Donald Menzel and Ernest Taves had a sharper objection to the proportion of unknowns. All of them, they thought, were explicable, although 'some are indeed so trivial as to scarcely warrant the attempt'.[10] And in 28 crisply argued pages they demolished the 23 reports listed overtly as unexplained in the study.

Not all are as finally dismissable as these arch-skeptics would have us believe. But it is worth mentioning that their solution to one 'classic', the radar/visual reported from an RB-47 reconnaissance aircraft near Biloxi, Mississippi, in 1957, was accepted by the crew of the plane as correct. They

Case #14

The Schirmer Experiment

ASHLAND, NEBRASKA, USA
3 December 1967

Sgt Herbert Schirmer was at the junction of Highways 3 and 63 on the outskirts of Ashland when he saw a football-shaped UFO on the ground, displaying red lights and standing on a tripod. After the sighting, Schirmer realized he seemed to have 'lost' a period of about 20 minutes, and he had an inexplicable red weal on his neck.

The case came to the attention of the Condon study, and Dr Leo Sprinkle was asked to regress the officer hypnotically, in the hope of learning more about the encounter. The essential purpose of this exercise, the Condon Report notes, was 'to determine whether or not hypnotic techniques might have value in developing otherwise inaccessible information about UFOs.' Before being hypnotized Schirmer was given a battery of psychological tests. Condon did not publish the results, nor did he ever divulge them to Dr Sprinkle.

In the first session, on 13 February 1968, Dr Sprinkle felt that Schirmer – with his chief of police present, plus as many as nine members of the Condon team looking on – would not respond to hypnosis, and used a 'pendulum technique' to relax him and probe his subconscious. In this, Schirmer held a pendulum and was asked to give details of his experience ('Do you remember having an impulse to take your gun out of its holster?... Do you believe there is a relationship between the object and the engine failure?' and so on). Schirmer then silently repeated the question to himself, and the way the pendulum swung was interpreted as a 'yes', 'no', 'don't know' or 'don't want to say'. While being questioned, Schirmer said later, he felt that he was 'in direct mental contact' with the UFO entities.

Schirmer was hypnotized in the second, afternoon session, but after describing his sighting said he felt it would be wrong to say more. He was then brought out of the trance. In answer to questions from those present, Schirmer said the craft was driven by a force that could control gravity, and had taken its power from nearby electricity lines. It belonged to a 'sister ship' that was like an aircraft carrier and came from another galaxy. The occupants intended to 'prevent earth people destroying the earth'. At no time did Schirmer suggest that he had been on board the UFO or that he had been abducted.

Dr Sprinkle's report to the Condon study ended: 'I believe that the additional information [about Schirmer's sighting, provided under hypnosis] serves as a basis for explaining the apparent "loss of time"... In my opinion, the events described by Sgt Schirmer are "true" in his experience; however, I believe the present evidence does not answer [further] questions regarding the source, method and purpose of communicating the additional information.' The Condon Report's judgement was: 'Evaluation of the psychological assessment tests, the lack of any evidence, and interviews with the patrolman, left project staff with no confidence that the trooper's reported UFO experience was physically real.'

Details of Schirmer's 'abduction' emerged only when he was hypnotized at the instigation of Warren Smith, by Dr Loring G. Williams on 8 June 1968. In this session he said that entities about 4ft (1.5m) tall came from the UFO and surrounded his patrol car. Terrified, Schirmer went to draw his revolver, but was prevented by a telepathic command. One alien was holding a 'box-like thing' that covered the car with green light or gas. When another touched his neck he felt a distinct pain. He admitted he was 'the watchman of this town' and was taken into the UFO. Here he was told the craft operated by 'reversible electromagnetism'. The aliens had been watching Earth for a long time; they had several bases on Earth. Schirmer asked if the aliens kidnaped people. They replied that they 'had a program known as "breeding analysis" and some humans had been used in these experiments'. This appears to be the first overt reference in an abduction case to a genetic program conducted by aliens.

Case #15

Zond and the Airship

EASTERN STATES, USA

3 March 1968

At about 9.45 p.m. hundreds of witnesses in the eastern USA from Kentucky to Pennsylvania saw what the Condon Report called 'a majestic procession of fiery objects with sparkling golden orange tails' moving across the sky.

Witnesses varied considerably in their descriptions of the event. Of 30 reports analyzed by William K. Hartmann, 17 said the objects – two, three or more in number – were flying in formation, while 12 witnesses saw them as rocket, cigar or disk shaped, six said they changed direction, three saw windows on the 'craft', and two perceived its sharp, well-defined outline. One witness described one object pursuing another, 'as if it was making an attempt to shoot the other one down'. Another described 'a long jet airplane-looking vehicle without any wings... many windows... If there had been anybody in the UFO near the windows I would have seen them.' Another saw a fuselage 'constructed of many pieces or flat sheets' with a 'riveted-together look' with 'rather square shaped windows' that 'seemed to be lit up from the inside'. One thought the UFO was 'at about treetop level'. Another tried to communicate with the UFO by signaling in Morse with her flashlight.

The 'UFO' was in fact already identified to those in the know. On that day TASS, the Soviet news agency, had announced that the spacecraft Zond IV had been placed in a low 'parking orbit' and would then be launched further into space. The attempt to move Zond IV failed, and it fell back to Earth. The flaming debris of Zond IV's re-entry was what the witnesses were reporting.

Hartmann used these reports and similar misperceptions of other known causes of UFO events to illustrate how witnesses inject prior conceptions into their experiences. He noted that the longest and most detailed reports received by the Condon study were also the least accurate, which he ascribed to an 'excitedness effect'. He also identified an 'airship effect', which 'causes some observers to conceive of a shape surrounding light sources.' In particular Hartmann observed that about a quarter of the reports would suggest a spacecraft re-entry to anyone familiar with such an event, while another quarter were misleading. The remainder were 'insufficiently detailed to be diagnostic'. A reporter or investigator 'coming upon the case in innocence' would find it hard to tell the accurate from the inaccurate reports. To show how interpretations might differ, Hartmann offered two parallel accounts of the event, one written for saucer believers, the other by 'a more sober investigator'. Hartmann concluded that the 'airship effect' had seized the pilots Chiles and Whitted during their famous sighting of 1948 (see Chapter One), creating an impression of a structured craft when a fireball flashed by their aircraft.

note that Nick Mariana, photographer of the Great Falls, Montana, UFOs (see Case #11) was a journalism graduate and 'publicity-minded', and find it remarkable that the two USAF jets in the air at the time of the sighting detected no UFOs. They disposed effectively too of several claimed sightings by astronauts that Condon's team had failed to explain.

As perhaps the fattest 'government file' on UFOs ever produced, the Condon report was a landmark in ufology. Its careful arguments were, sadly, ignored for the most part for the sake of some ill-founded gibing and scoffing, but it ended the USAF's official, overt interest in flying saucers. On 17 December 1969, Secretary of the Air Force Robert C. Seamans Jr announced the closure of Blue Book.

The reaction of ufologists was almost one of relief. NICAP said, as if Condon had never issued his report:

'UFOs can now be given the serious scientific attention they require, free from military considerations.' The organization told the *New York Times* that the Air Force decision opened the way for 'a fresh look at the UFO problem'. It did. The 1970s would see a free-for-all among ufologists vying for the most intriguing way to account for the phenomenon. It also saw the uncovering of some intriguing government files.

Chapter Four

MUTILATING THE EVIDENCE

DISINFORMATION, MISINFORMATION, MISPERCEPTIONS AND HOAXES

1969–1982

WITH THE CLOSURE of Blue Book, ufology was, so to speak, left to its own devices. Looked at from one angle, the following decade appears to be a chaotic, directionless mess – a broiling pool in the river of history into which ufology crashed after being damned by the Condon Report.

From this disarray the study of UFOs only slowly recovered, and eventually re-emerged whole, if very different, in the 1980s. From another point of view the 1970s was the most refreshing decade in the history of ufology, as a fine spray of new ideas sparkled on all sides. And while many of their authors were skeptical of the

---

A mutilated cow found at Morrill farm, Piermont, New Hampshire, on 27 September 1978. Such 'mysteriously' disfigured animals were found over about a third of the area of the continental USA in the 1970s, but especially in the Southwest. The cattle 'mutes' soon featured in a host of anti-government conspiracy theories.

---

traditional ETHers' approach, none dismissed the idea that UFOs were a mystery of some kind, whether that mystery was social, psychological, paranormal, political, geological or technological in origin.

From yet a third angle, the chaos and the ferment of ideas were facets of the same thing.

The long shadow of the Air Force in its aspect of Giant Despair had gone: there was no one to wag a stern finger and tell unruly ufologists that their quest was futile. Which left ufologists not so much grieving after Condon's destruction of the ETH, as rejoicing and ready to come out to play in the sun. Most of those doing the playing were also born after World War II, and were no respecters of authority or 'the older generation' and its outmoded antagonisms.

They were not only free of the Air Force. Donald Keyhoe, the leading propagandist against the government, and the chief evangelist of the ETH, had left the scene as well. He had been ousted from NICAP in 1969, just days

before Blue Book closed, for financial mismanagement. In 1971, James McDonald shot himself with a .38 pistol. Some have implied that this tragedy was connected with McDonald's interest in flying saucers, but the real causes were entirely personal. Without these two overbearing figures trying to keep them on another kind of straight and narrow path, the new ufologists would be able to feel entirely free of the stale animosities of the past.

J. Allen Hynek became the undisputed leader – or father-figure – of ufology. A courteous, considerate and thoughtful man, his trusting nature could, it is true, sometimes lead him into gullibility. But for the next 15 years Hynek stood for tolerance and restraint in ufology.

Power and corruption

For the first half of the 1970s, the activities of the US government, whether in the shape of the USAF, the CIA, the FBI or some more shadowy

Astrophysicist J. Allen Hynek parted company with the USAF when Blue Book closed. In 1973, he founded the Center for UFO Studies, based in Chicago. Hynek's endorsement of a UFO case was widely regarded as the ultimate seal of approval within ufology.

for so little; while the war itself ground relentlessly on. A year later, President Richard Nixon was daily losing credibility over his part in the Watergate affair; and within eight months he had resigned to avoid impeachment.

America's despair

Americans savored a profound disillusionment with their institutions, and with their leaders in particular. By the middle of the 1970s it seemed that everything of importance that those leaders had done during recent years, much of it in the names of democracy and the American people, had been hidden or had been lied about, from the Gulf of Tonkin incident that first took US troops to Vietnam to the bombing and invasion of Cambodia – and far beyond.

The feeling that power had gone frighteningly out of control at every level of government was deepened by the exposure – and the sheer scale – of the CIA's history of illegal activities. The revelations began in 1973 with the publication of Victor Marchetti's *The CIA and the Cult of Intelligence*, and from 1974 became a veritable flood as Frank Church's Senate investigation took off.

CIA wrongdoing ran from illegal domestic surveillance to horrific mind-control experiments involving LSD, brain surgery, hypnosis, and dubious sexual practices. One CIA-funded researcher had had the brilliant idea of 'locking someone in a light-proof, soundproof box indefinitely –

agency, were of little interest in the new debate that was taking place about the real meaning of UFOs.

By the middle of the decade, however, a quartet of notions had begun to crystallize. During the 1980s they would contribute to a new consensus about both the saucers and the government. They were: a growing acceptance of abduction claims; a cluster of beliefs about some ostensibly mysterious mutilations of livestock; a revival of stories about crashed flying saucers; and a new conviction that whatever the government told the public about UFOs, it was all a pack of lies.

Several factors contributed to this gloomy view of government. The major one was the war in Southeast Asia, a war that shattered the cohesion of American society as thoroughly as it destroyed the lives of many of the combatants. Few of the draftees who fought it understood why they were fighting and, to judge from the secret 'Pentagon Papers', leaked in 1971, neither did the US government.

The Paris Peace Agreement of January 1973, which finally extricated American troops from the battlefields, brought no sense of victory, or even relief. There was rather a feeling of terrible waste, that so many had died

to see what would happen.'[1] Happily, the proposal was turned down. But it was shocking enough that CIA operatives had entertained such an idea at all.

The bitterness and cynicism bred by these disclosures, by the defeat in Vietnam and by the Watergate crisis are vital keys to understanding the development of mainstream ufology in the 1970s and 1980s. And it is not hard to see why the CIA was always voted the prime mover in every cover-up and conspiracy theory that followed, whether it involved assassinations, drug-running, the Mafia – or UFOs and aliens.

Klass act

Without the Air Force to throw cold water on the extremes of UFO belief, the subject attracted a number of severely rational critics like moths to a flame. The flap of 1973 – the last in UFO history – produced two notable cases that drew the attention of aviation journalist Philip J. Klass, who was taking over the mantle of debunker-in-chief from Donald Menzel. While both cases have since become classics in the annals of the believers, Klass has remained adamant that one was a hoax and that the other has a more prosaic explanation.

On 11 October 1973, Charles E. Hickson, aged 45, and Calvin R. Parker Jr, aged 19, were spending the evening fishing off the pier of the abandoned Shaupeter shipyard in Pascagoula, Mississippi. At about 9.00

Charlie Hickson's sketch of one of the strange, lobster–clawed, elephant–skinned creatures that abducted him in 1973. No other abductees have reported such features among aliens, although the case, and J. Allen Hynek's limited acceptance of it, helped to make abduction claims acceptable within mainstream ufology.

p.m. Hickson turned to get fresh bait, and heard a 'zipping sound'.

Hovering close to the ground nearby, Hickson said, was an egg-shaped blue-gray craft. Three small creatures with gray, wrinkled skin and pincers for hands floated out of it, gathered up the two fishermen and

floated them into the craft. Hickson then found himself suspended in a brightly-lit room while a free-floating object resembling a gigantic eye moved back and forth above his body, as if examining it.

After 20 minutes or so, the pair were floated back to the pier. Hickson

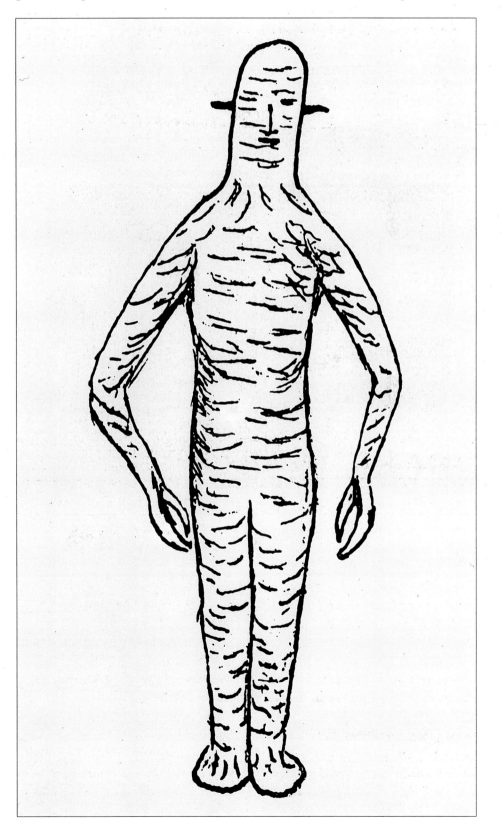

landed on his feet. The UFO vanished 'in less than a second'.

When the two men reported their experience to the sheriff's office, the interview was taped. The pair were then left alone while, unknown to them, the recording continued. Their agitated discussion convinced the law officers that they had told the truth. The following day the two men were medically examined at Keesler AFB at Biloxi; no radiation or other physical problems were found. Shortly afterward, Parker was hospitalized with a nervous breakdown.

In New Orleans on 30 October, Hickson passed a polygraph test. But

then his story began to come apart. His accounts of the size of the UFO and the time of its arrival changed from interview to interview, as did his description of the aliens' features.

A month after the incident, he claimed a serious eye injury, caused by the lights in the UFO, had troubled him for days. No injury had been detected by the USAF doctors. Klass discovered that the New Orleans polygraph operator was both inexperienced and unqualified. Neither drivers nor a bridge attendant on the busy US Route 90 near the pier where the abduction allegedly occurred saw anything unusual at the

time. And Hickson was in serious financial difficulty, having filed for bankruptcy on 6 July, and needed funds. He and Parker soon signed a local attorney to sell their story, hoping for a million-dollar deal.[2]

Hynek's analysis

APRO endorsed the account. Hynek contented himself with observing that the men had unquestionably had a 'very terrifying experience'. This cautious remark undoubtedly helped to make abduction claims respectable to many who might otherwise have ignored them. The USAF stuck to its post-Blue Book guns, and rebuffed all attempts to involve it in evaluating the story, declaring nothing had taken place 'to jeopardize national security'.

Likewise, the US Army took little interest in an encounter, a week later, between a Reserve medical unit's Bell Huey helicopter and a UFO near Mansfield, Ohio (see Case #16). Klass was sure that the object was a fireball from the seasonal Orionid meteor shower, then at its peak. There were some odd aspects to the case. While the UFO was overhead, the chopper apparently rose some 1800ft (550m) although its pitch controls were still down; there was a 10-minute radio blackout; and the UFO had shone a green beam into the cabin.

Klass concluded that in the stress of the encounter (which was undoubtedly unnerving) the pilot had instinctively and unconsciously pulled out of a 2000ft (600m) per second dive to avoid hitting the ground, by

Veteran aviation journalist Philip J. Klass, who in the 1970s became ufology's foremost critic. Believers appear to resent the way Klass's minute dissections of their favorite cases tend to discredit them, and have often simply ignored his findings when writing ufological history.

Case #16

A Helicopter in Ohio

Near MANSFIELD, OHIO, USA

18 October 1973

Captain Lawrence J. Coyne was in command of US Army Reserve Bell UH-1 ('Huey') helicopter 68-15444 on a return flight at night from Cleveland to Columbus, Ohio. Co-pilot First Sgt A.D. Jezzi was at the controls. Also on board were crew chief Staff Sgt Robert Yanacsek and the flight medic, Staff Sgt John Healey. Just after 11.00 p.m., the Huey was flying at 2500ft (760m) on a heading of 30 degrees.

Yanacsek then reported that a red light was running parallel to the aircraft to the east. Moments later he yelled that it had turned and was on a collision course with the Huey, flying at perhaps 625mph (1000km/h). Coyne, thinking it was a military jet, took the controls and went into a power dive to 1700ft (520m). Coyne was then amazed to see the altimeter was registering an altitude of 3500ft (1050m), although his collective pitch control remained fully 'down'. Next, the object stopped and hovered over the chopper. A beam of green light swung from the UFO and lit up the Huey's interior. Then the object slowly continued on west until it had passed Mansfield airport, seven miles (11km) away, when it accelerated sharply and then turned onto a northwest heading. Attempts to raise Mansfield by radio failed: both the UHF and the VHF channels on the Huey's radio were dead until about 10 minutes after the encounter.

then only some 400ft (120m) below. The same stress had probably caused the radio operator to change frequencies too quickly for the relatively old set to respond to Mansfield's signal, and the aircraft was anyway too near the ground to pick up other control towers (as the pilot himself confirmed in a later experiment). The 'green beam' was the fireball seen through the green plexiglass of the Huey's canopy. For Klass, the case was closed, but the helicopter's crew shared the *National Enquirer's* annual $5000 prize for the 'best' UFO account of 1973.[3]

The rise of the mutes

For the Army, the Mansfield case never even opened. But 1973 saw the first in a long wave of events that dragged in a government agency that had scarcely looked at UFO reports since the early days of the phenomenon – the FBI.

In spring 1973 the first reports of apparently mysterious animal mutilations were garnered from Minnesota, South Dakota, Iowa, Kansas, Nebraska, and southern border states. In Iowa, Federal Attorney Allen Danielson asked the FBI to investigate, but the Bureau agreed only to 'co-operate' with local agencies. More reports came in from the prairie states in

What the crew of a US Army Reserve helicopter saw hovering over them on 18 October 1973. Believers point out that if it was really a fireball, as claimed by skeptics, it traveled unusually slowly. Skeptics reply that time seems to slow down in a crisis, and suggest the crew's perception was distorted by fear and surprise.

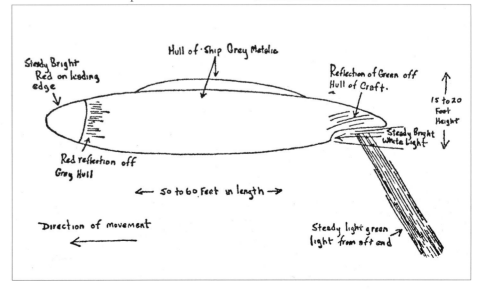

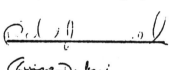

DISPOSITION FORM

For use of this form, see AR 340-15; the proponent agency is The Adjutant General's Office.

ERENCE OR OFFICE SYMBOL	SUBJECT
	Near Midair Collision with UFO Report

Commander
83D USARCOM
ATTN: AHRCCG
Columbus Support Facility
Columbus, Ohio 43215

FROM Flight Operations Off
USAR Flight Facility
Cleveland Hopkins Airport
Cleveland, Ohio 44135

DATE 23 Nov 73   CMT 1

1. On 18 October 1973 at 2305 hours in the vicinity of Mansfield, Ohio, Army Helicopter 68-15444 assigned to Cleveland USARFFAC encountered a near midair collision with a unidentified flying object. Four crewmembers assigned to the Cleveland USARFFAC for flying proficiency were on AFTP status when this incident occurred. The flight crew assigned was CPT Lawrence J. Coyne, Pilot in Command, 1LT Arrigo Jezzi, Copilot, SSG Robert Yanacsek, Crew Chief, SSG John Healey, Flight Medic. All the above personnel are members of the 316th MED DET(HEL AMB), a tenant reserve unit of the Cleveland USARFFAC.

2. The reported incident happened as follows: Army Helicopter 68-15444 was returning from Columbus, Ohio to Cleveland, Ohio and at 2305 hours east, south east of Mansfield Airport in the vicinity of Mansfield, Ohio while flying at an altitude of 2500 feet and on a heading of 030 degrees, SSG Yanacsek observed a red light on the east horizon, 90 degrees off the flight path of the helicopter. Approximately 30 seconds later, SSG Yanacsek indicated the object was converging on the helicopter at the same altitude at a airspeed in excess of 600 knots and on a midair collision heading. Cpt Coyne observed the converging object, took over the controls of the aircraft and initiated a power descent from 2500 feet to 1700 feet to avoid impact with the object. A radio call was initiated to Mansfield Tower who acknowledged the helicopter and was asked by CPT Coyne if there were any high performance aircraft flying in the vicinity of Mansfield Airport however there was no response received from the tower. The crew expected impact from the object instead, the object was observed to hesitate momentarily over the helicopter and then slowly continued on a westerly course accelerating at a high rate of speed, clear west of Mansfield Airport then turn 45 degree heading to the Northwest. Cpt Coyne indicated the altimeter read a 1000 fpm climb and read 3500 feet with the collective in the full down position. The aircraft was returned to 2500 feet by CPT Coyne and flown back to Cleveland, Ohio. The Flight plan was closed and the FAA Flight Service Station notified of the incident. The FSS told CPT Coyne to report the incident to the FAA GADO office a Cleveland Hopkins Airport MR. Porter, 83d USARCOM was notified of the incident at 1530 hours on 19 Oct 73.

3. This report has been read and attested to by the crewmembers of the aircraft with signatures acknowledgeing this report.

FORM 2496

REPLACES DD FORM 96, EXISTING SUPPLIES OF WHICH WILL BE ISSUED AND USED UNTIL 1 FEB 63 UNLESS SOONER EXHAUSTED. ☆U.S. GPO: 1972 - 473-663 P.O. 1

239

The Ohio helicopter crew's official report of their sighting to their unit commander.

1974. With them came accounts of unmarked, often black, helicopters hovering near the carcasses (soon dubbed 'mutes') and stories that the creatures had been drained of blood. Typically, the stomach, eyes (or just one eye), tongue, sexual organs, udder and rectum were missing, cut away with 'surgical precision'.

By the summer of the following year, the phenomenon had accrued all the elements that were to cling to it thereafter. Ranchers were shooting at helicopters venturing over their land, as rumors spread that the government was testing biochemical weapons on their livestock.

The *Colorado Springs Gazette Telegraph* claimed that an immensely wealthy, nationwide Satanic cult was responsible. It became part of the lore that coyotes and even domestic dogs, both notorious scavengers, would refuse to approach the carcasses. In Colorado, cattlemen's organizations offered rewards totaling $11,000 for the arrest and conviction of the cul-

prits. And UFOs were now reported appearing with disturbing frequency in conjunction with the discovery of mutilated animals, mostly cattle but also including horses, goats, sheep and even cats.[4]

The connexion with UFOs was sometimes somewhat tenuous, although the reported experiences may have been genuinely anomalous. Sheriff Richards of Cochran County, Colorado, told researcher Linda Moulton Howe: 'The people who have been reporting this all tell the same story. [The UFO] is about as wide as a two-lane highway, round, and looks the color of the sun when it is going down and has got a blue glow round it. When these people see this thing, in two or three days we hear about some cows that have been mutilated.' Almost anything can happen within two or three days of anything else, but that does not forge a link between them.

Steering in a new direction

Sheriff Richards also checked the ground around a mutilated steer with a Geiger counter, got a low reading, and thought it mysterious. Just as the self-appointed mute experts were too ignorant of rural life to know that coyotes don't bother to go near carcasses that have nothing left to eat on them, Richards seemed unaware of the existence of natural background levels of radiation. 'Where did it come from in the first place?' he asked.[5]

By 1979 all kinds of strange assertions had been made about the mutes. Among the weirdest was the claim that 'VX toxin', a biological weapon allegedly designed to kill only Orientals and intended to be used in Vietnam, was being secretly tested on range cattle, to sidestep a 1969 international ban on research into offensive biochemical weapons. One theory said the mystery choppers were looking

Senator Harrison Schmitt of New Mexico asks the Department of Justice to put the FBI on the trail of mutilated cattle. A personal request for action from the Attorney General noted that the Senator 'is a friend of ours'. Politics may have had more to do with official investigation of the apparent mute epidemic than practical need.

for the effects of seepages from nuclear and biological weapons tests and environmental pollution.

A related claim was that oil companies were maiming the animals in a clandestine (and economical) prospecting program; it was said that traces of oil or gas, taken in with their food, could be found in their carcasses. Some mutes were said to show the symptoms of having been dropped from a considerable height – from a helicopter, it was inferred.

Mutes were now turning up in northern New Mexico, especially around Dulce, and there was a wave in Arkansas in 1978 and 1979. Harrison Burgess, a former Sandia National Laboratories employee, had calculated that from 1973 to 1979, some 10,000 animals had been mutilated.

Various psychics had pronounced on the phenomenon. So had New Mexico Senator Harrison Schmitt, who on 21 December 1978 wrote to the US Attorney General Griffin Bell to ask the Justice Department – which meant the FBI – to investigate the matter of the mutes.

On 24 April 1979, the Law Enforcement Assistance Administration granted $50,000 to the District Attorney, First Judicial District of New Mexico (in Santa Fe), to fund an investigation into whether a crime had been committed. Kenneth M. Rommel, a 28-year veteran of the FBI, retired to direct the enquiry.

On 6 March, the Albuquerque FBI office had begun a probe of mutes reportedly found on the Santa Clara

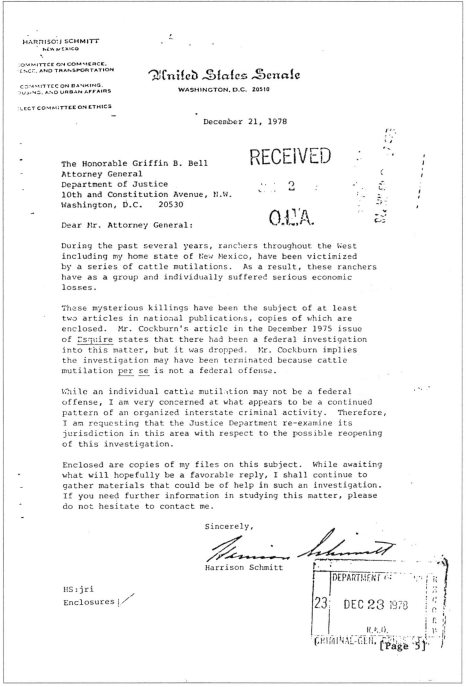

Pueblo and Jicarilla Apache reservations in New Mexico. These were the only mute cases that the FBI felt were within their jurisdiction to consider.

The investigator's report

The FBI discovered that the law officers on the spot, along with the New Mexico Livestock Board, had already established that the animals that had been found dead on the Santa Clara and Jicarilla reservations had been the victims of predators. There were no signs on the animals that anything

inexplicable, unnatural or abnormal had ever occurred.

In January 1980 Kenneth Rommel delivered his 297-page report, *Operation Animal Mutilation*, to the District Attorney in Santa Fe. He too had found nothing to suggest that anything besides natural predators, scavengers and decomposition was responsible. The prime symptom of a mutilation, the striking neatness of the incisions, was not strange; only a microscope revealed the difference between the work of an animal and that of a scalpel. Rommel actually asked a Santa Fe surgeon what was meant by 'surgical precision'. The distinguished doctor replied: 'Well, it means I try to cut in a straight line.'

Lack of blood in the bodies resulted from the blood draining to the bottom of the carcass, coagulating and drying out. Claims that the mutes

---

A daylight disk photographed by Warren Smith on 3 July 1967. Smith and two companions were in the foothills of the Rocky Mountains, southwest of Calgary, Alberta, returning from a weekend prospecting trip. J. Allen Hynek and the Royal Canadian Air Force Defense Photographic Interpretation Center considered the picture genuine. Skeptics might note the difference in sharpness between the disk's image and the images in the background.

---

showed signs of being dropped proved groundless. Only the eye facing upward – the one exposed to scavengers – was removed.

'Flakes' believed to have come from a UFO seen coincidentally with a mute turned out to be house paint. It was impossible for traces of oil or gas, 3000–5000ft (900–1500m) below ground, to enter the animals' food chain. Many ranchers, Rommel found, reported carcasses as 'mutes' even though they showed none of the alleged symptoms. They could not, in fact, tell a naturally savaged animal from an unnatural one.

Other parts of the mute legend took longer to be dismantled. In a classic study, Daniel Kagan and Ian Summers showed that the 'VX toxin' story had been invented by a petty criminal and con-man (apart from

being scientifically absurd, which should have been obvious). They asked another obvious question: why would the government not simply buy cattle on which to test biochemical weapons? As for the numbers involved, Kagan and Summers found the figure of 10,000 mutes had been produced by speculation and guestimates, and over-represented the dead animals by at least 75 per cent. [6]

Mutes, I might add, were found in an area covering about one third of the continental USA. Even natural predators were therefore not exactly gorging themselves by consuming only 500 carcasses a year over such a vast expanse of land. It's also worth pointing out here something else the skeptics failed to note: the damage done to the mutes was highly variable. This should have made it clear that no

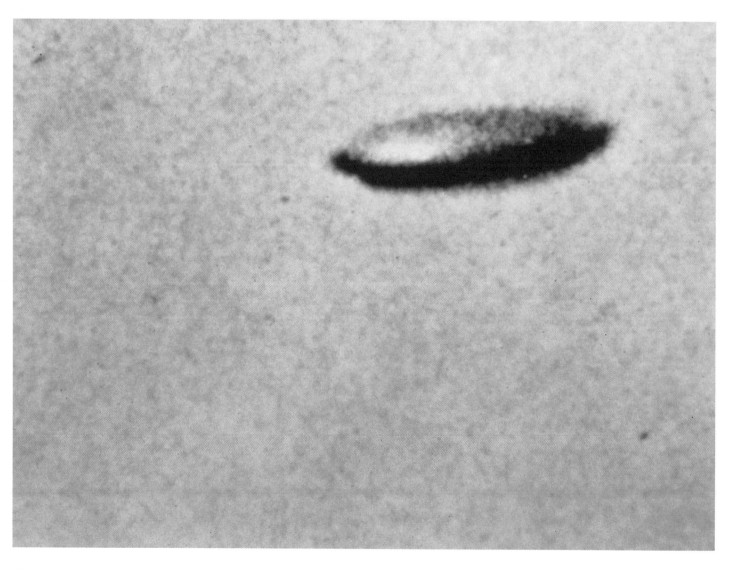

Kenneth Rommel, Director of the official Animal Mutilations Project, requests analysis of 'flakes' associated with a UFO sighting allegedly connected to cattle mutilations.

scientific agenda lay hidden behind the phenomenon.

Kagan and Summers found not one mute report from large ranching operations. Those 'affected' were small, part-time ranchers – relatively powerless people who also might feel most vulnerable to 'big government', giant corporations and the military, the FBI and the CIA, which were then under attack from all quarters.

The mute legends, Kagan and Summers argued, were really a means to vent distrust and distaste for these demons of the era. The point was illustrated by the reception the mute believers gave Rommel's report. There were ritual cries of cover-up, of course, but Rommel was also libeled as 'mentally ill', a liar and a fraud, and was accused of taking bribes to publish false findings.

Surprise material

While the cattle mutilation stories were gathering steam, US researchers were handed a new tool with which to try to uncover the government's UFO secrets – an amendment, in 1974, of the 1966 Freedom of Information Act (FOIA). This made it possible for the public to acquire documents from government files, provided they could identify their subject and source with reasonable accuracy. Documents might, however, still be withheld (subject to appeal) on certain grounds, mainly national security and personal privacy.

One of the first to take advantage of the new law was William H. Spaulding, director of the Phoenix, Arizona-based Ground Saucer Watch

---

Office of the District Attorney
First Judicial District

Kenneth M. Rommel, Jr.
Director

Diana S. Moyle
Coordinating Secretary

LOCAL & STATE

Animal Mutilation Project
Post Office Box 1209
Espanola, New Mexico 87532

Cipriano Padilla
Investigator

Telephone: (505) 753-7131
827-2195

March 5, 1980

Director
Federal Bureau of Investigation
J. Edgar Hoover Building
Washington, D.C.

Attention: F.B.I. Laboratory

Gentlemen:

For background information, I refer to your Albuquerque origin matter entitled as follows:

Mutilations of Animals on Indian Lands in New Mexico --
Crime on Indian Reservation.

Enclosed for examination is one vial containing several flakes of an unknown material which this office would like to have identified in connection with an official investigation.

For your information, since approximately 1975, New Mexico and other states, primarily those located in close proximity to New Mexico, have had incidents referred to by many as "the cattle mutilation phenomena." Stock animals, primarily cattle, have been found dead with various parts of the carcass missing such as one eye, one ear, the udder, and normally a cored anus. Most credible sources have attributed this damage to normal predator and scavenger activity. However, certain segments of the population have attributed the damage to many other causes ranging from U.F.O.s to a giant governmental conspiracy, the exact nature of which is never fully explained. No factual data has been supplied supporting these theories.

In May, 1979, responding to pressure from his constituents, the District Attorney, First Judicial District of New Mexico, applied for and was awarded a one year L.E.A.A. grant to investigate these mutilations.

I retired after twenty-eight years as a special agent of the F.B.I. to direct this investigation.

As previously stated, there are those that have attempted to make a connection between cattle mutilations and U.F.O. sitings.

In July, 1978, a U.F.O. was reportedly observed by a resident of Taos, New Mexico, reportedly hovering over a pickup truck. The next morning, the enclosed powder flakes were reportedly recovered from the roof of the aforementioned pickup.

Some of the individuals that are most vocal to the media have inferred that these flakes are identical with a substance that was taken from cowhides in a controlled test conducted in the Dulce, New Mexico area.

Dulce, New Mexico, which has been the site of several reported mutilations, is located approximately seventy miles from Taos, New Mexico. I have not been able to locate a sample of the substance reportedly collected in the Dulce test, but it has been described as a florescent material.

I have, to-date, been able to confirm any connection between these two substances, and have been told by those that have seen both that they are not identical.

However, I would appreciate it if through the use of a G.S. Mas spectroscopy test or any other logical test, that these flakes can be identified. This in itself would go a long way to assisting me to discredit the U.F.O. -- Cow Mutilation association theory.

If need be, the flakes can be destroyed during your examination.

Your cooperation in this investigation is appreciated.

Sincerely,

KENNETH M. ROMMEL, JR.

Right and Far Right: Three pages from the notorious top-secret affidavit presented to a federal court by the National Security Agency, defending its decision not to release certain UFO-related files in its possession. Seven-tenths of the document remain secret, which is taken by some as evidence of a cover-up about UFOs, and by others as prudence on the part of intelligence agents.

(GSW). Believing that the CIA was at the center of secret research into UFOs, Spaulding requested, and on 30 June 1975 was given, the complete, unexpurgated text of the minutes and report of the 1953 Robertson Panel (see Chapter Two). To dig as deep as possible into the CIA's archives, GSW filed suit under the FOIA for 'all records relating to UFOs' belonging to the CIA.

GSW were somewhat taken aback when the CIA's attorney suggested they amend their motion, to ask the CIA to conduct 'a reasonable search' for its UFO-related papers. This done, the US District Court in Washington DC so ordered the CIA, which on 15 December 1978 released 879 pages of documents. Parallel requests by GSW, Citizens Against UFO Secrecy (CAUS) and others secured the release of hundreds more documents from the National Security Agency (NSA) and the Defense Intelligence Agency (DIA). By 1981 approximately 3000 pages of previously classified papers had come to light through FOIA requests to these sources, the Army, Navy and Air Force, the Department of State and the FBI.

The CIA withheld 57 documents; the NSA retained 135 more. On 23 January 1980, CAUS appealed to the NSA to release its cache of material. The NSA denied the appeal, and CAUS took the case to court. On 18 November, Federal Judge Gerhard Gesell upheld the NSA's denial. An appeal against the decision, filed the

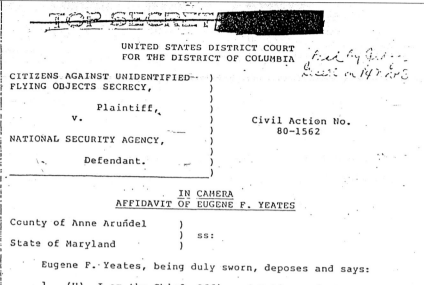

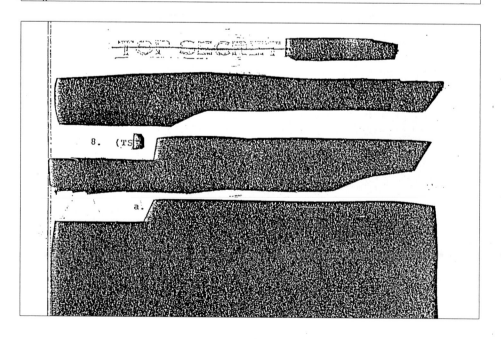

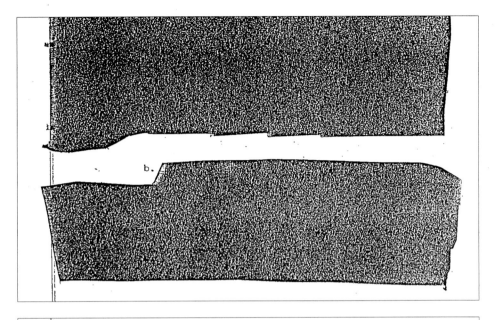

following January, failed on 3 November 1981. CAUS next petitioned the Supreme Court which, on 8 March 1982, announced its decision not to hear the case of CAUS v. NSA. The ufologists were stonewalled.

At the heart of these denials was a 21-page affidavit written by the NSA's Director of Policy, Eugene Yeates. It was classified TOP SECRET (CODEWORD), and only the judge(s) and the NSA's lawyers saw it. Judge Gesell was not cleared to view the files to which it referred, and that CAUS wanted released.

On 27 April 1982, CAUS made an FOIA request 'for all or any portion' of the affidavit. Twenty-one days later, the NSA released it. The document was 582 lines long; 412 of them had been blacked out. Eleven pages had vanished entirely under the heavy hand of the censor. A further attempt to prise the lid open a little further resulted in some minor changes and exposure of an interesting reference to UFOs as 'surprise material'.[7]

Obvious conclusions

The NSA affidavit has become a *cause celebre* among ufologists. What is it hiding? The NSA produced a public affidavit as well as a secret one. Its description of the documents, and its reasons for not releasing them, boiled down to this:

The COMINT [communications intelligence] reports being withheld... are all based on intercepted foreign communications. The disclosure of these records would identify the communications that had been successfully intercepted and processed for intelligence purposes. No meaningful portion of any of the records could be segregated and released without identifying the communications underlying the communications intelligence report. ...Disclosing them would permit foreign intelligence officials to draw inferences [and] to take countermeasures... to defeat the capabilities of NSA's intelligence gathering techniques.

Case #17

Phantoms Chase Phantoms

TEHERAN, IRAN

19 September 1976

A number of Teheran residents reported seeing UFOs at about 12.30 a.m. At 1.30 a.m. an F-4 Phantom was scrambled from the Imperial Iranian Air Force (IIAF) base at Shahroki, about 130 miles (200km) to the southwest.

According to a report filed by the US military attaché in Iran, the F-4 was within 25miles (40 km) of the UFO when the jet's communications systems failed. When the jet turned away, the systems came back to life. A second F-4 took off at 1.40 a.m., and its radar return from the UFO showed it to be the size of a Boeing 707 airliner. Visually, the UFO showed flashing colored strobe lights in a rectangular pattern.

When the F-4 came within a distance of 25 miles (40km) of the UFO, the object sped away, thereafter maintaining the distance between the two. A second object then came from the UFO at high speed toward the F-4. The pilot attempted to fire an AIM-9 missile, but his weapons-control panel went off and his radios failed. The second UFO rejoined the first, then another small object streaked from it at the ground. It came to rest and lit up the surrounding dry lake bed. The F-4 descended to observe the area, then flew to Mehrabad airport. As it approached to land, another, cylindrical UFO passed over it and was seen by Mehrabad controlers, and a civil airliner's communications failed. A helicopter searching the dry lake the next day picked up a strong beeping radio signal, but the crew found nothing on the ground.

It transpired that only the second F-4 had had any electronics failures, and had a history of such faults. Philip J. Klass discovered that the IIAF aircrew had no night-flying experience and were scrambled from a deep sleep, and therefore easily confused. He put the events down to radar and radio malfunction due to bad maintenance, aircrew errors (going in pursuit of a star) and meteors – the Aquarid and Southern Piscid showers were at their peak that night. The mystery beeping was probably caused by a crash-locator beacon accidentally ejected from a military transport plane. The cylindrical UFO that passed over Mehrabad airport remains unexplained, although the 'airship effect' discussed in Chapter Three may have been responsible.

'If the prosaic explanation seems strained,' wrote Klass, 'consider the alternative: that the "UFO" was an extra-terrestrial spaceship with the remarkable ability to selectively disable many avionic systems on the F-4 [but not, for instance, its flight-control system], only the radio... on an airliner, [but not] any IIAF air-defense radars or the Mehrabad radio equipment. Despite this remarkable defensive capability, the "UFO" decided to fire an "old-fashioned" rocket-missile... which missed... and landed without causing an explosion. And the next morning this rocket-missile mysteriously disappeared, leaving behind only a mysterious beeping radio signal, similar to that emitted by crash-locator beacons.'

Nearly four hours after the encounter over Teheran, the standard accounts say that this same UFO was seen flying parallel to the Atlantic coast over Morocco.

For an hour from about 1.00 a.m. local time a bright UFO trailing sparks flew slowly at an estimated altitude of 3300ft (1000m) from the south to the north of Morocco. Reports came from Agadir, Kalaa Sraghna, Essaouira, Casablanca, Rabat and Fez. The UFO looked like a disk at a distance, resolving to a cylinder when closer.

The US Ambassador in Morocco requested a response from the State Department on the sightings. Secretary of State Henry Kissinger replied that both meteors and a satellite re-entry had been ruled out and concluded: 'It is difficult to offer any definitive explanation as to the cause or origin of the UFOs.' Klass suggested that the same meteor showers were the most likely causes of the reports.

Even among moderately skeptical ufologists, there is a nagging belief that the documents must hold some major secret about UFOs. British ufologist Jenny Randles reasons that the secret affidavit was censored 'not for reasons of NSA procedure but precisely because of the UFO content'. Diehard ETHers believe the NSA will not release the documents because they prove there has been contact with aliens. Timothy Good feels that the NSA has told 'only half the truth', and smoothly asserts: 'By July 1947, when sightings proliferated throughout the United States, and a disc crashed at Roswell, it must have become obvious that the 'flying saucers' were of extra-terrestrial origin.'[8]

This statement slides over both Good's defective logic and gaping holes in his evidence. The largest flaw in the believers' case is that they have no more seen the documents than they can produce a crashed, or even working, UFO for inspection. Ufologist Tom Deuley, who did see the documents when an NSA employee, and recommended continued denial, has said they contained nothing of scientific interest, no indication of follow-up activities, and no evidence of NSA interest in UFOs as such.[9]

There is another difficulty. If the withheld documents contain 'proof' of the 'reality' of flying saucers, why are there so few of them? A cover-up of a matter so fundamental and so challenging as genuine alien contact, and as vast as believers say it is, would generate a mountain of paper to match. No such paper trail seems to exist. But none of these arguments persuade those who are already convinced that the NSA has more to hide than its own tradecraft.

Crashed saucers rise again

The release of formerly classified documents under the FOIA did reveal some ostensibly interesting UFO cases, however. Reports of encounters with UFOs at Loring AFB, Maine, Wurtsmith AFB, Michigan, and Malmstrom AFB, Montana (see Case #19) were tagged evidence of 'cover-up'. Garbled versions had already appeared in the press, strongly implying an extra-terrestrial intervention. If the USAF's silence was covering anything up, it was a clearer and more accurate account than reported there.

That the Air Force attached no great significance to the sightings was indicated by the lack of analytical documents among those released (the issues could have been cleared up in a few telephone calls). Philip Klass, as ever, dissected the reports minutely, and produced credible physical and psychological alternative explanations for the events.[10]

Another case that surfaced in the released documents and generated intense interest was a pursuit by Imperial Iranian Air Force F-4 Phantom jets of a UFO seen over Teheran in September 1976 (see Case #17). Once again, it was Klass who would dig deeper, revealing that the original report from the US military attaché was uninvestigated, and inaccurate, hearsay. There was also no attempt to hush the event up in the Iranian press.

McDonnel Douglas F-4 Phantom of the Imperial Iranian Air Force. Two of these aircraft went aloft in September 1976 to intercept a UFO over Teheran, Iran. The failure of the mission remains a matter of debate between believers and skeptics.

```
PAGE  2                                                    12343
12. (U) USDAO, TEHRAN, IRAN
13. (U) FRANK B. MCKENZIE, COL, USAF, DATT
14. (U) NA
15. (C) THIS REPORT FORWARDS INFORMATION CONCERNING THE
SIGHTING OF AN UFO IN IRAN ON 19 SEPTEMBER 1976.
     A. AT ABOUT 1230 AM ON 19 SEP 76 THE IMPERIDAL IRANIAN
AIR FORCE (IIAF) COMMAND POST RECEIVED FOUR TELEPHONE CALLS
FROM CITIZENS LIVING IN THE SHEMIRAN AREA OF TEHRAN SAYING
THAT THEY HAD SEEN STRANGE OBJECTS IN THE SKY. SOME REPORTED
A KIND OF BIRD-LIKE OBJECT WHILE OTHERS REPORTED A HELICOPTER
WITH A LIGHT ON. THERE WERE NO HELICOPTERS AIRBORNE AT THAT
TIME. THE COMMAND POST CALLED BG YOUSEFI, ASSISTANT DEPUTY
COMMANDER OF OPERATIONS. AFTER HE TOLD THE CITIZEN IT WAS ONLY
STARS AND HAD TALKED TO MEHRABAD TOWER HE DECIDED TO LOOK FOR
HIMSELF. HE NOTICED AN OBJECT IN THE SKY SIMILAR TO A STAR
BIGGER AND BRIGHTER. HE DECIDED TO SCRAMBLE AN F-4 FROM
SHAHROKHI AFB TO INVESTIGATE.
     B. AT 0130 HRS ON THE 19TH THE F-4 TOOK OFF AND PROCEEDED
TO A POINT ABOUT 40 NM NORTH OF TEHRAN. DUE TO ITS BRILLIANCE
THE OBJECT WAS EASILY VISIBLE FROM 70 MILES AWAY.
AS THE F-4 APPROACHED A RANGE OF 25 NM HE LOST ALL INSTRUMENTATION
AND COMMUNICATIONS (UHF AND INTERCOM). HE BROKE OFF THE
INTERCEPT AND HEADED BACK TO SHAHROKHI. WHEN THE F-4 TURNED
AWAY FROM THE OBJECT AND APPARENTLY WAS NO LONGER A THREAT
TO IT THE AIRCRAFT REGAINED ALL INSTRUMENTATION AND COM-
MUNICATIONS. AT 0140 HRS A SECOND F-4 WAS LAUNCHED. THE
BACKSEATER ACQUIRED A RADAR LOCK ON AT 27 NM, 12 O'CLOCK
HIGH POSITION WITH THE VC (RATE OF CLOSURE) AT 150 NMPH.
AS THE RANGE DECREASED TO 25 NM THE OBJECT MOVED AWAY AT A
SPEED THAT WAS VISIBLE ON THE RADAR SCOPE AND STAYED AT 25NM.
     C. THE SIZE OF THE RADAR RETURN WAS COMPARABLE TO THAT OF
A 707 TANKER. THE VISUAL SIZE OF THE OBJECT WAS DIFFICULT
TO DISCERN BECAUSE OF ITS INTENSE BRILLIANCE. THE
LIGHT THAT IT GAVE OFF WAS THAT OF FLASHING STROBE LIGHTS
ARRANGED IN A RECTANGULAR PATTERN AND ALTERNATING BLUE, GREEN,
RED AND ORANGE IN COLOR. THE SEQUENCE OF THE LIGHTS WAS SO
FAST THAT ALL THE COLORS COULD BE SEEN AT ONCE. THE OBJECT
AND THE PURSUING F-4 CONTINUED ON A COURSE TO THE SOUTH OF
TEHRAN WHEN ANOTHER BRIGHTLY LIGHTED OBJECT, ESTIMATED TO BE
ONE HALF TO ONE THIRD THE APPARENT SIZE OF THE MOON, CAME
OUT OF THE ORIGINAL OBJECT. THIS SECOND OBJECT HEADED STRAIGHT
TOWARD THE F-4 AT A VERY FAST RATE OF SPEED. THE PILOT
ATTEMPTED TO FIRE AN AIM-9 MISSILE AT THE OBJECT BUT AT THAT


PAGE  3                                                    12343
INSTANT HIS WEAPONS CONTROL PANEL WENT OFF AND HE LOST ALL
COMMUNICATIONS (UHF AND INTERPHONE). AT THIS POINT THE PILOT
INITIATED A TURN AND NEGATIVE G DIVE TO GET AWAY. AS HE
TURNED THE OBJEAZ FELL IN TRAIL AT WHAT APPEARED TO BE ABOUT
3-4 NM. AS HE CONTINUED IN HIS TURN AWAY FROM THE PRIMARY
OBJECT THE SECOND OBJECT WENT TO THE INSIDE OF HIS TURN THEN
RETURNED TO THE PRIMARY OBJECT FOR A PERFECT REJOIN.
     D. SHORTLY AFTER THE SECOND OBJECT JOINED UP WITH THE
PRIMARY OBJECT ANOTHER OBJECT APPEARED TO COME OUT OF THE
OTHER SIDE OF THE PRIMARY OBJECT GOING STRAIGHT DOWN, AT A
GREAT RATE OF SPEED. THE F-4 CREW HAD REGAINED COMMUNICATIONS
AND THE WEAPONS CONTROL PANEL AND WATCHED THE OBJECT APPROACH
THE GROUND ANTICIPATING A LARGE EXPLOSION. THIS OBJECT APPEARED
TO COME TO REST GENTLY ON THE EARTH AND CAST A VERY BRIGHT
LIGHT OVER AN AREA OF ABOUT 2-3 KILOMETERS.
THE CREW DESCENDED FROM THEIR ALTITUDE OF 26M TO 15M AND
CONTINUED TO OBSERVE AND MARK THE OBJECT'S POSITION. THEY
HAD SOME DIFFICULTY IN ADJUSTING THEIR NIGHT VISIBILITY FOR
LANDING SO AFTER ORBITING MEHRABAD A FEW TIMES THEY WENT OUT
FOR A STRAIGHT IN LANDING. THERE WAS A LOT OF INTERFERENCE
ON THE UHF AND EACH TIME THEY PASSED THROUGH A MAG. BEARING
OF 150 DEGREE FROM EHRABAD THEY LOST THEIR COMMUNICATIONS (UHF
AND INTERPHONE) AND THE INS FLUCTUATED FROM 30 DEGREES - 50 DEGREES.
THE ONE CIVIL AIRLINER THAT WAS APPROACHING MEHRABAD DURING THIS
SAME TIME EXPERIENCED COMMUNICATIONS FAILURE IN THE SAME
VICINITY (KILO ZULU) BUT DID NOT REPORT SEEING ANYTHING.
WHILE THE F-4 WAS ON A LONG FINAL APPROACH THE CREW NOTICED
ANOTHER CYLINDER SHAPED OBJECT (ABOUT THE SIZE OF A T-BIRD
AT 10M) WITH BRIGHT STEADY LIGHTS ON EACH END AND A FLASHER
IN THE MIDDLE. WHEN QUERIED THE TOWER STATED THERE WAS NO
OTHER KNOWN TRAFFIC IN THE AREA. DURING THE TIME THAT THE
OBJECT PASSED OVER THE F-4 THE TOWER DID NOT HAVE A VISUAL
ON IT BUT PICKED IT UP AFTER THE PILOT TOLD THEM TO LOOK
BETWEEN THE MOUNTAINS AND THE REFINERY.
     E. DURING DAYLIGHT THE F-4 CREW WAS TAKEN OUT TO THE
AREA IN A HELICOPTER WHERE THE OBJECT APPARENTLY HAD LANDED.
NOTHING WAS NOTICED AT THE SPOT WHERE THEY THOUGHT THE OBJECT
LANDED (A DRY LAKE BED) BUT AS THEY CIRCLED OFF TO THE
WEST OF THE AREA THEY PICKED UP A VERY NOTICEABLE BEEPER
SIGNAL. AT THE POINT WHERE THE RETURN WAS THE LOUDEST WAS
A SMALL HOUSE WITH A GARDEN. THEY LANDED AND ASKED THE PEOPLE
WITHIN IF THEY HAD NOTICED ANYTHING STRANGE LAST NIGHT. THE
PEOPLE TALKED ABOUT A LOUD NOISE AND A VERY BRIGHT LIGHT


PAGE  4                                                    12843
LIKE LIGHTENING. THE AIRCRAFT AND AREA WHERE THE OBJECT IS
BELIEVED TO HAVE LANDED ARE BEING CHECKED FOR POSSIBLE RADIATION.
RO COMMENTS: (C) ACTUAL INFORMATION CONTAINED IN THIS REPORT
WAS OBTAINED FROM SOURCE IN CONVERSATION WITH A SUB-SOURCE, AND
IIAF PILOT OF ONE OF THE F-4S. MORE INFORMATION WILL BE
FORWARDED WHEN IT BECOMES AVAILABLE.

BT
#9575
ANNOTES
JEP 117
```

During the late 1970s, however, disturbing experiences of lights-in-the-night and daylight disks were moving from the center of the ufological stage. Besides abductions, researchers were increasingly preoccupied by accounts of crashed UFOs. In July 1978 Len Stringfield presented a dossier of what he called 'retrievals of the third kind' at a Mutual UFO Network (MUFON) conference in Dayton, Ohio. Most of the 19 cases were second-hand accounts, and several of the original witnesses were dead.

Stringfield continued to collect these stories until his death in 1995, publishing them in seven 'Status Reports'. The anonymity of the vast majority of his informants was their most conspicuous feature. Those acquainted with folklore noticed striking patterns in both the structure and detail of the accounts that suggested they were more fable than fact.[11]

But so attractive were the crashed saucer/alien retrieval (C/R) stories that there were even attempts to rehabilitate the long-discredited Frank Scully. The C/R anecdotes, no matter how inaccessible their sources, fulfilled all the conditions of the cover-up scenario. In this climate of acceptance Charles Berlitz and William L. Moore published *The Roswell Incident*, reviving the story of an alleged 'flying disk' that was retrieved from the New Mexico desert in July 1947 and the US Army Air Force's subsequent clamp-down on the news.

The book, largely written by Moore and researched by Stanton Friedman, launched a small ufological industry and a monumental and labyrinthine rumpus over what really happened. Both were still going strong in the 1990s (see Chapter Eight).

For ufology, which had been directionless for a decade, Berlitz and Moore's book gave an anchorage in fact to all the unverifiable C/R tales and intimations of a cover-up, and provided a much-needed focus for researchers' energy. Here, at last, was something that, given enough digging, could be proven one way or the other. As we shall see, evidence was not long in coming forth.

At the end of 1980 the theme of crashing saucers and clandestine knowledge of aliens and their craft was given fresh, factual impetus by a spectacular encounter with a flaming, diamond-shaped UFO, apparently out of control near Huffman, Texas (see Case #18). The craft didn't quite crash, but it was surrounded by military helicopters; and the military denied all knowledge of the affair.

The Grudge 13 affair

One of the most elaborate, and most prophetic, claims concerning retrieved alien bodies and crashed saucers surfaced on tape-recordings made by William S. English in the early 1980s. Len Stringfield referred to the case in 1987, and another version was published by George C. Andrews.[12]

English's version of his story, as told in interviews with the author, is this. In May 1970 he was an officer with US Army Special Forces in Vietnam. His A-team was sent to locate a Boeing B-52 Stratofortress bomber that had crashed in dense jungle in Laos, and if possible to rescue the crew. The B-52 had come down after a hostile encounter with a UFO, described as a 'large white light'.

English and his A-team located the B-52 by helicopter. It was lying among the trees 'like a great big giant hand had grabbed it and just set it down' – there was no damage at all to either the aircraft, its bomb load, or the vegetation around it. All the crew were on board, in their seats, but hideously mutilated – although there was no blood anywhere. The team took dog tags from the corpses and removed the code books, then blew up the aircraft (still with its bombs on board), and left. Some weeks later most of the A-team were wiped out in an ambush. English was taken prisoner but killed his guard and escaped, and was found in the jungle by US forces.

English left the Army in 1973. By 1976 he was working as an intelligence analyst at RAF Chicksands, a major USAF/NSA electronic listening post, in England, where his wife was teaching at the base school. On 29 June 1976 he was given a 625-page document to assess. Named Grudge/Blue Book *Report #13*, it detailed captured alien craft, including their armaments, autopsies performed on alien bodies, and close-encounter reports (see Document 4-01 for the account English gave to researcher John Lear in 1988). The document contained notes by Dr J. Allen Hynek, and others in Cyrillic handwriting.

Also included were photos English had taken of the dead crew of the downed B-52 in Laos, and the fact that the bomber had crashed after being attacked by a UFO. Seeing his own photos helped convince English that the report was genuine.

A few weeks after this, English was summarily dismissed from his post (either because of his positive rating of

Mrs Hannah Roberts took this picture of the scenery near the Eve River, north of Kelsey Bay, Vancouver Island, on 8 October 1981 without noticing the UFO in the sky. Nor did her husband or daughter, who were also present. After extensive research Dr Richard F. Haines could find no evidence of fakery, and the picture has yet to be fully explained.

Case #18

The Cash/Landrum Encounter

Near HUFFMAN, TEXAS, USA

29 December 1980

Betty Cash, Vickie Landrum and her seven-year-old grandson Colby Landrum were driving home to Dayton, near the city of Houston, Texas, on the evening of 29 December 1980, after a meal in nearby New Caney. Around 9.00 p.m. the trio, with Betty at the wheel, were on Highway FM1485, which runs through a forest of oak and pine. Then Colby pointed to a bright light moving over the trees ahead of them. The light grew larger and larger – until it became 'like a diamond of fire', in Vickie Landrum's words – while every so often flames burst from beneath it. Suddenly, it was right in their way.

Betty braked hard. The three watched as the UFO hovered above the road about 180ft (55m) away. From treetop level it sank to within 25ft (7.5m) of the highway, gave out a blast of fire, and rose again. It did this several times, mesmerizing the car's occupants. They climbed out to see the object, which was lighting up the trees and the highway all around it, more clearly. It seemed to be made of dull aluminum, and the four points of its diamond shape were rounded. A row of blue dots ran across its center. Now and then it emitted a beeping sound. A terrific heat was coming from the UFO, and Colby begged his grandmother to get back in the car (a Buick Cutlass). She and he both did, but Betty stayed outside until the object moved up and away. The car was now so hot that she could not touch the door with bare hands.

Then a crowd of helicopters appeared. 'They seemed to rush in from all directions,' said Betty. 'It seemed like they were trying to encircle the thing.' They drove on another 5 miles (8km) and stopped at a spot where they could see the UFO in the distance, and the swarm of helicopters around it. One, a giant, twin-rotor CH-47 Chinook, roared right over them. They counted a total of 23 machines of various types apparently in pursuit of the clearly visible UFO.

Worse was to follow. Over the next few hours, the trio developed painful swellings and blisters on their skin and had severe headaches and stomach upsets. Vickie's hair began to fall out. Colby suffered a sunburn-like rash. Over the following week or so, Betty's eyes also became swollen to the point that she could not see, and she had to be hospitalized. In a few weeks all three had lost some hair and were developing eye problems. Their hair eventually grew again, although it was different from their original hair. Since their experience, none has entirely recovered their former good health. Doctors said that the symptoms shown by the three victims were consistent with exposure to intense electromagnetic radiation in the ultra-violet, microwave and X-ray bands.

Investigators later established that other witnesses could confirm the UFO's flight path and appearance, and the presence of unusual numbers of CH-47 helicopters – which are quite distinctive – in the sky that night. Yet local civil airfields and military airbases deny that such a fleet used their facilities or showed on their radar. Vickie Landrum was convinced that a secret military device run haywire was responsible for her injuries, and she and Betty Cash sued the US government for $20 million in that belief. In 1986, the case was dismissed on the grounds that 'no such object was owned, operated or in the inventory' of the US Army, Navy, Air Force or NASA.

The origin and nature of the Huffman UFO remains an enigma. To ufologists, the Cash/Landrum case is perhaps the most baffling and frustrating of modern times, for what started with solid evidence for a notoriously elusive phenomenon petered out in a maze of dead ends, denials, and perhaps even official deviousness. (The Army and Navy made no reference to the presence of the Chinooks, for example, although both fly these helicopters.)

Skeptics have always asked a blunt and fundamental question: what was the trio's state of health before their alleged encounter?

Boeing B-52 Stratofortresses pound targets in Vietnam. William S. English claims a UFO downed one of these dreadnoughts of the sky over Laos in May 1970. Operating as part of a US Special Forces team he found it, absolutely intact, in the jungle. The official records contradict English's story – it is doubtful whether he had ever been to Southeast Asia – and only the most extreme UFO conspiracy theorists support his version of events.

the *Report #13* document or because he had not been intended to see it) by the base commander, Colonel Robert Black, and deported the very same day to the USA.

In about 1980, in Tucson, Arizona, he was approached by Col Black, who said he had also been released from the USAF for reasons connected with *Report #13*. He told English he had evidence that a large UFO was buried somewhere on White Sands Missile Range, and invited him to join an expedition to find it. English, Black, and a former USAF sergeant, financed by the sale of English's leather-goods business, equipped a 4x4 van and infiltrated it onto the range.

One evening on this trip English was about 3000ft (1000m) from the vehicle when helicopters came into view and rocketed the van, destroying it and killing his companions, who were in the vehicle. English escaped to

Tucson on foot, where he rested at the home of UFO researcher Wendelle Stevens. He then found his own home under surveillance and left Tucson by a series of subterfuges. Eventually he settled in Lynchburg, Virginia, for some years, working as a cameraman at WSET television.

Some eight years later he 'came out of the woodwork' and began to tell his story. Additional details included claims that some 15 attempts had been made on his life while he was in hiding. In one attack, he said, two men with sub-machine guns fired on his home for 15 minutes solid. (My conservative estimate is that they would have loosed off at least 2000 rounds in this time.) Yet no help came, even though, English said, the local police station was only about 600ft (200m) down the street. English's other claims were outlandish enough, but this defied all belief.

Common sense, general knowledge and some simple detective work disposed of almost all of English's tales.

The story of the crashed but intact B-52 echoes the Soviet 'Sverdlovsk case' of 1961. Most of the details are the same, except that the aircraft was an Antonov AN-2P mail plane. Heliborne troops found the plane intact in a tiny glade in dense forest, but there was no sign of the seven

Document 4-01

Grudge/Blue Book Report #13

Excerpts from William S. English's description of the document
received for analysis on 29 June 1976

In Box, diplomatic pouch under lock and key system. Lock had been opened, pouch was easily accessed. Standard diplomatic courier's pouch marked American Embassy Couriers, contained pouch serial number JL327Delta. Inside a publication with red tape which indicated code red security precautions and an Air Force disposition form. Disposition form was standard white page copy, title was 'Analysis Report'. Further down was 'Analyze enclosed report under code red measures. give abstract breakdown and report on validity. Observe all code red measures. Analysis required immediately'. Underneath were a series of dashes then the letters NDF then another series of dashes. Below that, lower left hand corner were the initials WGB.

Publication was withdrawn from pouch. It measured approximately 8" by 11" with gray cover. Heavily bound, paper back style similar to technical manuals. Across the center front it read, *Grudge/Blue Book Report No. 13*. It was dated 1953-(1963). In the lower right hand corner was AFSN 2246-3. In upper left hand corner was the word 'annotated'. Across the front upper right hand corner to lower left hand corner was red tape indicating Code Red security measures. Across the front was stamped in red ink 'Top Secret Need To Know Only Crypto Clearance 14 Required'. Inside front cover upper left hand corner were hand written notations in ink which were blacked out by black felt pen.

Inside cover sheet was basically the same information as the cover. Second page was title page. Next page after that was an appendix with numerous notations made in it. Notations dealt with inserts of what appeared to be photos and additional notes. At bottom of third page it read G/BV Page 1 of 624 pages. Title page was subject letter. Complete list of appendix not remembered. Title. Some notes on the practical applications of the Worst Nemo equations.

Table of Contents, Part 1. 'On the design of generators to accomplish strain free molecular translation'. Part 2, 'The generation of space time discontinuums, closed, open and folded'. Part 3, 'On the generation of temporary pseudo acceleration locas'. Part 1, Chapter 1, 'Design criteria for a simple generator and control system referring to equation 17 appendix A'. Part 2 Chapter 1, 'Continuation of Einstein's Theory of Relativity to final conclusion'. Part 3, Chapter 1, 'Possible applications of Einsteinian theory of relativity at conclusion'.

Part 1, chapter 2, reports of UFO encounters, classification 'Close Encounters of the 1st kind', subtitle 'Sightings and witnesses'. Part 2, Chapter 2, 'Close Encounters of the 2nd kind', subtitle 'UFO sightings witnessed within close proximity'. Part 3, Chapter 2 'Close Encounters of the 3rd kind', subtitle 'UFO encounters and extraterrestrial life forms witnessed and personal encounters'. Subtitle, 'Colonies relocation thereof'. Case histories. Chapter 3 Part 1, titled 'Military Encounters with UFOs'. Part 2 Chapter 3, 'Military Reports Concerning sightings on Radar and Electronic Surveillance of UFOs'. Subsection 2, Analysis Report, J. Allen Hynek, Lt Col. Friend. Appendix continued on for about 5 pages. Opening subject page consisted of a report of the findings as written by Lt Col. Friend and his analysis.

Must stress that the version seen was annotated. There were inserts that were added to this copy after it had been initially printed. Sections remembered very vividly are the photographs and the reports concerning captive sights of various UFOs to include Mexico, Sweden, United States and Canada. There were also what was then classified Close Encounters of the 3rd kind. It was made very clear that these people whom it was determined had genuine CE 3s were moved in the middle of the night by Air Force personnel and relocated to various sites in the midwest and northwest parts of the United States. In many cases these people experienced physical ailments from exposure to various types of radiation.

In this section of the report it also indicated that there were numerous occasions in which a UFO tracked alongside of a fired missile and on one occasion said missile was observed being taken aboard a UFO while in flight. The speeds indicated were absolutely phenomenal.

The report also indicated that there were a number of recovery teams that were activated specifically for the purpose of recovering any and all evidence of UFOs and UFO sightings. Most notably recorded in publication was what they called Recovery Team Alpha. It was reported that Alpha had been extremely active in a number of areas and on certain occasions had travelled outside of the continental United States. Alpha was based out of Wright-Patterson Air Force Base and was on the move constantly.

Further information in the report consisted of such things as reported sightings and where air force planes had been destroyed or had combat encounters or had been attacked by UFOs. Also there were autopsy reports of various human mutilations.

About midway through the report came a section which dealt specifically with photographs. Each photo was labeled and appendixed to certain reports. The photos dealt with special teams that were called in to recover a crashed UFO. It also dealt with alien bodies and autopsy reports, autopsy type photographs, high quality, color, 8 x 10, 5 x 7.

Photo number 1 showed an alien being on an autopsy table... A report by Dr. J. Allen Hynek was recalled vividly which indicated that he had also studied the information provided by this particular case and that he felt that it was indeed a genuine UFO capture and subsequently the alien was part of UFO. Dr. Hynek was non-committal but did however sign the report. Also indicated in report that he did not view bodies personally, but viewed photographs and accompanying reports from autopsies.

Numerous photos of flesh of the being starting with cutaneous and subcutaneous microphotographic plates. Appeared to be cellular studies done under microscope and electron microscope type photos. Extreme magnification of tissue samples.

people on board. English claimed he had never heard the story.

A false trail

Air Force records show unequivocally that no B-52 crashed anywhere in Southeast Asia between July 1969 and July 1972. English was unable to give the tail number of the B-52 he investigated, but he could quote chapter and verse from *Report #13*.

Nor was he able to recall the number of his A-team, and claimed that it had been based 'north of Phnom Penh, at Dien Bien Phu' – that is, 'north' of the capital of Cambodia(!), in North Vietnam. English is in fact too young to have served in Special Forces when he claimed he did. And in one interview

he was shown a Colt CAR-15, Special Forces' personal weapon of choice, and actually failed to recognize it. It is doubtful whether English was ever in Southeast Asia.

The existence of *Report #13* has always been denied by the USAF; its material was included in *Project Blue Book Special Report #14*. It is possible that English was at Chicksands in 1976 and was given the dossier he describes, to test his ability to detect disinformation (a test he failed, which would explain his dismissal).

However, Col Robert Black was not the commander of RAF Chicksands in 1976 (that was Col James W. Johnson), or at any other time; two retired USAF colonels named Robert Black are still alive today. The British Home Office has no record of anyone

bearing the name William S. English being deported from the United Kingdom. White Sands Missile Range authorities categorically deny patrolling the range with armed helicopters, let alone having rocketed any intruders' vehicles.[13]

Bill English's story, one may safely conclude, is fantasy. This did not prevent it joining forces, in due course, with the mute legend and the reviving crashed-saucer stories, to buttress a particularly dark version of the UFO myth that was to dominate ufology by the end of the 1980s. Before that was to happen, more government files (real and false) would be unearthed, more – increasingly bizarre – abduction cases come to light, and more disputes would divide ufologists than ever before.

Chapter Five

FEAR, FRAUD AND LOATHING

THE FRAGMENTATION OF UFOLOGY
1982–1995

THE PERIOD from 1982 to 1995 saw ufology begin to tear itself apart into separate, angry factions who attacked one other with even more gusto and vitriol than traditional skeptic-vs-believer squabbles had displayed. Some of the discord was between schools of thought – extraterrestrialists against proponents of the

At sunrise on 27 October 1979, Lou Blackburn took three shots of June and Norman Neilson's new cray-fishing boat as it slipped from the mouth of the Hurunui River near Motunau, South Island, New Zealand. Blackburn noticed nothing unusual at the time. The shots were too dark to use, as intended, in promoting the Neilsons' business. It was not until January 1980 that a friend noticed the mysterious lights beneath the clouds in the second picture (seen here). Former Royal New Zealand Air Force photo analysts judged the picture to be genuine. Skeptics have suggested a lens flare and an advertising plane as a source for the image.

earthlights hypothesis, for example – and often the protagonists were former young rebels of the 1970s, now defending their own fiefdoms. But those were as nothing compared to the ructions over abductions, over one or two specific sightings, and over Roswell and the increasingly tangled series of claims and counter-claims that flowed from it. Through this heated debate, like a dark and disturbing undertone, was a constant theme: official deceit and government cover-up.

One of the first to produce a conspiracy theory in the 1980s was William H. Spaulding, who had pioneered the ufological onslaught on government files using the FOIA. Indeed it was probably the only coherent and even remotely plausible conspiracy theory of the era. Spaulding had rejected the ETH and, with it, most of ufology, which he called 'looking for something that wasn't there in the first place'. But the documents he had obtained under the FOIA clearly showed that the USAF's

and CIA's interest in UFOs had continued long after they had claimed to have abandoned the subject. There had to be a reason.

The Federal hypothesis

Spaulding noted that areas of high UFO activity in the USA were also near proving grounds for secret weapons and aircraft – with most reports coming from within a radius of 100 miles (150km) of test areas. He also observed that waves of American UFO sightings often followed times of crisis for the US government. As an especially egregious example, he cited the 'flap' in New Mexico and West Texas, in November 1957, following the Soviets' successful launch of Sputnik II, only 30 days after Sputnik I. At the time, the US space program was suffering repeated, ignominious and nationally televised failures of its own satellite launch rockets. The UFO events, Spaulding believed, were set up to distract attention from the huge

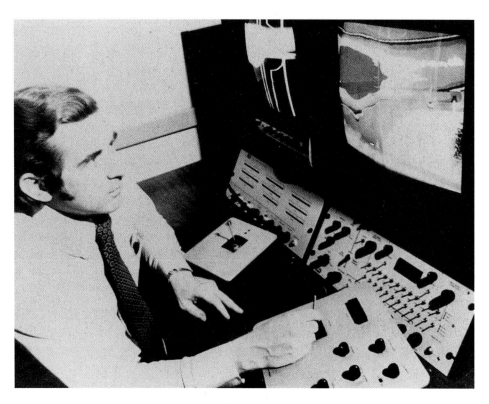

William H. Spaulding of Ground Saucer Watch and the hardware he used for digital enhancement of UFO photographs.

embarrassment on Capitol Hill and at the Pentagon and NASA.

Spaulding began to suspect that many aspects of the UFO phenomenon were attributable to interference run by the CIA, even if only by a small rogue cell within the organization. Close encounter and abduction experiences might be the result of illicitly administering mind-expanding drugs to the unwary – as in the known mind-control experiments the CIA admitted having run until the late 1960s. Through such tests, the agency could monitor victims' reactions, and media and general public reaction to accounts of events that were 'real in the mind of the witness' – in the ufologist's cliché – but incredible to almost anyone else.

In thinking such experiments could explain some abduction, contactee and close-encounter cases, Spaulding echoed Dr Leon Davidson, whose voluminous CIA file was in the papers released to GSW. In the late 1950s Davidson had proposed that former bootlegger George Adamski's contacts with 'Venusians' were hoaxes – perpetrated by the CIA upon the gullible Adamski. Psychological testing might also lie behind one of the weirder 'side-effects' of UFO sightings: the visits that some witnesses say they have received from sinister 'men in black' or MIB (see Case #20).

MIB typically resemble G-men from a 1940s or 1950s B-movie, and may produce ID and claim to be from a government department or the Air Force. They tend to travel in threes, and nearly always know all about a witness's experience before he has reported it to anyone else at all. They may threaten that the witness or a member of his family will suffer if they reveal anything about it, and do so in wonderfully 'Hollywooden' language – 'If you want your wife to stay as pretty as she is...' for example.

Another odd aspect of the MIB is their transport – not standard government-issue wheels, but usually Cadillacs that are brand-new but have been out of production for years, even decades. Still more bizarre, MIB often

seem unable to walk or talk properly, ask surreal and improper personal questions, and even vanish into thin air. Most importantly, the threats they make are never fulfilled: it is as if they were actually testing the effectiveness of empty menaces.

Public experiments

Only a few cases, set up years apart, would be enough to fuel the mystery and the media, and keep ufologists busy, Spaulding felt. Creating a series of such unlikely events would serve two purposes. First, the events that witnesses describe are so outlandish that most people tend to dismiss them as incredible, while the media make fun of them. No scientific body will investigate them closely, and nor will the military, but the CIA would be learning much about the social effects of highly publicised improbable stories. Second, the carefully nurtured folklore provides a smokescreen behind which secret technology, unusual aircraft designs and psychological manipulations can freely be tested (see Case #21); an indoctrinated public would instantly translate any contact with them into UFO-related experiences. In saying this, Spaulding was a good deal subtler than Leon Davidon had been.

Spaulding justified his 'Federal Hypothesis' by citing repeated references to recruiting UFOs for psychological warfare that he found in CIA documents from the early 1950s. He gave several illustrations of how (as he believed) the UFO phenomenon had been used as a cover for some secret operations. One was the 'NORAD flap' of November 1975 (see Case #19). Another involved Stealth technology, which had been under development since 1966, and which can be seen in the USAF's B-2 bomber and F117A Nighthawk fighter, and in the US Navy's A12-ATA attack aircraft (now canceled).

Case #19

The NORAD Flap

USAF BASES, NORTHERN UNITED STATES

27 October–11 November 1975

At around 8.00 p.m. on 27 October, a whirring UFO showing a white strobe and reddish orange lights came within 1000ft (300m) of a nuclear weapons store at Loring AFB, Maine. During the 90 minutes of the UFO's visit, it was tracked on radar as it flew over and around the base. On 29 October, radar detected an 'unknown' heading once more toward the weapons store. A helicopter failed to make visual contact with the UFO. The following night, a UFO was seen on three separate occasions but a helicopter sent to intercept it failed to make contact.

Also on 30 and 31 October, UFOs flew in formation over a weapons store at Wurtsmith AFB, Michigan. A KC-135 tanker aircraft sent to intercept them likewise failed to make contact. The crew picked them up visually but 'painted' the UFO on radar only once. (The aircraft's AN/APN-59 radar was in fact designed for navigation and storm-detection, not to track fast-moving, low-flying targets.)

On four consecutive nights from 7 November, UFOs reconnoitered Malmstrom AFB, Montana, ICBM launch sites (silos) in the state, and also visited Minot AFB, North Dakota. On 8 November, two F-106 jets from Great Falls AFB, Montana, went in pursuit of seven UFOs flying at altitudes from 9500ft (2900m) to 15,500ft (4700m). The interceptors' speed proved a disadvantage, as the UFOs accelerated and decelerated rapidly from as little as 3.5mph (6km/h) to 170mph (270 km/h). To ground observers, the UFOs became invisible while the jets were present, and reappeared when the interceptors left the area. At no time did the F-106s make radar contact with the UFOs.

A secret NORAD memo admitted that when the flap ended on 11 November, Air Guard helicopters, Strategic Air Command helicopters and NORAD F-106s had 'failed to produce positive ID'. William H. Spaulding contended that the UFOs were Special Forces helicopters and other aircraft, equipped with silencing and stealth technology. He noted that the F-106 fighters from Great Falls were instructed to fly no lower than 12,000ft (3650m) and at moderate speed (the F-106 was capable of Mach 2, or about 1500mph (2400km/h). Spaulding said the 'entire November flap represents a contrived military exercise, possibly involving both US and Canadian Special Forces, to covertly test detection capability and response... The whole "crisis"... reeks of a military mission [in which] a few individuals [know] the facts and the operators within the military system are kept in the dark.'

Philip J. Klass suggested a still more down-to-earth explanation. The object at Loring AFB may well have been a helicopter, probably straying over the base by accident. It may have been a prospectors' aircraft known to have been in the area, or may have belonged to smugglers.

A general alert was then issued to other bases in the NORAD region. Extra vigilance and anxiety may then have fired the imaginations of those on watch at the other bases. Several of the reports are consistent with sightings of 'bright celestial objects', while the slow-moving UFOs on radar were possibly birds, migrating through the region at that season. Klass also noted many inconsistencies and confusions in the reports made to various headquarters, as if observers were changing their minds about the nature of the events. The F-106s launched on 8 November, incidentally, were unable to fly below 12,000ft (3650m) 'because of the mountainous terrain', according to a report by NORAD to the National Military Command Center, that was made within minutes of the events.

In 1975, according to Spaulding, a USAF mobile radar unit picked up an aircraft leaving Edwards AFB, California, traveling at over 460mph (740km/h). In one sweep of the radar, the 'blip' had vanished – a feat possible, in theory, only if the target had accelerated to over 2000mph (3200km/h).

To the ufologist, this looked like another case of a UFO spying on a military installation, and was reported as such. And in a sense, it was exactly that – a plane testing the effectiveness of Stealth technology against a military unit that had deliberately been

Case #20

Men In Black Start Here

NEW HAVEN and BRIDGEPORT, CONNECTICUT, USA
August–September 1953

In April 1952, 31-year-old factory worker Albert Bender, from Bridgeport, Connecticut, founded the International Flying Saucer Bureau (IFSB). In October 1952 the first issue of its magazine *Space Review* appeared. By September 1953 IFSB had over 1500 members, with representatives in the UK, Europe, Australia and New Zealand. The following month, Barker announced the closure of IFSB in *Space Review* with this enigmatic 'Statement of Importance':

The mystery of the flying saucer is no longer a mystery. The source is already known, but any information about this is being withheld by orders from a higher source. We would like to print the full story in Space Review, *but because of the nature of the information we are very sorry that we have been advised in the negative. We advise those engaged in saucer work to please be very cautious.*

Bender told close associates that he was retiring from the UFO business because three intimidating men, dressed all in black, who were 'members of the United States government' had visited him after he had discussed a theory about the origin of flying saucers with an unnamed 'someone'. The three men in black had told Bender the true origin of the saucers, which would be revealed to the world in either five months or four years. Bender was so distressed by the experience that he was sick for three days. In 1962 Bender published *The Flying Saucers and the Three Men*, in which he revealed that the three men were aliens in disguise, who had bases in Antarctica and were on Earth to refine seawater (after which the story went downhill).

Those who knew Bender were sure something had genuinely terrified him. But what? In 1992, Professor Michael D. Swords proposed a solution to the 'Bender mystery'. In August 1953, a 'fireball' tore through a billboard in New Haven, Connecticut. It then changed course, and disappeared over a hill half a mile away. August Roberts, an investigator on IFSB's research team, arrived on the scene, found some metal fragments, and sent them to a research chemist for analysis. They turned out to be mostly copper. Shortly after Roberts, a team from US Naval Ordnance arrived to inspect the ventilated billboard.

Swords reasons that the Navy team's presence indicated that a shell or missile had holed the billboard, rather than a UFO – and the military were less than impressed that a civilian saucer researcher had got there first and made off with the evidence. Swords believes that Navy intelligence agents 'decided to tell Bender something so scary that he would never peep anything but nonsense about saucers again', and suspects that the Bender affair was 'an intelligence game or experiment to see how effectively operatives could manipulate the fledgling UFO "research" community.'

Men In Black have been considered to be hallucinations, apparitions, projections, and impersonations (perhaps by aliens) of government agents. It would be ironic if Swords were right, and so rich a source of ufological speculation and myth-making should have been, all the time, three somberly dressed but altogether fleshly human beings in the pay of the US government.

given absolutely no hint of its presence. The aircraft switched on its electronic counter-measures systems in that sweep of the radar, and became 'invisible'. Spaulding wondered: how many civilian air traffic controlers seeing UFOs on their screens had been the unwitting victims of such top-secret tests? [1]

The difficulty with the Federal Hypothesis is that, like all UFO conspiracy theories, it cannot be conclusively proven. Skeptics would say that Spaulding read more into the CIA's interest in UFOs after 1953 than can be justified by what the documents really say. All indications are, indeed, that after 1953 the CIA's involvement with UFOs was passive, and amounted to little more than collecting information for its own sake.

The startling silhouette of the Northrop B-2 bomber. First unveiled in November 1988, in the same month as the equally unorthodox F-117A Nighthawk fighter, the aircraft uses 'low observability' technology that had been in development since 1966. Some UFO reports may stem from 'stealth' program tests.

The Federal Hypothesis was also markedly unpopular with ufologists, who much preferred their conspiracies to revolve around crashed saucers and dead aliens than have them come to a dead halt on the desks of spies and generals, no matter how devious and duplicitous. At the same time there do exist a few UFO cases that look suspiciously as if they have a military bungle at their core – grit around which a ufological pearl has been spun. In these instances the military have let the mythology grow, and may even have encouraged it to grow. It is easier to be accused of taking part in a cosmic cover-up than it is to admit to an embarrassing foul-up. And the military know perfectly well that investigative journalists, prying politicians and the like will probably disregard anything that looks like the obsession of a minority faction.

The Majestic Twelve

Documentary proof of a cover-up of gigantic proportions had always been missing from the ufologists' armory of accusations against the powers that be. When it arrived – or seemed to arrive – it was greeted with a barrage of doubt, criticism and outright condemnation, and became one of the breaking-points in the fragmentation of ufology in the 1980s. The purported proof was, of course, an ostensibly authentic government document.

On 11 December 1984 TV producer Jaime Shandera allegedly received a double-wrapped, heavily sealed package in the mail at his Burbank, California, home. Inside was an undeveloped 35mm film. Some time before this, Shandera had been approached by Roswell researcher William L. Moore, who claimed to have made contact with a group of dissidents in USAF intelligence. This small circle – whom Moore later dubbed 'the Aviary' – allegedly wanted to make public the military's involvement with aliens and crashed saucers (see Chapter Six). Shandera at once took the film to Moore, who developed it.

The film pictured two documents, one dated 18 November 1952, the other 24 September 1947. If genuine, they were of world-shaking importance. The first was a briefing document addressed to President-Elect Dwight D. Eisenhower by Rear Admiral Roscoe H. Hillenkoetter. Each page was stamped TOP SECRET/MAJIC EYES ONLY. The

TOP SECRET / MAJIC

EYES ONLY

* TOP SECRET *
••••••••••••••

EYES ONLY   COPY ONE OF ONE.

SUBJECT: OPERATION MAJESTIC-12 PRELIMINARY BRIEFING FOR
   PRESIDENT-ELECT EISENHOWER.

DOCUMENT PREPARED 18 NOVEMBER, 1952.

BRIEFING OFFICER: ADM. ROSCOE H. HILLENKOETTER (MJ-1)

NOTE: This document has been prepared as a preliminary briefing
only. It should be regarded as introductory to a full operations
briefing intended to follow.

• • • • • •

OPERATION MAJESTIC-12 is a TOP SECRET Research and Development/
Intelligence operation responsible directly and only to the
President of the United States. Operations of the project are
carried out under control of the Majestic-12 (Majic-12) Group
which was established by special classified executive order of
President Truman on 24 September, 1947, upon recommendation by
Dr. Vannevar Bush and Secretary James Forrestal. (See Attachment
"A".) Members of the Majestic-12 Group were designated as follows:

                Adm. Roscoe H. Hillenkoetter
                Dr. Vannevar Bush
                Secy. James V. Forrestal*
                Gen. Nathan F. Twining
                Gen. Hoyt S. Vandenberg
                Dr. Detlev Bronk
                Dr. Jerome Hunsaker
                Mr. Sidney W. Souers
                Mr. Gordon Gray
                Dr. Donald Menzel
                Gen. Robert M. Montague
                Dr. Lloyd V. Berkner

The death of Secretary Forrestal on 22 May, 1949, created
a vacancy which remained unfilled until 01 August, 1950, upon
which date Gen. Walter B. Smith was designated as permanent
replacement.

On 24 June, 1947, a civilian pilot flying over the Cascade
Mountains in the State of Washington observed nine flying
disc-shaped aircraft traveling in formation at a high rate
of speed. Although this was not the first known sighting
of such objects, it was the first to gain widespread attention
in the public media. Hundreds of reports of sightings of
similar objects followed. Many of these came from highly
credible military and civilian sources. These reports resulted in independent efforts by several different elements
of the military to ascertain the nature and purpose of these
objects in the interests of national defense. A number of
witnesses were interviewed and there were several unsuccessful
attempts to utilise aircraft in efforts to pursue reported
discs in flight. Public reaction bordered on near hysteria
at times.

In spite of these efforts, little of substance was learned
about the objects until a local rancher reported that one
had crashed in a remote region of New Mexico located approximately seventy-five miles northwest of Roswell Army Air
Base (now Walker Field).

On 07 July, 1947, a secret operation was begun to assure
recovery of the wreckage of this object for scientific study.
During the course of this operation, aerial reconnaissance
discovered that four small human-like beings had apparently
ejected from the craft at some point before it exploded.
These had fallen to earth about two miles east of the wreckage
site. All four were dead and badly decomposed due to action
by predators and exposure to the elements during the approximately one week time period which had elapsed before their
discovery. A special scientific team took charge of removing
these bodies for study. (See Attachment "C".) The wreckage
of the craft was also removed to several different locations.
(See Attachment "B".) Civilian and military witnesses in
the area were debriefed, and news reporters were given the
effective cover story that the object had been a misguided
weather research balloon.

•••••••••••••••
* TOP SECRET *
•••••••••••••••

EYES ONLY TOP SECRET / MAJIC   T52-EXEMPT (E)
       EYES ONLY
                                              003

Part of the 'MJ-12' papers, almost universally regarded as a hoax. Among objections to the authenticity of the papers are the curious form of dating used throughout (with a zero before single digit numbers), the failure of Rear Admiral Hillenkoetter to observe military etiquette in not using his precise rank, and the presence of lawyer and newspaper publisher Gordon Gray on a panel of scientists and military men.

second, an attachment to this, was perhaps more momentous. It purported to be a TOP SECRET memo – referred to as Special Classified Executive Order #092447 in the briefing, but not so marked – signed by President Harry S Truman to Secretary of Defense James Forrestal.

Interpreted in light of the briefing to Eisenhower, it authorized Forrestal, after due consultation with nuclear scientist Dr Vannevar Bush, to establish a board of suitably qualified persons to be answerable directly and only to the President, and to be known as 'Majestic 12'. Their job, the presidential briefing made clear, was to investigate a crashed saucer that had been recovered near Roswell, New Mexico, in July 1947.

The briefing for Eisenhower described the members and progress of the MJ-12 group. The MJ-12 panel consisted of 12 eminent scientists, engineers, military men and intelligence experts – some of whom, such as Hillenkoetter, combined more than one of these roles. It even included Harvard astronomer Dr Donald Menzel, who in his public utterances was an intransigent opponent of any suggestion that UFOs were 'real'.

To scholars of UFO conspiracy theories, Hillenkoetter's involvement was hardly less fascinating. The Rear Admiral had not been purely a Navy man. He was the first Director of the CIA, which was also established in September 1947; Hillenkoetter had

Case # 21

Island Of Disguises?

VARIOUS LOCATIONS, PUERTO RICO

July 1989-December 1990

Since the late 1980s there has been a string of reports from Puerto Rico that feature aircraft, notably US Navy F-14 Tomcats, chasing UFOs. The reports may represent instances of William Spaulding's Federal Hypothesis in action. At around 8.30 p.m. on 4 July 1989, F-14s from Roosevelt Roads Naval Air Station at Ceiba were seen by several witnesses from the nearby town of Luquillo, in hot pursuit of 'a very big and brilliant blue-white star' that performed several bizarre maneuvers near Mt El Yunque before heading south-east across the Sierra de Luquillo, with the jets still trailing it.

On the evening of 22 June 1990, three witnesses saw four F-14s chasing 'a round ball of yellow light with a very bright red light in its center' that was flying in a southwesterly direction over the Rio Guyate near Route 52, in the eastern part of the island. Behind the F-14s came an AWACS radar surveillance aircraft.

At 5.30 p.m. on 19 December 1990, residents of Caguas, also in eastern Puerto Rico, saw 'unmarked' military helicopters apparently in pursuit of a similar yellow and red light, which was 'as big as a 747' and flew 'totally noiselessly' before it disappeared among the mountains.

The US Navy's Atlantic Fleet Weapons Training Facility (AFWTF) has its headquarters hard by Roosevelt Roads NAS, and controls two huge ocean firing ranges – Alfa, some 120,000sqmiles (310,000sqkm) in area, to the north and east of the island, and Bravo, 74,000sqmiles (192,000sqkm) in extent, to the south-east. Among the hardware tested by AFWTF are cruise missiles and electronic warfare devices. The US Navy has also funded development of advanced fighters using unconventional airfoils – swept-forward wings, for instance.

Some of these may actually look like UFOs or could easily be mistaken for a 'flying saucer' by an untutored observer – especially when flying at dusk, and especially if of unconventional shape. The military does not have to encourage UFO sightings in either case. It merely takes advantage of belief in UFOs as a cloak for its activities. These may include tests that the local populAtion might otherwise find objectionable (such as flying a cruise missile over populated areas, which is not without precedent). According to skeptical ufologist James Oberg, the Soviets did encourage interest in UFOs among citizens living near space launch sites and military installations so that details of activities or hardware there would get lost in accounts of apparently anomalous events. Much the same strategy may be at work around the notorious Area 51 in Nevada, USA.

---

headed its predecessor, the Central Intelligence Group, since 1 May that year. He retired from the US Navy in June 1957, and soon afterward joined the Board of Governors of Donald Keyhoe's NICAP, possibly the most influential UFO organization of the 1950s and 1960s. Conspiracy theorists have always maintained that Hillenkoetter – once a spy, always a spy – was a fifth columnist of the first water. William Spaulding, for example, had made much of the heavy presence

of ex-CIA members in NICAP's higher echelons.

Two and a half years later, on 29 May 1987, Shandera, Moore and nuclear physicist Stanton T. Friedman made the MJ-12 papers public. They claimed they had spent the intervening time trying to verify the documents, and released them only because British ufologist Timothy Good had announced that he, too, had copies, and was about to display them to the press. Moore and Shandera said

they then received cryptic postcards which suggested they look in a certain file in the National Archives. And there, in July 1985, Shandera found a 1954 memo to Lt General Twining – former head of Air Materiel Command, now USAF Chief of Staff, and an MJ-12 member, according to the 'briefing'. The note referred to a briefing by the MJ-12 panel during a National Security Council (NSC) meeting with President Eisenhower on 16 July 1954.

TOP SECRET
EYES ONLY
THE WHITE HOUSE
WASHINGTON

September 24, 1947.

MEMORANDUM FOR THE SECRETARY OF DEFENSE

Dear Secretary Forrestal:

As per our recent conversation on this matter, you are hereby authorized to proceed with all due speed and caution upon your undertaking. Hereafter this matter shall be referred to only as Operation Majestic Twelve.

It continues to be my feeling that any future considerations relative to the ultimate disposition of this matter should rest solely with the Office of the President following appropriate discussions with yourself, Dr. Bush and the Director of Central Intelligence.

TOP SECRET
EYES ONLY

President Harry S Truman supposedly sets up the MJ-12 panel in the wake of the Roswell UFO crash. On all his other correspondence, Truman's signature cuts into the typed text, but not on this one. The signature exactly matches that on a letter to Dr Vannevar Bush dated 1 October 1947, but for a slight increase in size, consistent with photocopying, and a slight thinning of the top of the capital 'T' – a sign that the original surrounding text had been whited out.

The trio soon claimed to have contacted a 'highly placed military intelligence operative' who could authenticate the story. But the 'highly placed' intelligence source turned out to be a lowly USAF sergeant – one Richard L. Doty, an AFOSI agent who in 1980 had been involved in a bogus UFO sighting report while at Kirtland AFB, New Mexico. He had already passed a doctored (and fake, the USAF says) AFOSI document to Moore that referred to 'MJ Twelve'. Also, in April 1983 Doty had shown the mute researcher and TV director Linda M. Howe a 'presidential briefing' (which president was not stated) on 'unidentified flying vehicles' that described at length 'extra-terrestrial biological entities' (EBEs) that had been retrieved from crashed UFOs.

In the course of the meeting he also mentioned MJ-12. 'MJ', he said, stood for 'Majority'. The 12 were a policy-making body in charge of contacts with extra-terrestrials and directing the cover-up. Doty then, to put it mildly, gave Howe the runaround for months on end, while promising her official footage of alien contacts and even a face-to-face interview with a live alien. In July 1986, Doty was removed from AFOSI for faking reports of contacts with communist agents while stationed in West Germany. In October 1988, he left the Air Force. It is notable that documents emanating from Doty, and the MJ-12 papers themselves, share a specific grammatical error – following plural nouns with singular verbs, as in 'Several government agencies... actively investigates legitimate sightings'.

MJ-12 meets the critics

The MJ-12 papers themselves soon began to take a battering from skeptics. Philip J. Klass revealed that the machine used to type the Truman 'executive order' of 1947 was a Smith-Corona model that had not been manufactured until 1963.

Hillenkoetter had dated his memorandum to Eisenhower in an odd hybrid of civilian and military styles and signed himself 'Roscoe H. Hillenkoetter'. Neither of these forms had appeared before or since in any of his voluminous surviving correspondence, Klass said.

Klass's close inspection of the signature on the Truman document showed beyond reasonable doubt that it was a photocopy of the signature on a letter from Truman to Vannevar Bush, written on 1 October 1947. And as the Hillenkoetter memo of 1952 refers specifically to the Truman 'special classified executive order' of 1947, it follows that both were fakes.

Klass was not alone, for once, in rubbishing the documents. The National Archives took the 1954 memo to General Twining to pieces almost line by line. There was no NSC meeting with Eisenhower, on or off the record, on 16 July 1954. There was no Top Secret register number on the memo, and the TOP SECRET RESTRICTED INFORMATION classification it displayed was first used in the Nixon era.

Klass noted that the form of the date on the MJ-12 papers was the same as that used by Moore. CAUS noted that the TOP SECRET/ MAJIC stamp on the papers was in identical type to Moore's return address stamp, even down to a slightly out-of-line letter 'I'.

Curtis Peebles observed that the pages did not have the 'Page [#] of [#] Pages' numbering system standard in Top Secret documents. The Roswell air base is wrongly named. The Executive Clerk to the President, Ronald Geisler, called the number on the Truman memo 'impossible', 'absolutely not correct', 'not an Executive Order', 'dumb-looking', and commented that 'in 28 years I have seen nothing close to this'.

Stanton Friedman has addressed some of these objections – or, as Howard Blum put it, listened like a judge, and 'bellowed, Overruled.' Some of the critics' arguments he has refuted, but not all. His most intriguing discovery, during a trawl of some 15 libraries and archives, was that Donald Menzel led a double life – as UFO debunker and distinguished astronomer in public, and as a linguist, cryptographer and consultant to the NSA and CIA for more than 30 years, and held a US Navy TOP SECRET ULTRA clearance.

This only proves that Menzel would have been a likely choice for a panel like MJ-12 if such a panel had existed. And his anti-UFO writings were too trenchant – and time-consuming – to pass as a shoal of red herrings. If Menzel had known huge UFO secrets, his debunking would have been more subtle. Menzel's presence on the MJ-12 list smacks of revenge – or a joke – by whoever

created the forgery.

All of Friedman's 'evidence' for the reality of MJ-12, and thus the authenticity of the documents, is circumstantial at best. And while Friedman has shown that there are other documents in the archives that use the unusual dating style, the kind of paper, the system of stamping, and so on used in the MJ-12 papers, he has yet to produce a known genuine document that contains all the many eccentricities – which extend to using British, not American, punctuation – that the MJ-12 documents manage to pack into a few pages.

It does seem improbable that so many oddities should find a home in a single document and that the document should be genuine. And that is without even starting to address the even greater inherent improbability that the US government has the wreckage of an alien spacecraft, the corpses of 'EBEs', or even a live alien celebrity cached away somewhere in its vaults. [2]

The guardian of Carp

The uproar within ufology that the MJ-12 affair created had settled by the mid-1990s. Even Timothy Good, who had managed to base large parts of his monumental and exhaustive study of government documents, *Above Top*

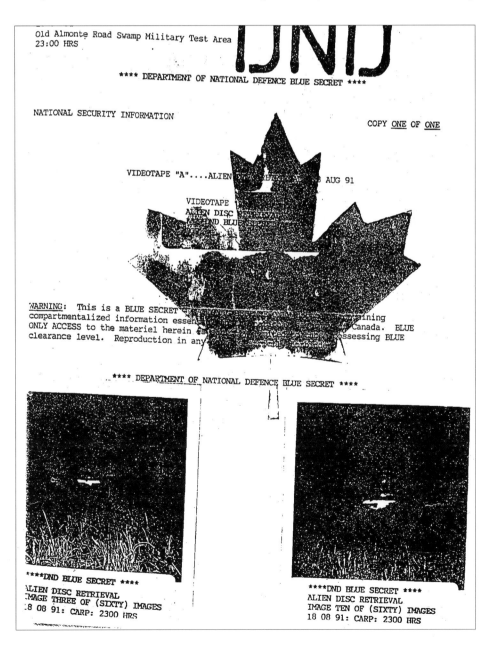

One of the crudely faked Canadian Department of National Defence documents sent out with a videotape supposedly showing the landing of a UFO in Ontario in August 1991.

Case #22

The Caper at Carp

MANION CORNERS, near CARP, ONTARIO, CANADA
4 November 1989 and 18 August 1991

In February 1992 an American ufologist, Ted Oechsler, received a package, postmarked Ottowa, Canada, at his Maryland home. It bore no return address, only the codename 'Guardian' and a fingerprint. Inside were Canadian Department of National Defense documents that largely concerned the Apocalypse and the prophecies of Nostradamus, a 16th-century seer. Also in the packet was a 30-minute videotape. The material on it, Oechsler thought, was 'exceptional'.

The first six minutes were moving images of what appeared to be a rotating disk-shaped object seen at night. The UFO had a dome with a pulsating light on top, and showed various other bright blue, red and white lights. The remaining 24 minutes of the video show still pictures of the same event and what seems to be an alien entity with a luminous face – with large, slanting black eyes – and glowing hands.

With the help of local UFO researchers in Canada, Oechsler found a witness to a UFO event that Guardian had earlier reported to him through the mails. Mrs Diane Labanek said she had witnessed the crash of a UFO that had allegedly been tracked on radar over Carp before falling into a swamp near her house, on 4 November 1989. According to Guardian, the craft was powered by a 'pulsing electromagnetic field', and was constructed from 'matrix-dielectric magnesium alloy'. Its crew of three were descendants of the dinosaurs, who had fled into space 60 million years ago but were now returning to reclaim the Earth.

Oechsler visited the crash site and discovered disturbed ground and plants that he concluded had been dried out by microwave radiation. At this point he told Diane Labanek about the video. She told him of seeing, on 18 August 1991, red 'fires' among the trees visible from her children's bedroom window. Next, a UFO had come down among the fires – which, at the time, she had thought must be landing flares – and put on a display of lights like those in the video. This lasted between five and eight minutes, and then the UFO took off. A little later, she saw helicopters cruising around the area.

Oechsler claimed that the Guardian video had been analyzed exhaustively by Dr Robert Nathan of the NASA Jet Propulsion Laboratory in Pasadena, California, who had found no evidence of trickery, and that NBC-TV had spent up to a quarter of a million dollars attempting, and failing, to replicate the film.

Secret, on the assumption that the papers were genuine, had come to consider them a hoax. Only Stanton Friedman among leading ufologists seemed to lay much store by the MJ-12 papers any more, and defended them with his customary energy and ebullience at every opportunity.

The willingness of many of ufology's leading lights to take extreme claims to their bosoms without pausing for sober reflection was illustrated once again, in the late 1980s, by another case – the famous Gulf Breeze photographs taken by Ed Walters. The case crumpled somewhat when a model of the celebrated UFO turned up in Walters' house and one of his accomplices admitted to assisting in the hoax, but it too had caused huge rifts in the UFO community: a number of long-serving and highly respected members of MUFON resigned because the organization's director had persistently backed the genuineness of the pictures despite the lack of supporting evidence.

One of the champions of the Gulf Breeze pictures had been Bruce Maccabee, an optical physicist who had made a reputation as an expert analyst of UFO photographs. It seems the Gulf Breeze fiasco did not make Maccabee any more cautious about endorsing another set of flying saucer pictures, which even included shots of aliens. The affair at Carp, west of Ottowa, Ontario, might have alerted suspicion because an early scene in the case was so similar to the curtain-raiser to the MJ-12 affair, with its anonymous packages and suspect 'official' documents (see Case #22). But Maccabee lost no time in 'analysing' the video footage that came in the package and declaring his belief that it showed an 'extraordinary craft'. On an *Unsolved Mysteries* telecast, he said it was the 'best footage of a landed UFO' he'd ever seen.

MUFON Ontario (MO) investigators came to different conclusions. The Canadian Depart-ment of National Defense documents were soon proven to be crude for- geries. MO learned the Royal Canadian Mounted Police had investigated the video with the help of local pilots and the Canadian military, and saw not a UFO but a helicopter visible among all the lights.

MO made a still more prosaic interpretation: the 'UFO' was a pick-up truck, precisely like the one owned by the chief witness's nephew, with its wipers upright and reflecting light. When Maccabee snorted that no ordinary pick-up would have Day-glo wipers, MO responded: 'There are thousands of sets on vehicles around Ontario.' It was not hard to agree with their opinion of the alien: 'suspiciously like a man in a mask'.

Real explanations

MO's visit to the alleged landing site generated yet more skepticism. Damage to the ground that Oechsler believed was caused by the UFO was deemed to be the work of skunks, and not microwave radiation but the hard Canadian winter had affected juniper trees. And how, they wondered, had the anonymous witness – the self-styled 'Guardian' – managed to shoot very smooth video film after walking more than 1000ft (300m) across very uneven ground in the dark, take several 35mm and over 20 Polaroid stills, and even (in Oechsler's opinion) get abducted – all in the 5-8 minutes that Diane Labanek said the event lasted?

'Perhaps the Guardian is a large octopus,' MO suggested. And significantly missing from the video were shots of the UFO either landing or of it taking off.

The landing site was on an abandoned 200-acre (80-ha) farm. Dotted around were notices reading DEFENCE CANADA KILLING TECHNOLOGY TEST AREA. Labanek denied all knowledge of either. In fact, she and her husband owned the property and had a shack full of such paramilitary signs. Labanek also denied knowing anything about either the Guardian or UFOs.

The Guardian turned out to be one Bobby Charlebois, a UFO devotee (as was Labanek's nephew), and a family friend who visited her several times a week. MUFON Ontario's verdict: a hoax. And, they suggested, Maccabee and Oechsler knew it, but had hoped to make money from the story. Maccabee strenuously denied the allegation.[3] Others recalled he had had

The 'alien' seen on the video of the Carp landing. Skeptics may be forgiven for thinking most children make a better showing in a mask on Hallowe'en, and that the film was certainly more trick than treat.

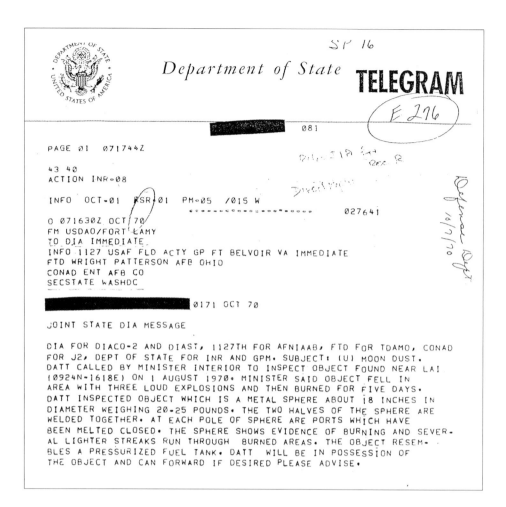

PAGE 01   071744Z

43 40
ACTION INR-08

INFO OCT-01 SSR-01 PM-05 /015 W
O 071630Z OCT 70
FM USDAO/FORT LAMY
TO DIA IMMEDIATE
INFO 1127 USAF FLD ACTY GP FT BELVOIR VA IMMEDIATE
FTD WRIGHT PATTERSON AFB OHIO
CONAD ENT AFB CO
SECSTATE WASHDC

0171 OCT 70

JOINT STATE DIA MESSAGE

DIA FOR DIACO-2 AND DIAST, 1127TH FOR AFNIAAB, FTD FOR TDAMO, CONAD
FOR J2, DEPT OF STATE FOR INR AND GPM. SUBJECT: (U) MOON DUST.
DATT CALLED BY MINISTER INTERIOR TO INSPECT OBJECT FOUND NEAR LAI
(0924N-1618E) ON 1 AUGUST 1970. MINISTER SAID OBJECT FELL IN
AREA WITH THREE LOUD EXPLOSIONS AND THEN BURNED FOR FIVE DAYS.
DATT INSPECTED OBJECT WHICH IS A METAL SPHERE ABOUT 18 INCHES IN
DIAMETER WEIGHING 20-25 POUNDS. THE TWO HALVES OF THE SPHERE ARE
WELDED TOGETHER. AT EACH POLE OF SPHERE ARE PORTS WHICH HAVE
BEEN MELTED CLOSED. THE SPHERE SHOWS EVIDENCE OF BURNING AND SEVER-
AL LIGHTER STREAKS RUN THROUGH BURNED AREAS. THE OBJECT RESEM-
BLES A PRESSURIZED FUEL TANK. DATT WILL BE IN POSSESSION OF
THE OBJECT AND CAN FORWARD IF DESIRED PLEASE ADVISE.

A telegram from the US Embassy in Chad, relaying news of unidentified space debris to the State Department and Defense Intelligence Agency, refers to 'Moon Dust'. Believers claim Moon Dust was a super-secret project, charged with picking up alien hardware – but the message was entirely unclassified.

a share of the royalties from Ed Walters' best-selling book about his encounters at Gulf Breeze.

Moon Dust

When it came to real government documents that appeared to concern UFO retrievals, ufologists were less excitable, but could still read into them more than the words seemed to bear. CAUS leaders Lawrence Fawcett and Barry J. Greenwood, for example, made much of Projects Moon Dust and Blue Fly in their newsletter *Just*

Cause (Issue 8, June 1986).

A long letter to a Col Betz from a Lt Col Norman M. Rosner at the Pentagon written on 3 November 1961 (but not released until 1979) makes it verbosely clear that Blue Fly 'has been established to facilitate expeditious delivery... of Moon Dust or other items of great technical intelligence interest'. In other words, it was 'a project for the acquisition of airlift for a quick reaction capability', as Col A.W. Schumann described it in response to an enquiry.

In short, it consisted of some transport aircraft and their crews who should be ready to move at short notice. Fawcett and Greenwood had noticed that the codeword 'Blue' was often attached to projects (such as Blue Book, for example) concerned with high-altitude vehicles. As Moon Dust was set up to retrieve space debris – whether it was American or foreign didn't matter, the point was to lay hands on it – this should not come

as a great surprise.

But *Just Cause* cited this segment of the letter:

Peacetime employment of AFCIN intelligence team capability is provided for in UFO investigation (AFR 200-2) and in support of Air Force Systems Command (AFCS) Foreign Technology Division (FTD) Projects Moon Dust and Blue Fly. These three peacetime projects all involve a potential for employment of qualified field intelligence personnel on a quick reaction basis to recover or perform field exploitation of unidentified flying objects, or known Soviet/Bloc aerospace vehicles, weapons systems, and/or residual components of such equipment. The intelligence team capability to gain rapid access, regardless of location, to recover or perform field exploitation, to communicate and provide intelligence reports is the only such collection capability available to AFCIN, and it is vitally necessary in view of current intelligence gaps concerning Soviet/Bloc technological capabilities.

And commented on it thus:

And what did Moon Dust material include? Among other things, it included things acquired from the recovery and/or field exploitation of UFOs! Note how UFOs are set apart from Soviet/Bloc aerospace vehicles. Since the Soviets were the only other real space power in the world at the time, besides the U.S., what could have been meant by setting off UFOs as a separate subject of investigation? If they were British, or another nation's space vehicle, why not say this, as it was said for the Soviets?

Soviet interpretation

With a less stimulated eye it is not difficult to read 'UFOs' in the Betz letter to mean 'unknown Soviet vehicles' or 'unidentified debris of any kind', as exemplified in Case 23, for instance. Fawcett and Lawrence seem surprisingly keen here to interpret 'UFOs' as 'flying saucers'; and reckon that Moon Dust 'likely dates from the beginnings of Blue Book at least'.

Case #23

Moon Dust in August

KUTUM, SUDAN; LAI, CHAD; and LA PAZ, BOLIVIA
3 August 1967, 1 August 1970 and 21 August 1979

References to Project Moon Dust turn up in a number of State Department telegrams from US embassies overseas and in internal teletypes of the Department of Defense. These are copied automatically to the CIA, DIA, NASA, AFOSI, NSC and other potentially interested branches of the US security establishment. A trio of the more intriguing reports is summarized here.

KUTUM, SUDAN, 1967: A cube-shaped 'satellite' weighing about 3 tonnes was found about 50 miles (80km) from Kutum. It consisted of numerous smaller cubes fastened together with a 'silky material'. The local authorities took photographs and 'with difficulty cut samples'. No inscriptions were evident on the outer surface.

LAI, CHAD, 1970: The US Defense Attaché was called by Chad's Minister of the Interior to inspect an object that was found near Lai. There were three loud explosions as the object fell, and it burned for five days. The remains consisted of a metal sphere about 18in (450mm) in diameter and weighing 20–25lb (45–57kg). The Defense Attaché thought it resembled a pressurized fuel tank.

LA PAZ, BOLIVIA, 1979: A fireball fell with a whistling sound and exploded in the suburb of Bue Retiro. There was no impact crater, however. The two objects recovered were metal spheres, similar to copper, and 'dark with light spots'. They were both about 3ft (1m) in diameter, 3lb (1.5kg) in weight, and each had a 9in (230mm) hole in it. A Bolivian officer considered they seemed to be designed for space flight.

Two attachments to the Pentagon letter are dated 23 January 1957, and 4 March 1957, which ought to be better clues. In this period the US and the USSR were competing directly to be the first to get a satellite into space, and this was the obvious time to establish a quick-reaction force to sweep up space debris. It would serve two purposes – to find out what the opposition was up to, and to keep US material out of Soviet hands.

The Manhattan apartment block from whose 12th floor Linda Cortile claimed she was abducted one night in November 1989. The UFO that hovered outside was supposedly three-quarters the width of the building across. Despite its size, workers at the busy night-loading bays of the **New York Daily Post** *(right foreground) noticed nothing unusual.*

Case #24

The Abductee and the Secret Service

LOWER EAST SIDE, MANHATTAN ISLAND, NEW YORK CITY, USA

30 November 1989

In April 1989, 45-year-old New Yorker Linda Cortile (a.k.a. 'Linda Napolitano') began regressive hypnosis with researcher Budd Hopkins. She suspected that she had been abducted by aliens in her twenties. Then, at the end of November, she was apparently abducted again.

She had gone to bed at about 3.00 a.m.; her husband was already asleep. She began to feel a paralyzing numbness creeping from her feet up her body, which from previous experience she knew was a prelude to an abduction. She tried unsuccessfully to wake her husband. When a gray entity appeared in the room, she threw a pillow at it. Then she became totally paralyzed, and her mind went blank, although she vaguely recalled someone palpating her spine.

Under hypnosis, Mrs Cortile recollected that three or four aliens had come into the room. Then she had been 'floated' through the closed window of her 12th-storey apartment by the aliens, had entered a blue beam of light, and was taken aboard a craft that was hovering above the building. She was given a medical examination, then taken back and dropped onto her bed from mid-air. Her violent return failed to wake her husband. Fearing he and her two sons had been killed by the aliens, she checked their breathing with a mirror held under their noses. They were unharmed.

About 15 months later, in February 1991, Hopkins received a letter from two men claiming to be police officers. They said that they had seen Mrs Cortile's abduction, from a car parked under the FDR Drive, near her apartment house. She had floated 'like an angel' through the air into the UFO, which was 'about three quarters the size of the building across'. Then the UFO had gained altitude, flown over FDR Drive, and plunged into the East River not far from the Brooklyn Bridge. They had considered visiting the block to find the woman. They were particularly concerned to know if the victim were alive and well, for they had waited 45 minutes but not seen the UFO emerge from the river. The officers signed themselves Richard and Dan.

Hopkins warned Mrs Cortile that she might be visited by the pair. Some weeks later she reported that Richard and Dan had called on her, and were visibly relieved to find her safe and well. They refused to speak to Hopkins in person, for fear of public exposure, but agreed to contact him.

Soon afterwards Hopkins received additional letters, drawings of the event and a taped account from one of the officers. He explained that they could not meet Hopkins because he and his partner were in fact Secret Service agents. On the night of the abduction they had been taking Perez de Cuellar, then Secretary-General of the United Nations, to a heliport, when their limousine broke down. They had pushed it to within a couple of blocks of Mrs Cortile's apartment house. De Cuellar had also witnessed the entire episode. Hopkins concluded that the aliens had been deliberately demonstrating their powers and the reality of their presence on Earth, to a person of international standing and influence. In short, the limo's breakdown had been the aliens' doing, too.

Linda Cortile experienced two more abductions in 1991, but not by aliens. One afternoon in April, Richard and Dan forced her into a car while she was out walking and asked her a series of bizarre questions. They demanded that she remove her shoes to prove she had toes because, they said, aliens had no toes. Mrs Cortile somehow noted that the car was being followed. Hopkins traced the cars to the British and Venezuelan missions to the United Nations.

On 15 October, she was kidnaped by Dan, who shoved her into a red Jaguar and drove her to a beach house on Long Island. There, he made her disrobe and put on a white nightgown like the one she had been wearing when abducted. Mrs Cortile managed to tape-record some of this encounter, which was cut short when Richard arrived and managed to sedate Dan. She later received a letter from Dan. Written from a mental institution, it was clearly not the work of a sound mind.

In November 1991 Hopkins received a letter and drawings from a retired telephone operator in her sixties whom he calls 'Janet Kimble'. Her car had mysteriously, temporarily, failed as she crossed Brooklyn Bridge, within sight of the Cortile apartment, on the night Mrs Cortile was abducted. The bridge lights had blacked out, and the other cars on the bridge also broke down. Mrs Kimble claimed to have seen the UFO, the party of aliens and Mrs Cortile being floated into the craft, even though the UFO was shining so brightly that she had to shield her eyes from it. Drawings of the event by this witness and one of the alleged Secret Service agents matched in many major and minor details.

Just Cause's whole exercise in speculation bordered on futility, as both Moon Dust and Blue Fly were no longer active by 1979. The 1961 Pentagon letter looks like a lengthy plea for decently qualified personnel to fulfil Moon Dust's duties (and included the intriguing suggestion that field training should take place in Laos and Vietnam). It reeks, indeed, of a justification for keeping the project alive. Clearly a tour of duty in Moon Dust was not going to be onerous, once out of the jungle.

Nor was it particularly secret in its latter days: none of the State Department and DIA teletypes referring to it are classified. If the security services had thought there was any possibility that the various bits of metal and junk that dropped out of the sky might be extra-terrestrial, they would surely have been a good deal more circumspect in their communications about them.

What ufologists' toying with such half-hidden projects reveals is a desire to keep the notion of cover-up alive. *Just Cause* went so far as to quote a long and fatuous passage from one of Donald Keyhoe's books, and ended: 'Could an MJ-12-type committee have begun Moon Dust as a reaction to early UFO events like Roswell?' None of the documents, real or fake, supports the suggestion. [4]

What really caught ufologists' imag-inations in the 1980s and 1990s was the abduction phenomenon. Budd Hopkins published *Missing Time*, his first full-length essay into the subject, in 1981. By 1993 he was regaling the lecture and convention circuit with the story of Linda Cortile (see Case 24). MUFON dubbed it 'the case of the century' but a large portion of the so-called UFO-community thought it was preposterous drivel. Once more there was a massive falling-out among ufologists, with furious exchanges in journals and still more vitriolic letters and memoranda circulating privately and on the Internet.

The UN connection

Lost in the storm was the way the case latched on to the theme of a cover-up – without a solitary shred of documentary evidence – and enlarged it to its ultimate proportions. The chief witness, allegedly, to Linda Cortile's abduction was none other than the then Secretary General of the United Nations. Hopkins contended that 'the aliens' had been deliberately displaying their powers and their presence on Earth to the world's premier diplomat – who thus became the mediator between this world and the alien Otherworld.

This was a sublime version of the idea that the world's elite knew everything but were, like Brer Fox, saying nothing. And throughout the case ran another conspiratorial thread – the increasingly demonic behavior of those secular powers of darkness, the men from the Secret Service.

In due course, Linda Cortile even answered the rational response to her grandiose claim. Why did the aliens not abduct Perez de Cuellar from his car and have done with it? But they did: Cortile saw him aboard the spacecraft. And, inevitably, the UN insisted that Sr de Cuellar had no official business anywhere at that hour on 30 November 1989; he was at home in bed. If you believe everything you hear about abductions that, of course, would have been no great hindrance to the aliens.[5]

There are many points of detail that push holes in the Cortile case, even if one accepts in principle that alien abductions are genuine material events. If you visit the site of the Cortile event, as I have, its ludicrous aspects are immediately apparent. Hopkins had not even bothered to check the weather conditions on the night Cortile was 'abducted'.

But its real importance was not in its truth or even its falsity. It lay in making respectable some elements of ufology that bordered on the demented, and that had been gathering strength since the mid-1980s. That grim and truly paranoid episode we contemplate next.

Chapter Six

BEYOND DREAMLAND

THE DARK SIDE OF AMERICAN UFOLOGY

WHEN Donald Keyhoe claimed in the 1950s that the US government was concealing what it knew about UFOs, he could hardly have imagined the monster that would shuffle forth under the banner of 'cover-up' some 30 years later. From the early 1980s on, a small group of men by turns amazed, bemused and horrified UFO experts, while among the public they set in motion one of the most grotesque – some would say malignant – conspiracy legends of the entire flying-saucer era.

The fable they spun tells of secret deals between devious government agencies and treacherous alien entities, of alien bases hidden deep beneath the Southwestern desert, of gruesome genetic experiments. And underlying

---

The UFO that repeatedly visited Ed Walters in Gulf Breeze, Florida, in 1987 and 1988. The usual large claims were made that such pictures, shot with a Polaroid camera, could not be faked without a Hollywood-style budget, and, as usual, soon crumbled. A young man admitted helping Walters fake the photos, and others showed that Walters had previously produced double exposures with his Polaroid as a party trick.

---

it all was, apparently, a monstrous plot to rule the world. This bizarre saga had its immediate origins – as far as anyone can precisely pinpoint them – in an entirely innocent investigation into the alleged abduction of Ms Myrna Hansen and her six-year-old son in the spring of 1980 (see Case #25). It was conducted by one of the most benign and upright UFO researchers in the business, abduction specialist Dr Leo Sprinkle. From there on the story was to become as convoluted as it was fantastic.

Paul Bennewitz, as a representative of the Aerial Phenomena Research Organization (APRO) based in Tucson, Arizona, was present when Dr Sprinkle guided Ms Hansen through a series of hypnotic regressions. From parts of her account it was possible to infer that American, or at least human, scientists were colluding with the alien abduction program. According to researcher William L. Moore, Bennewitz became convinced that the aliens had implanted 'some sort of communication device in the woman's head', which they were using to control her actions. Jim Lorenzen, a founder of APRO, felt Bennewitz 'had already decided what he was going to find before he went looking for it' and

was 'prone to make great leaps of logic on the basis of incomplete data'.[1]

This may explain why Bennewitz did not pause to resolve an obvious logical conflict. For the implant, if it was present at all, seems to have been strikingly ineffective in preventing Myrna Hansen from divulging the aliens' grisly secrets. Rather than simply conclude that there was no device, or even make the attempt to detect one, Bennewitz decided on a grander stroke – to intercept the aliens' signals to their victims, and then to try to jam them.

Bennewitz was an electronics expert, the president of Thunder Scientific Laboratories, a supplier of humidity-control equipment to Kirtland Air Force Base, near his home in Albuquerque, New Mexico. He was aware of rumored UFO activity at the base, and proceeded to build and deploy scanning equipment to monitor radio signals from it.

The Beta report

Bennewitz succeeded in picking up a number of apparently coherent but mysterious pulsed signals, and some unusual magnetic emissions – which, he concluded, were evidence of

Case #25

The Cimarron Encounter

Near CIMARRON, COLFAX COUNTY, NEW MEXICO, USA
5 May 1980

Driving home on a road near Cimarron one evening in the spring of 1980, 28-year-old Myrna Hansen and her six-year-old son saw five UFOs descending into a cow pasture. Until hypnotically regressed, she had confused memories of a close encounter, and could not account for a period of 'missing time' of some four hours. She was regressed in sessions held between 11 May and 3 June by Dr Leo Sprinkle, in the company of Dr Paul Bennewitz, an electronics engineer who was also an investigator for the Aerial Phenomena Research Organization.

According to Ms Hansen's accounts under hypnosis, two white-suited figures emerged from one of the UFOs and mutilated one of the cows in the field, while it was alive, with an 18-inch (45 cm)-long knife. She remonstrated with them, and she and her son were captured and taken to separate ships. She continued to resist but was undressed and given a physical examination, including a vaginal probe that reportedly later produced a severe infection.

The procedure was interrupted by what appeared to be a tall, jaundiced human, who apologized and ordered the aliens punished. He then took Ms Hansen on a tour of this and possibly some other UFOs. The last seems to have taken flight, as she was next led out into a landscape that at one point she believed she recognized as being west of Las Cruces, and at another had the impression was near Roswell. Here she was taken into an underground base, where she managed to escape briefly. She found herself in a room full of what appeared to be water tanks, and was horrified to discover they were vats in which were floating human body parts, including an arm that had a hand attached to it.

Ms Hansen was then dragged out of this area, and she and her son were both put through a further painful process involving loud noises and blinding lights, before being taken back aboard the UFO and flown (with her car also aboard) back to the site of the abduction.

contact between the base and aliens. If the persistent reports that say the transmissions were at extremely low frequencies (ELF) are accurate, it's odd that Bennewitz did not ask himself why the 'aliens' would use a wavelength that is physically incapable of carrying highly detailed information, and has a negligible range in space. But – with the aid of the aliens, he said – he did devise a computer program that he believed could decode the signals. Apparently distracted from his original intention to shield abductees from alien mind control, he began a dialogue with the aliens themselves.

In the course of his research Bennewitz ultimately took some 6000

feet (1828m) of Super-8 film of UFOs around Albuquerque and northern New Mexico. And, partly through field trips, partly by examining NASA satellite photographs of the terrain, and partly from information gleaned from security agents in the US Air Force Office of Special Investigations (AFOSI), as well as, he said, from the aliens themselves, he assembled his 'data' into a grand pattern.

This not only revealed to him what the aliens were doing, but managed to explain the cattle mutilations that had plagued the Southwest for nearly 10 years and the entire abduction mystery too. And from around 1982 he began to tell everyone who would listen, and many who would not, from fellow

ufologists to congressmen and the US President, what he had found.

Bennewitz announced his findings in what he called *The Beta Report*. Here, edited for spelling and punctuation, are some of its main claims:[2]

● *Constant reception of video from alien ship and underground base view-screen; typical alien, humanoid and at times apparent homo sapiens.*

● *Established constant direct communication with the alien using a computer, and a form of hexadecimal code communication was instigated.*

● *Subsequent aerial and ground photographs revealed landing pylons, ships on the ground – entrances, beam weapons and apparent launch ports – along with aliens on the ground in electrostatically supported*

A minute by USAF Office of Special Investigations agent Richard C. Doty of a meeting between the Air Force and Paul Bennewitz in 1980. It is intriguing that a former Blue Book investigator was still on call for UFO cases. That he was brought in to the case, however, suggests that Blue Book was not merely a feeble public-relations front, as conspiracy theorists have long claimed.

vehicles; charging beam weapons, also apparently electrostatic.

● *It was learned... that two women and a boy near Austin, Texas were exposed to severe radiation at close range and the ship was last seen going west with helicopters. [This refers to the 1980 'Cash/Landrum' encounter – See Case #18].*

● *The computer communications and constant interaction with the alien in this manner without direct encounter has given a reasonably clear picture of the alien psychology, their logic and logic methods and their prime intent.*

The immediate intent, it turned out, was to construct a race of humanoid hybrids – part human, part alien. The ultimate purpose of this chilling program would be spelled out by others who were to take up Bennewitz's theme. For now, he was anxious to reveal that:

● *The total alien basing area apparently contains several cultures, (all under the designation 'Unity') and is approx 3km [1.9 miles] wide by 8km [5 miles] long and is located in the middle of nowhere on the Jicarilla Indian reservation west of Dulce, NM. Based on the number of ships presently in this area, the total alien population is estimated to be at least 2,000 and most likely more. More are coming or are on the way.*

● *Most importantly, the aliens will allow no one abducted to go without an implant. After insertion, knowledge of it is wiped out. All indications are that communication with the aliens cannot happen without the implant (with the exception of the use of the binary and the computer).*

MULTIPURPOSE INTER . OSI FORM
(Complete only applicable items)

	SUBJECT	FILE NO.
DO NO.(S) 17/IVO	KIRTLAND AFB, NM, 8 Aug - 3 Sep 80	8017093-0/29
CET NO.(S)	Alleged Sightings of Unidentified Aerial	TRANSMITTAL DATE
HEADQUARTERS	Lights in Restricted Test Range	28 Oct 80
DO NO. 17/UID		SUSPENSE DATE
DET NO.		
HEADQUARTERS		

ERENCE

AFOSI Fm 1, 8 Sep 80, Same Title

MINOR DISCREPANCIES NOTED ARE LISTED BELOW.
YOUR DISTRICT IS DESIGNATED OFFICE OF ORIGIN.
ATTACHED REQUIRES INVESTIGATION IN YOUR AREA
DETERMINE SUBJECT'S ACCESS TO CLASSIFIED INFORMATION AS REQUIRED BY OSIM 124-1, PARA 2-6-3.
FORWARD RESULTS DIRECTLY TO OFFICE OF ORIGIN, OR TO:
NO FURTHER INVESTIGATION CONTEMPLATED
OUR FILES REFLECT PRIOR INVESTIGATION BY _____, DTD. _____, FILE _____ (By copy of this form is requested to furnish _____ copies of prior investigation/letter summary, if applicable, to _____
REPORT OF PRIOR INVESTIGATION/SUMMARY ATTACHED.
INVESTIGATION CONTINUING AND YOU WILL BE FURNISHED FURTHER REPORTS.
DISCONTINUE INVESTIGATION. FORWARD RESULTS OF ANY INVESTIGATION ACCOMPLISHED.
DISCREPANCIES BETWEEN LEAD REQUEST AND DEVELOPED INFORMATION ARE SET FORTH.
REPORT OF COMMAND ACTION HAS NOT BEEN RECEIVED.
REQUEST STATUS OF THIS MATTER AND/OR DATE REPORT MAY BE EXPECTED. (Requester, forward 2 copies of this form.) (Recipient, use one received copy for answer with proper signature in remarks section unless OSI directives state reply not required.)
REFER ATTACHED TO INTERESTED COMMANDER FOR INFORMATION OR ACTION IF NOT PREVIOUSLY REPORTED
CHECK WORLD-WIDE LOCATOR FOR BELOW LISTED PERSON OR SUBJECT.
ATTACHED IS FORWARDED FOR INFORMATION AND/OR ACTION.
UPON REMOVAL OF ATTACHMENT(S) _____ THE CLASSIFICATION ON THIS CORRESPONDENCE WILL BE
☐ RETAINED. ☐ DOWNGRADED TO _____ ☐ CANCELED. ☐ MARKED "FOR OFFICIAL USE ONLY."
If classification is retained, with or without attachments, indicate reason for security classification and grouping per AFR 205-1.)

MARKS

On 24 Oct 80, Dr PAUL FREDRICK BENNEWITZ, Male Born 30 Sep 27, KS, Civ, SSAN: b7C b7C Albuquerque, NM, contacted SA RICHARD C. DOTY through Major NEST E. EDWARDS, Commander, 1608 SPS, Kirtland AFB, NM and related he had knowledge and idence of threats against Manzano Weapons Storage area. The threat was from Aerial enomena over Manzano.

On 26 Oct 80, SA DOTY, with the assistance of JERRY MILLER, GS-15, Chief, Scientific ivisor for Air Force Test and Evaluation Center, KAFB, interviewed Dr. BENNEWITZ at his me in the Four Hills Section of Albuquerque, which is adjacent to the northern boundary Manzano Base. (NOTE: MILLER is a former Project Blue Book USAF Investigator who was signed to Wright-Patterson AFB W-PAFB, OH, with FTD. Mr. MILLER in one of the most know dgeable and impartial investigators of Aerial Objects in the southwest). Dr. BENNEWITZ oduced photographs and over 2600 feet of 8mm motion picture film depicting unidentified rial objects flying over and around Manzano Weapons Storage Area and Coyote Canyon Test ea. Dr. BENNEWITZ has been conducting Independent research into Aerial Phenomena for e last 15 months. Dr. BENNEWITZ also produced several electronic recording tapes,

PIES TO: AFOSI/IVOS; File	ATTACHMENTS	FILE STAMP AND/OR OTHER
NAME GRADE, TITLE, SIGNATURE		
THOMAS A. CSEH, Major, USAF Commander ... Investigative Detachment	FOR OFFICIAL USE ONLY.	

OSI FORM 96
JAN 74

---

allegedly showing high periods of electrical magnetism being emitted from Manzano/Coyote Canyon area. Dr. BENNEWITZ also produced several photographs of flying objects taken over the general Albuquerque area. He has several pieces of electronic surveillance equipment pointed at Manzano and is attempting to record high frequency electrical beam pulses. Dr. BENNEWITZ claims these Aerial Objects produce these pulses.

3. After analyzing the data collected by Dr. BENNEWITZ, Mr MILLER related the evidence clearly shows that some type of unidentified aerial objects were caught on film; however, no conclusions could be made whether these objects pose a threat to Manzano/Coyote Canyon areas. Mr MILLER felt the electronical recording tapes were inconclusive and could have been gathered from several conventional sources. No sightings, other than these, have been reported in the area.

4. Mr MILLER has contacted FTD personnel at W-P AFB, OH, who expressed an interest and are scheduled to inspect Dr. BENNEWITZ' data.

5. Request a DCII check be made on Dr BENNEWITZ.

6. This is responsive to HQ CR 44.

7. Command was briefed but did not request an investigation at this time.

MULT. PURPOSE INTERNAL OSI FORM
(Complete only applicable items)

DO NO.(S)	SUBJECT	FILE NO
DET NO (S)	KIRTLAND AFB, NM, 8 Aug.- 3 Sep. 80,	8017D93-0/29
HEADQUARTERS IVOS	Alleged Sightings of Unidentified Aerial	TRANSMITTAL DATE
DO NO.	Lights In Restricted Test Range	26 Nov 80
DET NO.		SUSPENSE DATE
HEADQUARTERS		

REFERENCE

AFOSI Form 96, 28 Oct 80, Same Title

MINOR DISCREPANCIES NOTED ARE LISTED BELOW.

YOUR DISTRICT IS DESIGNATED OFFICE OF ORIGIN.

ATTACHED REQUIRES INVESTIGATION IN YOUR AREA.

DETERMINE SUBJECT'S ACCESS TO CLASSIFIED INFORMATION AS REQUIRED BY OSIM 124-1, PARA 2-6-3.

FORWARD RESULTS DIRECTLY TO OFFICE OF ORIGIN, OR TO·

NO FURTHER INVESTIGATION CONTEMPLATED.

OUR FILES REFLECT PRIOR INVESTIGATION BY _____ . DID _____ . FILE _____ . By copy of this form

_____ is requested to furnish _____ copies of prior investigative letter-summary, if applicable, to _____

REPORT OF PRIOR INVESTIGATION/SUMMARY ATTACHED.

INVESTIGATION CONTINUING AND YOU WILL BE FURNISHED FURTHER REPORTS

DISCONTINUE INVESTIGATION. FORWARD RESULTS OF ANY INVESTIGATION ACCOMPLISHED.

DISCREPANCIES BETWEEN LEAD REQUEST AND DEVELOPED INFORMATION ARE SET FORTH.

REPORT OF COMMAND ACTION HAS NOT BEEN RECEIVED.

REQUEST STATUS OF THIS MATTER AND/OR DATE REPORT MAY BE EXPECTED. *(Requester, forward 2 copies of this form.) (Recipient, use or received copy for answer with proper signature in remarks section unless OSI directives state reply not required.)*

REFER ATTACHED TO INTERESTED COMMANDER FOR INFORMATION OR ACTION IF NOT PREVIOUSLY REPORTED

CHECK WORLD-WIDE LOCATOR FOR BELOW LISTED PERSON OR SUBJECT

ATTACHED IS FORWARDED FOR INFORMATION AND/OR ACTION.

UPON REMOVAL OF ATTACHMENT(S) _____ , THE CLASSIFICATION ON THIS CORRESPONDENCE WILL BE

☐ RETAINED. ☐ DOWNGRADED TO _____ . ☐ CANCELED. ☐ MARKED "FOR OFFICIAL USE ONLY."

(If classification is retained, with or without attachments, indicate reason for security classification and grouping per AFR 205-1.)

REMARKS

1. On 10 Nov 80, a meeting took place in 1606 ABW/CC Conference Room attended by the following individuals: BGen WILLIAM BROOKSHER, AFOSP/CC, COL JACK W. SHEPPARD, 1606 ABW/CC, COL THOMAS SIMMONS 1606 ABW/CV, COL CRES BACA, 1606 SPGp/CC, COL FRANK M. HUEY, AFOSI Dist 17/CC, LTC JOE R. LAMPORT, 1606 ABW/SJ, MAJ THOMAS A. CSEH, AFOSI Det 1700/CC, Dr. LEHMAN, Director, AFWL, ED BREEN, AFWL.Instrumentations Specialist and Dr. PAUL F. BENNEWITZ, President Thunder Scientific Laboratory, Albuquerque. Dr. BENNEWITZ presented film and photographs of alleged unidentified Aerial Objects photographed over KAFB, NM during the last 15 months. Dr. BENNEWITZ also related he had documented proof that he was in contact with the aliens flying the objects. At the conclusion of the presentation, Dr. BENNEWITZ expressed an interest in obtaining financial assistance from the USAF in furthering his investigation regarding these objects. DR. LEHMAN advised DR. BENNEWITZ to request a USAF grant for research. DR. LEHMAN advised DR. BENNEWITZ he would assist him in filling out the proper documents.

2. On 17 Nov 80, SA RICHARD C. DOTY, advised DR. BENNEWITZ that AFOSI would not become involved in the investigation of these objects. DR. BENNEWITZ was advised

COPIES TO	ATTACHMENTS	FILE STAMP AND/OR OTHER
Dist 17/IVO, File		SO17D93-0/29 x 2
NAME-GRADE-TITLE-SIGNATURE		
THOMAS A. CSEH, Major, USAF		
Commander		
Base Investigative Detachment	FOR OFFICIAL USE ONLY	

AFOSI FORM 96 JAN 74   REPLACES OSI FORM 96 JUN 71 WHICH WILL BE USED

---

that AFOSI was not in a position to evaluate the information and photographs he has collected, to date or technically investigate such matters.

3. On 26 Nov 80, SA DOTY received a phone call from an individual who identified himself as U.S. Senator HARRISON SCHMIDT, of New Mexico. SEN SCHMIDT inquired about AFOSI'S role in investigating the aerial phenomena reported by Dr. BENNEWITZ. SA DOTY advised SEN SCHMIDT that AFOSI was not investigating the phenomena. SA DOTY then politely referred SEN SCHMIDT to AFOSI Dist 17/CC. SEN SCHMIDT declined to speak with 17/CC and informed SA DOTY he would request that SAF look into the matter and determine what USAF agency should investigate the phenomena.

4. It should be noted that DR. BENNEWITZ has had a number of conversations with SEN SCHMIDT during the last few months regarding BENNEWITZ'S private research. SEN SCHMIDT has made telephone calls to BGEN BROOKSHER, AFOSP/CC regarding the matter since Security Police are responsible for the security of Manzano Storage Area.

Left: *Doty's minute of Bennewitz's second meeting with the USAF at Kirtland AFB, to which the Air Force sent some impressive brass. Their involvement and the interest of Senator Schmitt (misspelled by Doty) did not succeed in raising public interest in Bennewitz's claims.*
Right: *A drawing of a huge 'alien base' that Bennewitz discerned from an aerial photograph taken near Albuquerque, New Mexico.*

● The victims' 'switch' [on the implant] can be pulled at any time. At the same time they are 'walking cameras and microphones', if the aliens choose to listen in with one of their beams. No classified area in the US is inviolate under such conditions. They are located and can be viewed by X-ray.
● Cattle mutilations – it appears that the humanoids are fed by a formula made from human or cattle material or both and they are made from the use of female encounter victims' ovum. The resultant embryos are referred to by the alien as an organ. Time of gestation appears to approximate 1 year.
● The aliens are picking up and 'cutting' (as the aliens call it) many people every night. Each implanted individual is apparently ready for the pull of their 'switch'. Whether all implants are totally effective I cannot predict, but conservatively I would estimate at least 300,000 people have been implanted in the US and at least 2 million worldwide.

Still worse, all of this was being done with the consent and co-operation of the US government and the USAF. The reason for that had yet to be explained.

Enemies within and without

Yet again, cracks in Bennewitz's capacity to apply logic to his data are apparent where he describes the aliens' armaments and transport. Their main 'electrostatic' weapon boasted:

plasma-generating voltages and an internal storage device – it is pulse powered. The

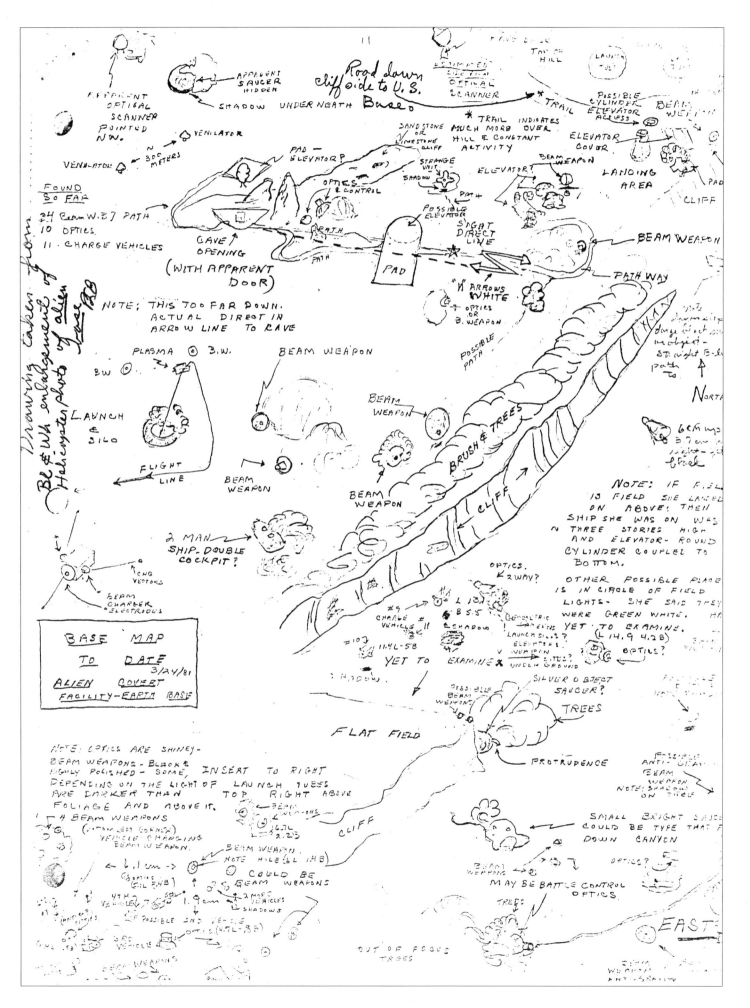

Document 6-01

LEAR.TXT

29 December 1987

EXCERPTS

During the period of 1969–971, MJ-12 representing the U.S. Government made a deal with these creatures, called EBEs (Extraterrestrial Biological Entities, named by Detlev Bronk, original MJ-12 member and 6th President of Johns Hopkins University). The 'deal' was that in exchange for 'technology' that they would provide to us, we agreed to 'ignore' the abductions that were going on and suppress information on the cattle mutilations. The EBEs assured MJ-12 that the abductions (usually lasting about 2 hours) were merely the ongoing monitoring of developing civilizations.

In fact, the purposes for the abductions turned out to be:

(1) The insertion of a 3mm spherical device through the nasal cavity of the abductee into the brain. the device is used for the biological monitoring, tracking, and control of the abductee.

(2) Implementation of Posthypnotic Suggestion to carry out a specific activity during a specific time period, the actuation of which will occur within the next 2 to 5 years.

(3) Termination of some people so that they could function as living sources for biological material and substances.

(4) Termination of individuals who represent a threat to the continuation of their activity.

(5) Effect genetic engineering experiments.

(6) Impregnation of human females and early termination of pregnancies to secure the crossbreed infant.

The U.S. Government was not initially aware of the far reaching consequences of their 'deal'. They were led to believe that the abductions were essentially benign and since they figured the abductions would probably go on anyway whether they agreed or not, they merely insisted that a current list of abductees be submitted, on a periodic basis, to MJ-12 and the National Security Council. Does this sound incredible? An actual list of abductees sent to the National Security Council? Read on, because I have news for you.

The EBEs have a genetic disorder in that their digestive system is atrophied and not functional. Some speculate that they were involved in some type of accident or nuclear war, or possibly on the back side of an evolutionary genetic curve. In order to sustain themselves they use an enzyme or hormonal secretion obtained from the tissue that they extract from humans and animals. (Note: Cows and Humans are genetically similar. In the event of a national disaster, cow's blood can be used by humans.)

The secretions obtained are then mixed with hydrogen peroxide and applied on the skin by spreading or dipping parts of their bodies in the solution. The body absorbs the solution, then excretes the waste back through the skin. The cattle mutilations that were prevalent throughout the period from 1973 to 1983 and publicly noted through newspaper and magazine stories and included a documentary produced by Linda Howe for the Denver CBS affiliate KMGH-TV, were for the collection of these tissues by the aliens. The mutilations included genitals taken, rectums cored out to the colon, eyes, tongue, and throat all surgically removed with extreme precision. In some cases the incisions were made by cutting between the cells, a process we are not yet capable of performing in the field. In many of the mutilations there was no blood found at all in the carcass, yet there was no vascular collapse of the internal organs.

The various parts of the body are taken to various underground laboratories, one of which is known to be near the small New Mexico town of Dulce. This jointly occupied (CIA-Alien) facility has been described as enormous, with huge tiled walls that 'go on forever'. Witnesses have reported huge vats filled with amber liquid with parts of human bodies being stirred inside.

During the period between 1979 and 1983 it became increasingly obvious to MJ-12 that things were not going as planned. It became known that many more people (in the thousands) were being abducted than were listed on the official abduction lists. In addition it became obvious that some, not all, but some of the nation's missing children had been used for secretions and other parts required by the aliens.

By 1984, MJ-12 must have been in stark terror at the mistake they had made in dealing with the EBEs. They had subtly promoted *Close Encounters of the Third Kind* and *E.T.* to get the public used to 'odd looking' aliens that were compassionate, benevolent and very much our 'space brothers'. MJ-12 'sold' the EBEs to the public, and were now faced with the fact that quite the opposite was true. In addition, a plan was formulated in 1968 to make the public aware of the existence of aliens on earth over the next 20 years to be culminated with several documentaries to be released during 1985-1987 period of time. These documentaries would explain the history and intentions of the EBEs. The discovery of the 'Grand Deception' put the entire plans, hopes and dreams of MJ-12 into utter confusion and panic.

Meeting at the 'Country Club', a remote lodge with private golf course, comfortable sleeping and working quarters, and its own private airstrip built by and exclusively for the members of MJ-12, it was a factional fight of what to do now. Part of MJ-12 wanted to confess the whole scheme and shambles it had become to the public, beg their forgiveness and ask for their support. The other part (and majority) of MJ-12 argued that there was no way they could do that, that the situation was untenable and there was no use in exciting the public with the 'horrible truth' and that the best plan was to continue the development of a weapon that could be used against the EBEs under the guise of 'SDI', the Strategic Defense Initiative, which had nothing whatsoever to do with a defense for inbound Russian nuclear missiles.

beam, totally effective in the atmosphere, can be loaded with hydrogen or oxygen. The maximum range appears to be about 2km [1.25 miles] if it is dry weather. It is capable of sustaining a limited number of full-power charges... so they must be recharged periodically. If it is raining the weapon becomes ineffective and is swamped and thus discharged.

It seems strange that a species capable of interstellar travel should carry weapons that are less effective than the average Sidewinder missile – which has a longer range and the enormous additional advantage of being impervious to rainwater. The alien craft too are surprisingly vulnerable. They are 'relatively fragile. They can be downed by lightning or any method that will interfere with their propulsion system,' Bennewitz reported.

Added to that, the alien command and control system was hardly designed to counter foes of a daring warrior mentality:

Because of the aliens' apparent logic system, a key decision cannot be made without higher clearance. ...Because of this apparent control, individual decision-making by the 'greys' are [sic] limited. If the 'plan' goes slightly out of balance or context, they become confused. Faced with this, possibly, the humanoids they have created would be the first to break and run.

Military reflections

It is interesting that in discussion papers published in Western military journals at about this time, much the same analysis was being made – not of alien commanders and humanoid slaves, but of the Warsaw Pact generals and their troops. And in *The Third World War*, published in 1978, General Sir John Hackett and others showed how superior technology combined with a greater capacity for initiative among junior officers would bring victory for NATO ground troops in any foreseeable European war against the Soviets. [3]

As late as June 1991 Bennewitz was still elaborating on this extraordinary scenario. In a letter to Ken Willoughby, which Bennewitz asked to be posted on the Internet, he wrote (verbatim):

The Archuleta Base was raided by a Delta Force, and [all?] of the Aliens within were killed outright. I can not vouch for some of this although I have absolute proof that it was [sic]. It is said that a General, a U.S. officer; he apparently got into an argument in that they, the Alien, were making Cocaine, instead of making humanoids. Supposedly there was 16 Tons of cocaine piled in one room. One of them, apparently, one he was talking to used a Blaze Gun, which is similar to a minature flame thrower and burned him severely.

He sent his Aide to call for help and the Delta Force was there in a very short time. When they saw what happened, knowing the General had one leg near burned off, attacked in a frenzy and killed at least 120 of them. Some of the Delta Force were also burned badly, and some were lost due to

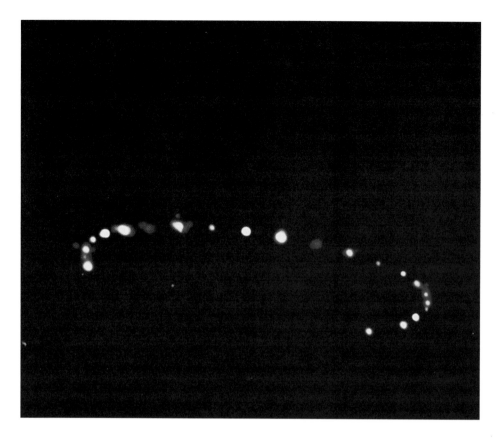

A strange circle of colored lights photographed (and seen by many witnesses) in the Hudson Valley between Southbury and Waterbury, Connecticut, on 26 May 1988 at about 9.30 p.m. The Federal Aviation Agency explained the sighting as low-flying ultra-light aircraft, an interpretation difficult to reconcile with the picture. Reports of unexplained lights and disks in the sky seemed to be on the wane in the late 1980s as ufologists concentrated on the exotic claims of abductees and cover-up specialists.

shock etc... They were apparently making the stuff so that they could sell it on the street. In the final count, later, apparently 8 Tons of the stuff was missing. There was a covert landing strip just North of Archeleta and they were flying it out of there. The troops blew the whole operation to hell bringing down all entrances and totally destroyed the so called plastic worms, killing those within. All instrumentation was destroyed. The whole area was closed and all people were barred from the mountain; it is now administrated by the Drug Administration (U.S.), so it is finished. The air strip was plowed and barricaded.

About 80 escaped taking their ships with them; ...a humanoid who is in charge by the name CARAUCHE is using a beam over the Four Hills area where I live and are hitting people in the nerve endings that control the stomach's Hcl, or hydrocloric acid causing the acid to come up the esophagus. Thus causing one to either throw up or become badly burned in the mouth and esophagus area. They hit at night and hit me last night. Fortunately, I had some anti acid Mallox so it reduced the pain. The odds are if they do it in this area, they will start elsewhere.

The reader may be forgiven for concluding that only a tropical case of self-delusion could make anyone mistake a severe attack of heartburn for alien 'beams'. For all that, Bennewitz was not alone in creating his horrific vision. He was, it seems, assisted by the US Air Force.

Skunks in the works

Kirtland AFB contains a number of highly secret units and installations, including the Manzano nuclear weapons storage area, the Sandia National Laboratory research facility and, nearby, the Coyote Canyon weapons-testing range. It is, consequently, one of the more security-conscious sites in the US defense establishment.

Electronics specialists there became aware that Bennewitz was listening to their activities, not least because he told them, although he ascribed the signals he had monitored to aliens. He also produced for their inspection some of the pictures he had taken of UFOs flitting around the Manzano

weapons store. Kirtland responded by sending one of their top regional UFO experts to interview Bennewitz on 26 October 1980. He was accompanied by AFOSI's own Special Agent, Sgt Richard L. Doty, whose extremely ambiguous role in the affair of the MJ-12 papers we have already observed (see Chapter Five).

The meeting was recorded in a minute signed by the commander of Kirtland's Investigative Detachment, Major Thomas A. Cseh. Bennewitz was invited to Kirtland to present his evidence to a group of officers and scientists on 10 November. On 17 November, Sgt Doty told Bennewitz that AFOSI had decided against any further investigation.

Bennewitz saw their resistance to his interpretation of things as proof that they had something that they wanted to hide. And indeed they did, for he had apparently tuned in to secret communications experiments. But those had nothing to do with UFOs, as he persisted in believing.

He refused to close down his electronic monitoring operation. AFOSI then decided that it would feed Bennewitz a mass of misleading information about aliens, subterranean bases and anything else they could think of – so that, should he leak any technical details of their work, he could and would be discredited as a crank by all and sundry.

At the 1989 MUFON Symposium, which took place in Las Vegas, William L. Moore, who is a long-time researcher into the 1947 'Roswell Incident', provided his version of what happened when Bennewitz started his eavesdropping on Kirtland's radio traffic.[4]

In September 1980, Moore was asked by what he called 'a well-placed individual within the intelligence community' to report on Bennewitz's activities. In this way AFOSI hoped to find out just how much Bennewitz, with his technical expertise, was learning about the secret research going on at the Kirtland complex. Moore accepted because (somewhat naïvely) he believed his contact, whom he called 'Falcon', was telling the truth when he claimed to be:

directly connected to a high-level government project dealing with UFOs. This individual... told me that he spoke for a small group of similar individuals who were uncomfortable with the government's continuing cover-up of the truth and indicated that... I might be able to help them find a way to change the prevailing policy and get the facts to the public...

A strange relationship

Moore swallowed this bait, and made and maintained contact with Bennewitz from 1981 until mid-1985. Bennewitz swallowed his bait, too. Exactly how much of Bennewitz's wild scenario was fed to him by AFOSI, or whether it was communicated to him electronically or otherwise, and how much he created out of his own imaginings, is not entirely clear. Moore said that 'the entire story' was derived from government disinformation.

Dr Sprinkle, however, says that when he made a second trip to New Mexico in 1980 for more regressions with Myrna Hansen, Bennewitz 'had rifle in hand and pistol on hip' to ward off the aliens he thought were about to invade his domicile at any moment, and 'was concerned that I [Dr Sprinkle] was with the CIA or worse! He asked me to leave before further sessions could be conducted.'[5]

Document 6-02

The Dulce Papers

EXCERPT FROM GENERAL DESCRIPTION CIRCULATED AMONG UFO RESEARCHERS

December 1987

These papers contain... documents that discuss copper and molybdenum, and papers that discuss magnesium and potassium, but mostly papers about copper. Sheets of paper with charts and strange diagrams. Papers that discuss UV light and gamma rays. These papers tell what the aliens are after and how the blood (taken from cattle) is used. The aliens seem to absorb atoms to eat. They put their hands in blood, sort of like a sponge, for nourishment. It's not just food they want; the DNA in cattle and humans is being altered.

The 'Type One' creature is a lab animal. They know how to change the atoms to create a temporary 'almost human being.' It is made with animal tissue and depends on a computer to simulate memory, a memory the computer has withdrawn from another human. Clones. The 'almost human being' is slow and clumsy. Real humans are used for training, to experiment with and to breed with these 'almost humans'. Some humans are kidnapped and used completely. Some are kept in large tubes, and are kept alive in an amber liquid.

Some humans are brainwashed and used to distort the truth. Certain male humans have a high sperm count and are kept alive. Their sperm is used to alter the DNA and create a non-gender being called 'Type Two'. That sperm is grown in some way and altered again, put in wombs. They resemble 'ugly humans' when growing but look normal when fully grown, which only takes a few months from fetus-size.

They have a short life span, less than a year. Some female humans are used for breeding. Countless women have had a sudden miscarriage after about three months' pregnancy. Some never know they were pregnant, others remember contact some way. The fetus is used to mix the DNA in types one and two. The atomic make-up in that fetus is half human, half 'almost human', and would not survive in the mother's womb. It is taken at three months and grown elsewhere.

Bennewitz came to believe that night-rescue exercises by helicopters were UFOs on abduction missions. According to Moore, who was colluding in the process, Bennewitz became insomniac and paranoid, believing the aliens 'were coming through his walls at night and injecting him with hideous chemicals that would knock him out for long periods of time'. He had guns and knives stashed 'all over his house'. Moore said that on one occasion he saw Bennewitz chainsmoke 28 cigarettes in 45 minutes. In the end, around late 1985, he had a nervous breakdown.

Yet, as noted, Bennewitz still believed in the 'Beta' scenario two years after Moore had shocked his fellow ufologists with these revelations. Whatever the cost to Bennewitz, the AFOSI strategy worked well. All but the most gullible of ufologists – and they had their own agenda to pursue – had refused to take his tales entirely seriously.

But AFOSI's duplicity and disinformation may not have ended there. For Moore's reward for his part in this wretched episode, some say, was the Majestic-12 documents which, in due course, were to be comprehensively denounced as fake – and accepted as such by all but a minority of ufologists (see Chapter Five).

The Lear document

During the mid-1980s few knew and fewer passed on Bennewitz's startling assertions. But around 1987 his story was to reach the ears of John Lear, who among other things was an airline pilot with 14,000 hours logged in the air, the holder of an impressive string of air speed records, the disinherited son of renowned executive-jet designer William P. Lear, and a recently-converted UFO buff of a distinctive order.

Lear met Bennewitz in August 1987, absorbed what he had to say, and

applied it to a highly selective version of UFO history, including what was then the hottest news in ufology. That was the release – by Timothy Good in the UK, and by Jaime Shandera, William Moore and Stanton Friedman in the USA – of the Majestic-12 papers (see Chapter Five).

Lear did not offer his conclusions to any of the dozens of specialist UFO journals published in the West. Instead, on 29 December 1987, he posted a 4000-word document – LEAR.TXT – on the Internet's Paranet bulletin board, thus bypassing the critical scrutiny of more experienced ufologists and, simultaneously, reaching a wider audience.

The 'Lear Document' was an elaboration of the Bennewitz story, mingled with yet more rumor and hearsay and outright fantasy about the MJ-12 papers, the supposed MJ-12 group itself and other choice items such as the compatibility of human and bovine blood (see Document 6-01). Among its more entertaining asides was a heavy hint that virtually every scientist who had publicly addressed the issue of extra-terrestrial intelligence was a fraud in the pay of the government. And guaranteed to offend almost anyone with a respect for the religious sensibilities of others, was this pearl:

The EBEs [Extraterrestrial Biological Entities, i.e. aliens] *have a type of recording device that has recorded all of Earth's history and can display it in the form of a hologram. ...The crucifixion of Christ on the Mount of Olives has allegedly been put on film to show the public. The EBEs claim to have created Christ....*

The following May, MUFON Deputy Director Dan Wright sent a series of questions to Lear about the sources of his 'information'. Lear responded on 10 June 1988, and a striking number of times he named his source as an unnamed 'confidential informant'. Also cited was the Project Grudge/Blue Book *Report #13* that

William S. English claimed to have seen at RAF Chicksands in the UK (see Chapter Four).

English became something of a minstrel to the medicine show put on by Lear and his associate Bill Cooper. Bennewitz wrote up an account of *Report #13* from tape recordings English had made in 1982, and passed the transcipt to Lear at their August 1987 meeting.

In October 1988, Bill Cooper put this transcript and Lear's account of a meeting with English the previous month into a single file. Within three months Cooper was issuing documents on the Internet that outdid anything so far produced by Lear, and he sidelined English's claim to fame by asserting that he too had seen the infamous *Report #13*, several years before English, and many other supersecret items besides.

The Dulce papers

Meanwhile, a description of another amazing document had turned up in researchers' mail. In December 1987, in LEAR.TXT, Lear claimed that 66 US Special Forces troopers were killed in a 1979 'altercation' at the Dulce laboratory, trying to free 'a number of our people trapped in the facility, who had become aware of what was really going on' and 'our people were not freed'. A month later, in contrast, Lear was saying on the Internet that:

I know of one person that did escape and he is the one that assembled what is known as 'The Dulce Papers'. These 'papers' contain a 6-minute video of the inside of the Dulce facility, 25 black and white photos and about a dozen documents explaining what went on inside there. I have not seen the Dulce papers themselves but I have seen drawings of the photographs.

The source of the Dulce Papers, it was later said, was a CIA agent, named as one Thomas Calabro, who had made notes and taken still photos and videotapes in the base and survived the melée in 1979 – along with 43 other humans. According to the rumor, the as-yet unnamed Thomas Calabro then distributed sets of his material to five trusted friends and went underground. He had been in hiding ever since, and every six months contacted each of the five. If he missed four successive contacts, then the five could do whatever they wanted with the material. The December 1987 description of the 'Dulce Papers' was supposed initially to have come from one of the caretakers of the papers.

The documents apparently included discussions of copper, molybdenum, magnesium and potassium; much medical terminology; and discussions of ultraviolet light and gamma rays, the true intentions of the aliens, the uses of cows' blood, DNA manipulation, 'almost human' beings, and the 'creation of nongender beings' (see Document 6-02). The last half of these discussions supposedly concerned a 'supercrystalline' metal used for UFOs' hull structure.

Second- or third-hand accounts of highly implausible documents were now replacing counterfeit papers in this strange saga – a strategy that more hoaxers could helpfully adopt, as they would then save both themselves and skeptics a vast expense of trouble and energy in, respectively, creating fake records and debunking them.

The last phoney 'official' paper to surface around this time was bombastically titled *A Situation Report on Advanced Technology and Interaction with Alien Cultures*, purportedly written by one O.H. Krill, to whom no reference could be found in any academic, military, business or industrial directory. His paper was a rambling, 19,000- word trawl through the least credible aspects of ufology, repeating Bennewitz's, Lear's and the Dulce Papers' claims, and including such gems as an interview allegedly given by a 'Nordic' alien to writer George C. Andrews, an account of a long-since-discredited 'anti-gravity' device made in the UK, and much about 'men in black' and sundry species of humanoid alien. The whole turgid Krill testimonial might have been swiftly forgotten but for the significance Bill Cooper was to attach to the name of its author.

And the stage was now set for the entry of this remarkable character into what was an increasingly surreal fray.

Operation Majority

On 10 January 1989 Cooper posted on the Internet a 'final release'

Document 6-03

Cooper On Krill

When the aliens landed at Holloman AFB in the '60s a basic communication was established between the United States Government and the aliens. During this communication a basic agreement was reached which was the precursor for the formal treaty and the diplomatic relations which followed.

The aliens left a hostage with the United States as a pledge of fulfillment of their part of the agreement. The name of that hostage was KRLL and was sometimes spelled KRYL. I will refer to him as KRLL as this was the spelling used in the MAJESTY documents which I saw. This hostage furnished much information about the aliens which became the foundation of the 'YELLOW BOOK' that was completed... at a later date.

In order that this information could be circulated and discussed among the military and the scientific community a pseudonym was coined as a code for information which had originated from KRLL. The code name for KRLL was Cril. The initials O.H. stand for 'ORIGINAL HOSTAGE'. All information thus circulated from the source KRLL was said to be authored by O. H. Cril. The information was usually of scientific or seemingly occult nature and was sanitized so that no inference to an alien race or culture occurred. This was done so that feedback and recommendations could be gleaned from those experts who were not privy to the secret. It was also used to pass technology from the aliens into the defense contracting community and the US space program.

KRLL became ill after a few years and almost died but was nursed by a physician who eventually became the government expert on alien medicine and pathology. My information is that KRLL did at some later date die. The pseudonym continued to be used for the same purpose for many years and may or may not be in use at this time.

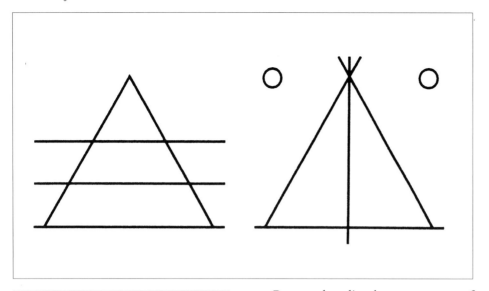

The 'Trilateral Insignia' (left) that, according to William Cooper, is on the flag of the aliens, and inspired the name of the international economic forum, the Trilateral Commission. Cooper alleges, on no evidence whatever, that the think-tank is part of a secret world government. At right is the insignia that supposedly appears on alien craft and uniforms.

('THERE WILL BE NO CORREC-TIONS TO THIS FILE' an opening rubrick proclaimed, although several further 'final' versions were to follow) concerning what he described as Operation Majority.

'This file contains the absolute true information regarding the alien presence on Earth and the US government's involvement with the aliens,' Cooper trumpeted, and soon worked up to a climax: 'This file is my death warrant if MJ-12 continues to operate in a manner consistent with its history.' Cooper next 'solemnly' swore that:

the information contained in this file is true and correct to the best of my knowledge. I swear that I saw this information in 1972 in the performance of my duties as a member of the Intelligence Briefing Team of the Commander In Chief of the Pacific Fleet as a Petty Officer in the U.S. Navy... The following is brief listing of everything that I personally saw and know from 1972 and does not contain any input from any other source whatsoever.

Cooper then listed a score or so of code words and brief descriptions of their supposed significance, mainly super-secret UFO- or alien-related government projects. Among the terms was this:

KRLL or KRLLL or CRLL or CRLLL pronounced Crill or Krill was the hostage left with us... as a pledge that the aliens would carry out their part of the basic agreement reached during that meeting... KRLL became sick and was nursed by Dr. G. Mendoza who became the expert on alien biology and medicine. KRLL later died. His information was disseminated under the pseudonym O.H. Cril or Crill.

Other, less easily excited, ufologists by now suspected that the Krill papers themselves were the combined effort of strictly terrestrial entities, John Lear and John Grace (a.k.a. 'Valdemar Valerian'), and Lear soon admitted as much. Cooper, however, insisted that he had seen this information (in fact all his information) among classified papers he had had examined in 1972 in Hawaii. But Cooper's unique spin on all this went deeper into paranoia and conspiratorial fantasy than anyone in ufology had ever gone before:

President Eisenhower commissioned a secret society known as THE JASON SOCIETY (JASON SCHOLARS) to sift through all the facts, evidence, technology, lies and deception and find the truth of the alien question. The society was made up of 32 of the most prominent men in the country in 1972 and the top 12 members were desig-

nated MJ-12. MJ-12 has total control over everything. ... The Director of the CIA was appointed J-1 and is the Director of MJ-12. MJ-12 is responsible only to the President.

MJ-12 runs most of the world's illegal drug trade. This was done to hide funding and thus keep the secret from the Congress and the people of the United States. It was justified in that it would identify and eliminate the weak elements of our society... MJ-12 assassinated President Kennedy when he informed them that he was going to tell the public all the facts of the alien presence.

A frightening theory

In May 1989, Cooper published *The Secret Government*, which took the notion that 'MJ-12 has total control over everything' to its logical, if unlikely, conclusion: the group really ran the country, and in a fashion that made nonsense of everything that everyone took for granted about life, liberty and the pursuit of happiness. The core of his 'argument' is this:

By secret Executive Memorandum, NSC 5410, Eisenhower... establish[ed] a permanent committee (not ad hoc) to be known as Majority Twelve (MJ12) to oversee and conduct all covert activities concerned with the alien question... Majority Twelve [included] six men from the executive committee of the Council on Foreign Relations known as the 'Wise Men'. These men were all members of a secret society of scholars that called themselves 'The Jason Society'; or 'The Jason Scholars'...

...A chosen few were later initiated into the Jason Society. They are all members of the Council on Foreign Relations and at that time were known as the 'Eastern Establishment'. This should give you a clue to the far reaching and serious nature of these most secret college societies. The Jason Society is alive and well today but now includes members of the Trilateral [sic] Commission as well. The Trilateralists existed secretly several years before 1973. The name of the Trilateral Commission was taken from the alien flag known as the Trilateral

Insignia. ...the Council on Foreign Relations and... the Trilaterial [sic] Commission not only control but own this country.

...The headquarters of the international conspiracy is in Geneva, Switzerland... Meetings are held by the 'Policy Committee' when necessary on a Nuclear Submarine beneath the Polar Ice Cap. The secrecy is such that this was the only method which would ensure that the meetings would not be bugged...

Throughout our history the Aliens have manipulated and/or ruled the human race through various secret societies, religion, magic, witchcraft, and the occult. The Council on Foreign Relations and the Trilaterial [sic] Commission are in complete control of the alien technology and are also in complete control of the nation's economy. [6]

The secret government (says Cooper) is in cahoots with the aliens and has a fiendish plan:

to exploit the alien and conventional technology in order for a select few to leave the earth and establish colonies in outer space. I am not able to either confirm or deny the existence of 'Batch Consignments' of human slaves which would be used for manual labor in the effort as part of the plan. The Moon, code named 'Adam', would be the object of primary interest followed by the planet Mars, code named 'Eve'. As a delaying action, [the plan] included birth control, sterilization, and the introduction of deadly microbes to control or slow the growth of the Earth's population. AIDS is only ONE result of these plans.

Towards Alternative 3

There was much more that was just as wild – about the self-destruction of

Earth 'by or shortly after the year 2000', plant life flourishing on the dark side of the Moon, a devious scheme to encourage street violence, generate revulsion against guns, and thereby disarm the American people, an assertion that in the 1960s future US president George Bush established the international drugs trade, plus claims that UFO skeptic Philip J. Klass is a CIA agent, that one in every 40 people carries an alien implant, and that the US space program is a gigantic hoax. Cooper maintains that when President Kennedy announced the plan to put a man on the Moon:

In fact a joint alien, United States, and Soviet Union base already existed on the moon at the very moment Kennedy spoke the words. On May 22, 1962 a space probe landed on Mars and confirmed the existence of an environment which could support life. Not long afterward the construction of a

colony on the planet Mars began in earnest. Today cities exist on Mars populated by specifically selected people from different cultures and occupations taken from all over the Earth. A public charade of antagonism between the Soviet Union and the United States has been maintained over all these years in order to fund projects in the name of National Defense when in fact we are the closest allies.

Navy intelligence

Cooper said that he saw secret documents (including the Grudge/Blue Book *Report #13*) containing all these choice details in 1972, when he was a Petty Officer in the US Navy, and a member of a permanent intelligence assessment team, attached to the headquarters staff of the Commander in Chief of the US Pacific Fleet in Pearl Harbor, Hawaii. Just what such papers

President John F. Kennedy in Dallas, 22 November 1963. William Cooper maintains Kennedy was assassinated by MJ-12 because he was about to tell the public 'the facts' about the disastrous alien presence on Earth.

Robert Lazar, who claims to be a physicist and to have worked for US Naval Intelligence at a secret facility connected to Nellis AFB, Nevada. There, he says, he inspected captured alien craft.

were doing in Hawaii, and how Cooper managed to see them, remains a mystery. The legendary POW-hunter Lt Col 'Bo' Gritz has stated that no one below the rank of commissioned officer would have had access to intelligence briefings of this kind; while serving officers have said there are no permanent intelligence assessment teams; their life is about two weeks at most.[7]

It may be significant too that most of Cooper's UFO-related claims had already been made by Paul Bennewitz, Bill English, and John Lear. And Cooper's most extravagant idea, the joint Western–Soviet plot to enslave humanity to serve an elite living on Mars, is pure fiction. It comes directly from a British television documentary, *Alternative 3*, which was shown in the UK on 20 June 1977.

Devilish doings

Weighty academics and other 'sources' were seen blowing the gaffe on this diabolical scheme, which was being prepared against the day the greenhouse effect made Earth uninhabitable. Many of the whistleblowers in *Alternative 3* were already well-known to viewers of British television, because they were all actors who appeared regularly in UK soap operas and drama series.

But the biggest clue to the nature of the film was in the copyright notice at the end – it did not specify just © 1977, but 1 April 1977. Indeed Anglia TV, the program's producers, had intended to air it on that date but had had to postpone the broadcast for nearly three months. In 1992, review-

ing the mythic dimensions the *Alternative 3* hoax had acquired over the years, Bob Rickard wrote in *Fortean Times* (Issue 64):

Anglia had originally announced that Alternative 3 *was to be transmitted in at least nine countries. Whether it ever was or not, conspiracy addicts worldwide... who missed the programme, saw its absence as evidence of the global conspiracy. One woman even thanked* [its creators] *for explaining the disappearance of her boy; it was a relief to her to know he was happy and on Mars.*

There were several rumors of heavy-handed interference from on high, too, when Leslie Watkins's book version of the film (Sphere 1978) of the story seemed to be hard to find only a few weeks after it had been published. In a 1980 letter to Mrs Anne Cooper [no relation], however, Watkins stated categorically: '*Alternative 3* is fiction. The so-called conspiracy is science-fantasy.'

Hard facts and limpid statements have never appealed much to full-blown conspiracy addicts, and Cooper was no exception. By the time he assembled his byzantine plot into a book – apocalyptically titled *Behold A Pale Horse* – he felt free to cite the notorious *Protocols of the Elders of Zion* as a respectable authority.

This demented anti-Semitic tract, which even Nazi Adolf Hitler had acknowledged to be a fake, appeared to represent nothing less than the shining light of truth to Milton William Cooper.

Lazar beams

During 1989 too there emerged another twist in the developing myth of secret alien-human co-operation. Starting in March, a number of programs put out by Channel 8 KLAS-TV in Las Vegas, Nevada, featured interviews with a mysterious

'Dennis' who, his face in shadows, claimed to be a physicist who had worked for the US Navy at the government's Nevada Test Site, about 65 miles (105 miles) north of Nellis AFB.

Base goings-on

In the northeast corner of this huge tract of land is an area known variously as 'Dreamland', 'Area 51', 'the Ranch', and 'the Skunk Works'. Dennis related that here, at a location he called 'S-4', a few miles south of Groom Lake, there were nine disk-shaped craft of extra-terrestrial origin. They were being analyzed, and some were occasionally flown, in the hope of reverse-engineering their technology. One day, being led by security men through a hangar in which the disks were parked, he gave security the slip, and rapidly inspected one saucer inside and out.

One of the disks, Dennis was startled to realize, resembled a craft, allegedly from the Pleiades star cluster, that had been photographed by contactee Eduard 'Billy' Meier in Switzerland during the mid-1970s.

Dennis had worked on their engines which, he said, were based on 'a gravity propulsion system: the power source is an anti-matter reactor'. (His statements were full of specious technicalities of this kind.) At some point the Soviets had been involved in the research, but 'were kicked out of the program rather abruptly'. Dennis thought he may have chanced on an alien at the site on one occasion.

On a KLAS-TV special report aired on 11 November 1989, 'Dennis' was revealed to be one Robert Lazar, and an associate of none other than John Lear. Over the following months, in further interviews, Lazar elaborated on his story. The fuel for each of the 'totally different' nine disks was 223 grams of the as-yet undiscovered element 115. But Lazar could never remember details like its atomic weight or what he called 'the resonant frequency of the gravity wave' other than that it was 'really odd'. And he was

prone to come out with opaque, not to say scientifically meaningless, statements such as this:

Everything seems to come down to 115. It's a super-heavy element. It seems that as you get into the heavier elements – and I'm sure this property extends into as-yet-undiscovered elements in excess of atomic number 115 – that the atomic gravity wave inside the atoms holding things together begins to extend outside of the atomic structure itself, and it's this wave that can be tapped off in quantity – small quantity, actually.

The top-secret military research center on the edge of Groom Lake, that is allegedly part of the legendary 'Area 51'. The huge tract of land in central Nevada that is officially designated the Tactical Fighter Weapons Center covers some 6000sqmi (15,500sqkm), is largely inaccessible, and is heavily guarded. Information on half the area, including the Coyote, Caliente, Elgin and Cedar divisions, is not available to the general public.

Then Lazar's personal résumé largely evaporated on close inspection. Colleges, universities and employers that Lazar claimed for his past denied all knowledge of him. The Los Alamos National Laboratory, where Lazar said he worked in the Weapons Division on highly classified Star Wars technology, conceded only that he had been involved with 'non-sensitive' projects. The Massachusetts Institute of Technology had never heard of him. Even the hospital where Lazar said he had been born had no record of him.

'It's as if someone has made him disappear,' said the Channel 8 commentator, suitably awed. On 20 December, on KVEG Radio in Las Vegas, Lazar was also claiming someone had shot at (but missed) his car 'six or eight months' previously. For those who wanted to believe, it all looked like a prelude to a comprehensive elimination.

But it is surprisingly easy to 'disappear' from the records of any institution, if you have never been on its books in the first place. And anyone can tell a tale about being shot at, if the would-be assassin leaves no bullet hole. Lazar's ultimate excuse for failing to recall items such as the atomic weight of element 115 (even though it has already been calculated by chemists) was that he had been subjected to some kind of 'mind control'.

Still more unfortunately, relevant documentation and the sample of element 115 that Lazar had (somehow) spirited out of Dreamland had been stolen from his house. It was all very inconvenient for a man hoping to per-

suade the world that one of the greatest yarns in history was authentic.

The sole survivor

In due course, the survivor of Dulce, Thomas Calabro, was reported to have come forward and told all.[8] Beneath the entire United States, it seems, and stretching on around the globe, runs a vast network of tube shuttle trains linking military bases and their super-secret underground facilities. (The only explanation of how these were so invisibly constructed is to credit the machinery and the spoil-disposal to the ever-superior aliens.)

Calabro alleged that he traveled from his home in Santa Fe to Dulce on a leg of this system. The Dulce complex had at least seven storeys below ground, and perhaps several more. The deeper the level, the more gruesome the particulars that were

contained therein. It was almost a technological parody of the nine circles of Dante's Hell.

On Level 4, Calabro reported, researchers investigate the human aura, telepathy, dreams, and hypnosis. On Level 6, Calabro said:

I have seen multi-legged 'humans' that look like half human/half-octopus. Also Reptilian-humans, and furry creatures that have hands like humans and cries like a baby; it mimics human words... also huge mixtures of Lizard-humans in cages. There are fish, seals, birds and mice that can barely be considered those species. There are several cages (and vats) of winged-humanoids, grotesque bat-like creatures, but 3½ to 7 feet [1 to 2m] tall. Gargoyle-like beings and Draco-Reptoids.

Level 7 is worse: row after row of thousands of humans and human-mixtures in cold storage. Here too are embryo storage vats of Humanoids, in various stages of development.

I frequently encountered humans in cages, usually dazed or drugged, but sometimes they cried and begged for help. We were told they were hopelessly insane, and involved in high risk tests to cure insanity.

We were told to never try to speak to them at all. At the beginning we believed that story. Finally, in 1978, a small group of workers discovered the truth. It began the 'Dulce Wars' [cf. Document 6-01].

The stories of the human–alien technological interface at the Skunk Works in Area 51/Dreamland in Nevada, and the legend of the honeycomb of horrors alleged to lurk beneath Archuleta Mesa in New Mexico, soon combined and took on a mythic life of their own.

In 1990 a New-Age channeling group named Cosmic Awareness Communications (CAC), based appropriately in Olympus, Washington State, put out an 18,500-word special report, titled *Nightmare Hall*, of a 'general reading' held on 12 May that year. CAC is shrewd enough to warn: 'The Interpreters interpret the energies as they see them in trance levels and are not personally responsible for what is said.' Cosmic Awareness itself opined that what it had to reveal about Dulce and Area 51 'is for the courageous, it is for the strong, it is for

the daring, it is for those who dare to be aware.' [9]

The 'Awareness' proceeded to confirm all the claims ever made about Dulce and Dreamland, and brewed them up with virtually every conspiracy theory ever proposed and every rumor and legend ever promulgated about UFOs, plus some wildness of its own. A couple of samples will give the flavor:

This Awareness indicates the Deros... are remnants of a humanoid species that were left underground for many generations. They have continued in their underground civilization which, through a network of caverns and tunnels extends throughout the United States, South America and in through Europe and other regions. These tunnels have been known by the Illuminati, which was formed in 1776 on May 1st, by Adam Weishaupt, which is the reason for the May 1st celebration in many countries; that this Illuminati as the foundation for many of the occult and conspiracy type organizations that have followed. It was based on the alien contact by these entities.

The cat and the pig were direct creations of Atlantean genetics.

This Awareness indicates that the pig having some human genes intermixed with earlier wild boar. The cat, being created from genes that had belonged to the Greys.

You will notice the cat-like eyes of the Greys; these were incorporated into the genes used for creating the cat. This also is a reason why there were cat societies, societies that worshipped the cat, thinking they were a kind of reflection of the gods of the time, many entities seeing these Grey aliens as gods.

Besides much else, 'this Awareness' also managed to link the Apocalypse and the Revelation of John the Divine; the ongoing, surreptitious replacement of corporate executives by 'synthetics' or 'robotoids' (as 'souls can be extracted from the physical body and transferred into other bodies or into replicas' by the aliens); the disclosure that as many as 200,000 aliens from Sirius, Zeta Reticuli, Orion [sic], Draco [sic], the Pleiades, and so on, live underground on Earth; and the announcement that no less than 40 million reptilian aliens were on their way to Earth from Draco inside a planetoid, and might well arrive by 1996 or 1997.

On the dark side

What can anyone make of this extraordinary collation of unsavory ingredients? While much of the detail seems to have been filtered by or through one man – John Lear – there are themes in the material whose entirely Earthbound sources are not difficult to discern.

Some of these motifs come from science fiction – we have already seen how Bill Cooper adopted the mock documentary *Alternative 3*. The mechanical wombs and genetically engineered horrors of Dulce's Nightmare Hall echo the 'axolotl

An alien/human hybrid child, born in the late 1950s. A scene from the British science-fiction film **Village of the Damned,** *which prefigured several ideas promoted by the Dark Side of ufology.*

tanks' of the secretive and amoral biotechnicians of the planet Ix, in Frank Herbert's *Dune* sagas. Still further beyond that lies a long science-fiction tradition of mad scientists, who seek to rule the world, or have murderous proclivities, or whose bio-genetic experiments go hideously wrong. One strand of that tradition stretches right back to Mary Shelley's *Frankenstein*, first published in 1818 and the subject of countless movies this century, and it always involves the creation of monsters, counterfeit humans, or ghastly hybrids. Examples run from *The Creature of the Black Lagoon* and *House of Wax* to *The Fly*.

Another strand, which happens to embrace aliens too, is typified in John Wyndham's novel *The Midwich Cuckoos*, Don Siegel's movie *Invasion of the Body Snatchers* (from the novel by Jack Finney), and the TV mini-series *V*: the dehumanization, takeover or subjection of Earth's population by mind control, mental invasion or deceit. *The Midwich Cuckoos* actually opens with six respectable ladies in an English village finding themselves inexplicably pregnant with, it turns out, super-intelligent and deadly alien/hybrid children.

The template for this theme can be found in ancient fairy lore and demonology. Wyndham's novel was published in 1957 and filmed in 1960 (as *Village of the Damned*) – still long before such ideas started to be recycled in ufological circles.

The mythic Dulce combines all these motifs. Whether presented as science fiction or alleged fact, they seem to reflect two underlying cultural anxieties. One is a widespread distrust of the unsupervised power of an impersonal and only vaguely understood discipline called Science; this is not the same as individual scientists, who are recognizably human. The other is a fear that someone or something is secretly, unpredictably and, more frightening, uncontrollably

manipulating public affairs, and by no means for the good of the people. One of the oldest and most vicious of these beliefs holds that there is a secret Jewish masterplan for world domination. It is supposedly being carried out through economic manipulation and skullduggery, underpinned with occult depravities that include cannibalism.

These charges are at least as old as medieval times, when few occupations were open to Jews in Europe besides banking and finance; and the theme of treacherous, money-loving Jews ultimately derives from the figure of Judas Iscariot, who was the treasurer of the twelve apostles.[10]

Jerome Clark and Jacques Vallée[11] have shown there are connections among several prominent ufological claimants and extreme right-wing political groups. In paranoid ufology the demonic aliens are allied with the 'Silence Group' and the 'international bankers' – code terms for 'the international Jewish conspiracy'; in Dulce lore, underscoring the point, the satanic number 666 crops up in access codes and uniform insignia.

Significantly, Bill Cooper abandoned ufology in the 1990s to take up far-right political demagoguery on radio, much of it in support of anti-Federal-government militias. Their mythology includes a similar anti-Semitic, apocalyptic scenario, and even shares with paranoid ufology the mysterious black helicopters that feature in so many cattle mutilation cases.

Explaining everything

The problem, as Jerome Clark has said, is that paranoia is 'a sign of societal as well as personal illness. And it is the ultimate unfalsifiable hypothesis: it explains everything.' Thus, to the paranoiac, themes in fiction that later find their way into ufological lore don't indicate how UFOs are bound up with the earthbound culture in which they appear. Instead, they are evidence

of the ETs' (or the government's) plan to educate the populace gradually about the long presence of aliens on Earth; and a persistent debunker like Philip J. Klass must be a CIA agent trying to keep the lid on a panoply of horrors, rather than a self-appointed partisan of militant skepticism.

Jerome Clark emphasizes the political environment that made it possible for the UFO paranoiacs – whom he calls the 'Dark Siders' – to find willing listeners to their ravings. Their audience, Clark says, 'assumed that if somebody said it, and it was awful enough, it must be true.' He continues:

I doubt, however, that before the traumas of the 1960s – the assassinations, the destructive and futile war in Vietnam, the agony of Watergate – the Dark Siders would have done as well... Americans emerged from the 1960s and the early '70s in a state of profound disillusionment. ...Many Americans came to see their society and their institutions as fundamentally flawed, cynical, manipulative, even evil. [And] some Americans could now imagine their government to be capable of anything, from complicity in the assassination of a president... to the betrayal of the whole human race to malevolent extraterrestrial intelligences.[12]

That analysis rings true. I think it is worth pointing out too that these beliefs also represent a kind of cannibalism. They are an extreme instance, and all the plainer because of their extremity, of the way ufology feeds off its own dead ideas. To begin with, the Darksiders treat as genuine 24-carat articles numerous claims and cases that have been debunked by skeptics, and are dismissed by most mainstream researchers too.

They also demonstrate the self-defeating and narrow-minded parochialism of ufology. No ufologist who introduced Bob Lazar to a media audience and implicitly endorsed his claims – such as George Knapp, Billy Goodman and Timothy Good – knew enough about physics to detect when

Lazar lapsed into (non)scientific gib-berish. Worse, they did not, apparently, bother to ask a physicist for an informed opinion: which would have been swift and deadly in coming.

But most parochially and cannibal-istically of all, the UFO paranoiacs have done little more than hijack, and usually (but not always) distort, notions that in one form or another have been floating around in ufology for decades. Mainstream ufologists have tended to give the Darksiders' batty notions some consideration exactly because they echo earlier ufo-logical ideas, regardless of whether those ideas have, or ever had, any intrinsic merit.

Through the mirror

Donald Keyhoe was, of course, the great-granddaddy of the belief that governments knew that UFOs were extra-terrestrial but dared not say so. To some extent his thesis was support-ed by Leon Davidson, who in the 1950s laid the responsibility for UFOs squarely at the feet of the CIA – who invented the flying saucer myth in 1947 to mislead the Soviets about the level of US technological achieve-ment. (At this time the US government was aware that the Soviets had already benefited from huge leaks about nuclear weapons development.) George Adamski was the subject of an elaborate hoax staged by the CIA, who also fostered belief in UFOs to encourage misperceptions of secret aircraft and weapons tests.[13] Like all single-issue, blanket explanations of UFOs, Davidson's was plausible as far as it went, but left a great deal unex-plained. And he framed his ideas well before documents obtained under the 1974 amendment to the Freedom of Information Act made it plain that between 1947 and 1953 the CIA was as confused and anxious as anyone else about what UFOs really were, and heartily recommended a comprehen-sive campaign of debunking. (Para-noics, of course, would turn this objection on its head and would say it simply confirms Davidson's essential correctness. The CIA could hardly reveal what its director, as an MJ-12 member, knew of UFOs and aliens.)

Pondering the contents – and, just as tellingly, the difficulty of obtaining – those papers led William H. Spaulding, founder of Ground Saucer Watch, to formulate the 'Federal Hypothesis' in the early 1980s. This developed the idea that secret military exercises, weapons tests and, perhaps most importantly, military blunders could be passed off as UFOs and further disguised by more (or less) credible mundane explanations by fronts such as Project Blue Book.

Innocent citizens of small-town America unload sacks of vegetables that, in truth, are creatures from space who will take over people body and soul - like the aliens of the Darksiders. A scene from Don Siegal's 1956 movie **Invasion of the Body Snatchers.**

Publisher Ray Palmer, 'the man who invented flying saucers'. He promoted Richard Shaver's tales of a bizarre and menacing underground alien civilization as non-fiction.

Spaulding put exotic UFO phenomena such as abductions and visitations by Men In Black down to covert psychological tests, possibly involving psychotropic drugs.

Meanwhile, from the mid-1970s, Jacques Vallée had begun to ruminate on the notion that the social and psychological impact of UFOs might be deliberately contrived, possibly to achieve social changes on Earth. UFO phenomena, Vallée said, represent a 'control system', although he has always been unwilling to commit himself to a statement of what or who the controlers are, or what their exact and ultimate purpose is.

The oldest and in some ways the strangest plank in the paranoics' platform reaches back to the 1940s, when Ray Palmer published a long series of stories by Richard Shaver in *Amazing Stories* magazine. Palmer said that 'flying saucers are a part of the Shaver Mystery – integrally so.'

It may be more accurate to say that Palmer is an integral part of the UFO mystery, as *Amazing Stories* published a picture of a flock of flying saucers on its back cover for August 1946, almost a year before Kenneth Arnold's sighting over Washington State launched the UFO era.

Shaver's stories, rewritten and expanded by Palmer for publication as non-fiction, described a hidden, terrestrial civilization of warring Deros and Teros – 'deranged' and 'integrated' robots, respectively – whose ancestors had lived on long-lost Atlantis and Lemuria. The Deros would occasionally venture forth to molest humanity.

Palmer claimed that on a visit to Shaver (who lived on a Pennsylvania farm) he heard the voices of Deros discussing their kidnap and dismemberment of a female human. And, crucially, Shaver said that Atlantis and Lemuria had been peopled by extraterrestrials whose robotic descendants live in an enormous, global complex of underground caverns.

All this illuminates an otherwise inscrutable remark that is contained in William Cooper's 1989 paper *Operation Majority*:

AQUARIUS is a project which compiled the history of alien presence and their interaction with Homo sapiens upon this planet for the last 25,000 years and culminating with the Basque people who live in the mountainous country on the border of France and Spain...

The Basques' language is unique in the world, and their national epic poem describes them as the remnants of the population of lost Atlantis.[14]

It hardly seems worth adding that hell is traditionally a netherworld, everywhere below us, and the habitat of monstrous, mindless entities who sometimes sally forth, or materialize, to tempt and torment humanity. The supposed treaty between the US and the aliens, in which human souls were exchanged for technological (worldly) advantage, is Faust's pact with Lucifer in contemporary garb and on an appropriately vast modern scale. As the 'Cosmic Awareness' put it:

those who at any time accept aliens as masters will be used by these aliens. That essentially is the harvest, wherein they collect those who have sold themselves to the aliens for some security, or monetary gain, or gain of power.

The paranoid vision has taken in myths from all quarters, it is plain: which tends to confirm one's suspicion that, however unconsciously, the Darkside nightmare is itself mythic in scope and intention.

The Government connection

It would be interesting to know where William Cooper found his connection between the Basques and the updated Deros of Dulce. Is he particularly well read, or was he fed the idea by someone more thoroughly versed in UFO lore – not to mention little-known epic poetry?

The question arises because the whole lurid Darkside panorama sprouted from seeds scattered by an admittedly unusual abduction narrative, which led an obsessive ufologist to intrude on secret government radio experiments, which led him into the noxious embraces of AFOSI.

A key figure in that disinformation operation, as we have seen, was AFOSI's Sgt Richard Doty, who crops up in more than one shadowy role in the long, tangled chronicle of attempts to unearth the real connection between the US secret establishment and UFOs.

In Chapter Five we saw how unlikely it is that Doty has ever told the whole truth about anything in the UFO field; nor is it clear how much of a freelance, or even rogue, operator he was within AFOSI. And it is certainly not clear from anything in the public domain how much of Paul Bennewitz's original *Beta Report* was his own fantasy, and how much was fed him verbally – or even piped to his video screen – by Doty acting on AFOSI's behalf, or behind its cover. It's not inconceivable that Doty's strange engagements with ufology were personal eccentricities that AFOSI tolerated and contained for its own convenience.

Doty, thus, has to be considered at least as a candidate, along with Bennewitz himself, for authoring the basic Dulce legend. But a pivotal figure in its later elaborations is John Lear. Within two years, and very soon after suddenly acquiring an interest in UFOs, Lear had disinterred Bill English, was enlarging on Bennewitz's tales, was encouraging Bill Cooper in his fantasies, and had made contact with Bob Lazar. He in turn may just have been an AFOSI puppet, if a remarkably naïve one.

Lear also claimed to have met Thomas Calabro, the renegade CIA agent who was supposedly the source of the Dulce Papers. Was Calabro sent to wind Lear up to further frenzy, or were he and his account both figments of Lear's imagination?

Lear himself once worked for the CIA, even if at something of a remove, as a pilot. Perhaps Lear was persuaded to continue the work so ably begun by Doty or AFOSI. Or did he become, through the military and intelligence contacts he claimed he maintained, merely the pawn of the Air Force and the CIA? Or was he none of those things?

My suspicion, for what it's worth, is that Lear has been credulous and gullible, and swallowed and repeated all that was fed him, wherever it came from, and invented a fair amount more. It's doubtful we shall ever know the whole truth of what is either a labyrinthine intrigue or a fantasy run riot. Perhaps that doesn't matter. But what does matter for political life in America is that many people believe that some cell of the US government was prepared to instigate and encourage these unhinged ideas and for a while, at least, large numbers of people believed those fantasies to be true. And some, no doubt, still do.

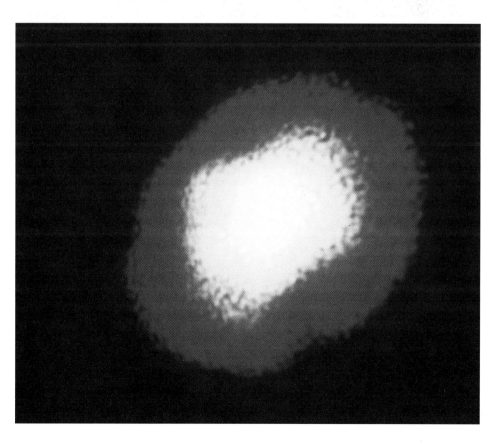

A genuine UFO – one of the mysterious lights that haunted the Hessdalen Valley in Norway during the 1980s. While Americans became enmeshed in conspiracy theories in this period, European ufologists sought more mundane explanations for the UFO phenomenon.

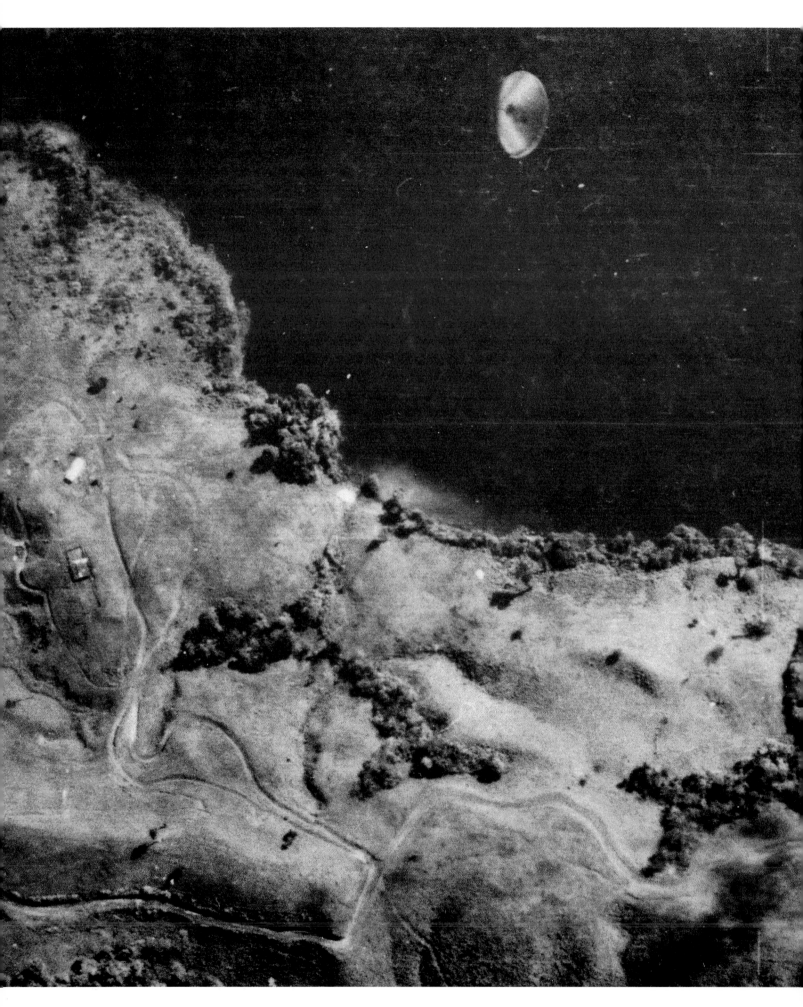

Chapter Seven

A WORLDWIDE WEB

EVIDENCE FOR AN INTERNATIONAL CONSPIRACY?

OVER THE half-century and more that UFOs have plagued, entertained and distracted the USA, they have gone through several changes in the minds of those curious to know what, exactly, they represent. Until late 1948, within the US military, they were largely believed to be secret weapons.

It was not until 1952 that the twin ideas took hold that they were both extra-terrestrial and the subject of a determined cover-up by the authorities. Both notions took a battering in the 1970s, then returned in strength to

This object appeared on a film used during an aerial survey by the Costa Rican Geographic Institute in 1971. Each frame was automatically exposed every 17 seconds: the UFO was caught on frame 300. Computer-aided analysis by Ground Saucer Watch concluded that the picture was a **bona fide** *image of an unknown object. The relatively straight 'trailing' edge was explained as the result of reflection, thin cloud cover masking part of the UFO, or 'someone' using a 'montage technique' – although GSW found no evidence of the latter.*

the USA in the 1980s and blossomed into the fevered vision of the Darkside Hypothesis. Meanwhile, from the late 1970s on, traditional sighting reports began to fall off. By the early 1990s few ufologists were paying them much heed. More exotic fancies had captured their imaginations.

The Darksiders' panoramic account of ufology connected crashed saucers, abductions, numerous sighting and encounter reports, and the overarching theme of the cover-up. The seductiveness of such a comprehensive 'explanation' became apparent during the 1990s, as mainstream ufologists such as Budd Hopkins embraced ideas of government involvement in abductions, while carefully avoiding the extremes of the Darkside.

However, one formerly respected abduction proponent, disbarred psychotherapist Richard Boylan, posted messages on the Internet early in 1996 yoking the Aviary with the Yellow and Red Books – 'alien-authored' works mentioned by Bill Cooper – and alleged alien predictions about an imminent Apocalypse and the return of Christ.[1]

The rest of the world was less inclined to revert to the ETH, although a hard core of believers remained. In Europe especially, many ufologists pondered other explanations for the phenomenon. Some related social, cultural and psychological contexts to UFO waves, flaps and sightings; some concentrated on linking UFOs to more or less obscure natural phenomena, from tectonic energies to ball lightning and mirages; others speculated that human psychic energies might be involved. Skeptics and debunkers also tended to be received more sympathetically in Europe than in the USA.

Foreign intelligence

Few governments actively investigated UFO reports beyond examining the immediate defense implications. Condon found that most were leaving detailed investigation to the USA; behind the Iron Curtain, UFO study was officially frowned on. Most, however, were less than forthcoming about their interest and for years none shared the data they had collected. In

1974, the French minister of defense, M. Robert Galley, revealed that his ministry had amassed a huge array of reports from the wave of 1954. Although it did not release those particular files, the French government did create a publicly accessible investigatory unit for UFOs.

In 1977, the Study Group on Unidentified Aerospace Phenomena (GEPAN) was established within the French National Center for Space Studies (CNES), and continues its work today. (Like Blue Book, GEPAN has been accused of being a public-relations front dealing only with minor events, while the strangest cases were being forwarded to less public agencies for study.)

Spanish shock

In Spain, UFO files were first released, unofficially, to journalist Juan Jose Benitez in 1976. The result was a sensationalizing book that shocked the military so much that it kept the lid on further releases for 15 years. In 1979, following representations by ufologists to King Juan Carlos, the Spanish joint chiefs of staff decided that the negative effect of this publication and the likely flood of media and public enquiries for information were enough to keep the UFO files classified. Leading ufologist Vincente-Juan Ballester Olmos tried again to have the files made public in 1984. He met with an immediate rebuff.

In May 1991, Ballester Olmos approached the chiefs of staff again, with a request for help with research he was conducting with Joan Plana into the relationship between UFOs and the Spanish military. In a long memorandum he highlighted the deterioration of the Air Force's image 'because of the growing belief in deliberate concealment of proof'. In July 1991, the Chief of Air Staff told Ballester Olmos that 'proper steps' had been taken to declassify UFO files. By

MANDO OPERATIVO AÉREO	ESTADO MAYOR SECCIÓN DE INTELIGENCIA

AVISTAMIENTO DE FENÓMENOS EXTRAÑOS

DESCLASIFICADO

ESCRITO	NUM.	REFERENCIA	FEC...
EMA/DOP	814	SESPA	16-4-94
OBSERVACIONES:			

EXPEDIENTE: - 761119.

LUGAR: - CANARIAS.

FECHA: - 1976 / día 19 de Noviembre.

RESUMEN:

- El día 19 de Noviembre a las 19:15Z los tripulantes del Buque Escuela de la Marina Española "JUAN SEBASTIÁN ELCANO", en viaje de instrucción desde Cádiz a Las Palmas, encontrándose a esa hora en posición 29º 04'N-014º 34'W con Rumbo 220º, observaron un punto luminoso algo mayor que una estrella de 1ª magnitud y algo menor que la luna llena; el punto luminoso, después de girar en espiral unos 4 giros, se agranda hasta alcanzar un tamaño de 2 a 3 veces el disco lunar; una vez que el borde inferior de dicho disco toca la superficie de la tierra queda como apoyado en el horizonte formando un semicírculo perfecto como trazado con tiralíneas, permaneciendo la esfera luminosa en el centro geométrico del fenómeno; en su expansión fue debilitándose en intensidad y aunque el espectáculo duró en su fase activa más de 20 minutos, se puede decir que hasta su total extinción, se prolongó por espacio de 2 horas.

- A esa misma hora un T-12 del 461 Escuadrón, que hacía un vuelo de Lanzarote a Gando, al sobrepasar punto "Sierra" (Punta Jandía de la Isla de Fuerteventura) observaron el mismo fenómeno que el buque pero ya en el momento en que el fenómeno estaba en proceso de expansión, aunque añaden un elemento nuevo a la declaración de los primeros al describir unos recuadros de color verde botella en el centro geométrico de la semicircunferencia. El fenómeno es localizado a la "1" de su posición y lo tienen a la vista durante 12 minutos, hasta que inician la maniobra de descenso, en la que lo pierden de vista al entrar en una capa de calima.

- La tripulación del Spantax BX-322 que viajaba desde LT a punto "Sierra", a nivel 280 en descenso para nivel 200, observa también a la misma hora el extraño suceso, contactando por radio con el T-12 para confirmar el fenómeno. El Comandante del avión declaró que el suceso tenía que estar detrás de la isla y lo apreció relativamente lejano.

- En la localidad de GUÍA, cercana a GÁLDAR, numerosos testigos observan, a la misma hora y en dirección AGAETE-TENERIFE, un disco

1

EJE.-C1.0 DEL AIRE

2 6 SET 1994

mid-1993, the process was well under way, and the Air Force had passed 66 files to Ballester Olmos for his study. There was a useful side-effect: the Spanish Air Force revised, improved and expanded its methods of investigating UFO reports.[2]

The Royal Australian Air Force began publishing summaries of UFO sightings, which it termed UAS ('unusual aerial sightings'), in 1960, and continued to do so until 1977. In 1980 industrial chemist Bill Chalker enquired about the sudden halt in the flow of information and was told that UFO files were still retained and available for inspection. Chalker negotiated a virtually exclusive arrangement with the Australian Defence Department to inspect all the RAAF's UAS archives. In 1982, the Australian parliament passed a Freedom of Information Act that, in theory, made the files available to anyone who cared to inspect them. In 1984, the RAAF abandoned taking UFO reports from the public, as they had 'proved not to have a national security significance'.[3]

Things were rather different in the United Kingdom. Americans in particular are often surprised at the secretive nature of government in the country that boasts of having the Mother of Parliaments. The reason is

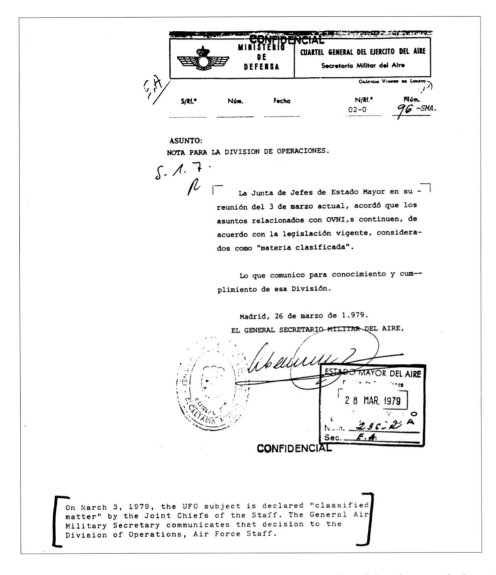

ASUNTO:
NOTA PARA LA DIVISION DE OPERACIONES.

La Junta de Jefes de Estado Mayor en su -
reunión del 3 de marzo actual, acordó que los
asuntos relacionados con OVNI,s continuen, de
acuerdo con la legislación vigente, considera-
dos como "materia clasificada".

Lo que comunico para conocimiento y cum--
plimiento de esa División.

Madrid, 26 de marzo de 1.979.
EL GENERAL SECRETARIO MILITAR DEL AIRE,

On March 3, 1979, the UFO subject is declared "classified matter" by the Joint Chiefs of the Staff. The General Air Military Secretary communicates that decision to the Division of Operations, Air Force Staff.

Left: *A formerly secret report by the Spanish Air Force on a 'UFO' seen in November 1976 from the Canary Isands, in the Atlantic Ocean, 60 miles (100km) off the coast of north-west Africa. The report runs to many pages: official Spanish UFO inquiries were admirably thorough.*
Above: *In 1979, the Spanish joint chiefs of staff, indignant after a limited release of files resulted in a sensational journalistic treatment of the subject, declare UFOs 'classified matter'.*

partly historic: despite enjoying full democratic rights, the British are not citizens of their country, but legally are still subjects of the sovereign. This subtle constitutional point relieves civil servants of any obligation to disclose anything to the public, as they are not employed by the people but by the Crown.

The 1911 Official Secrets Act made the disclosure of items as trivial as the menu at a government staff canteen a punishable offense unless duly authorized; under later legislation, a 'whistleblower' cannot use overriding public interest as a defense in any prosecution for leaking information. These arrangements suit both governments and the bureaucrats, who prefer to work with as little interference as possible, and they have resisted demands for freedom of information legislation for decades.

British government and military records are available for inspection, however, if they are at least 30 years old and neither affect national security nor embarrass (usually eminent) living people. Thus, many secrets from World War II remain under wraps, while the papers relating to the abdication of King Edward VIII in 1936 will remain classified until 2036.

These procedures are of no help to ufologists. Jenny Randles did succeed in persuading the Ministry of Defence (MoD) to release a number of UFO reports to her in the 1980s, but the cases were selected by the MoD, and the papers contained little useful data. Enquiries to the MoD about UFO reports are routinely answered in vague and dismissive terms, even when dealing with specific cases.

When investigating the Grudge *Report #13* affair (see Chapter Four) in 1993, I attempted to extract a simple Yes or No from the Home Office immigration service in answer to the question: 'Is William S. English telling the truth when he claims to have been deported from the UK?' Six letters to the relevant section met with obstructive answers; I managed to get some sense out of them only after enlisting the help of my member of parliament. Those with real grievances have fared a good deal worse from bureaucratic obliqueness.

The Brazilian connection

One of the earliest UFO reports outside the USA to have a proven government connection was the Trindade Island event of 1958. The sighting still arouses controversy, and several solutions have been offered to account for the four photographs taken by Almira Barauna from the Brazilian Navy survey ship NE Almirante Saldanha (see Case #26). The believers regard the pictures as among the best evidence available for their contention that UFOs are extra-terrestrial spacecraft, and cite as further 'proof' the Brazilian Navy's efforts to keep them secret. Over that latter aspect of the case there can be no doubt, although the reasons for the cover-up are not entirely obscure.

Those who have expressed doubts that the Trindade pictures actually show a UFO are divided over whether they represent a rare natural phenomenon or a hoax. In correspondence with NICAP's secretary Richard Hall in 1959, Donald Menzel suggested that what Barauna had photographed had in fact been an aircraft:

Above: *One of four pictures taken by Almira Barauna (left) from the deck of a Brazilian Navy ship in January 1958. To some, the photos merely add to the long line of hoaxes that litter ufology; others believe they show a genuine UFO; a few claim they show a mirage created by a rare combination of atmospheric conditions.*

I have in my possession one well-authenticated case of a saturn-like object... A plane, flying in a humid but apparently super-cooled atmosphere, became completely enveloped in fog, so about all one could see was a division where the stream lines were flowing up and down respectively over and under the wings. The cabin made a saturn-like spot in the center, and the wings closely resembled the appearance of the Brazilian photographs...

I do not have, of course, detailed meteorological phenomena [from Trindade] that would enable me to evaluate whether the air was indeed supersaturated. However, the conditions in a tropical atmosphere are more conducive to this sort of thing than a more temperate zone.[4]

However, in his book *The World of Flying Saucers* (1963), and again in *The UFO Enigma* (1977) [5] Menzel argued that the Trindade pictures were a hoax. He had discovered that Barauna was an accomplished trick photographer (his productions included both UFOs and treasures on the seabed), and pointed out that he also had ample opportunity, alone with his friend in the makeshift darkroom, to doctor the film.

He also noted that the size and appearance of the UFO in the photos differ considerably from the witnesses' descriptions and from picture to picture, and that of the many alleged witnesses only Barauna's two friends were prepared to speak to the press (and, he might have added, one of those did so only reluctantly).

Case #26

The Trindade Photographs

TRINDADE ISLAND (BRAZIL), SOUTH ATLANTIC OCEAN

16 January 1958

The Brazilian Navy's four-masted sail training ship NE Almirante Saldhana was converted to a hydrographic survey unit for International Geophysical Year, which opened in October 1957. With a crew of 300, commanded by Captain Jose Santos Saldanha da Gama, the vessel had been surveying the waters around Trindade, a Brazilian island about 750 miles (1200km) north-east of Rio de Janeiro. Among the civilian technical team on board were Almiro Barauna, an expert underwater photographer, and members of his diving club, including former Brazilian Air Force Captain Jose Teobaldo Viegas and Snr Amilar Vierira Filho. In October 1957, the Navy had set up an oceanographic post and meteorological station on Trindade itself, under Captain of Corvettes (Commander) Carlos Alberto Bacellar.

Just after noon, as the ship was preparing to get under way, Barauna was photographing the ship's launch being hoisted aboard. Standing 60ft (20m) away from him, Vierira Filho saw what he thought was 'a large seagull', and pointed it out to Capt Viegas – who immediately began shouting 'Flying saucer!' Barauna rushed over to photograph it. In less than 20 seconds, he snapped off six shots as the UFO approached, swung behind Mt Desegado, reappeared, then flew away. Two shots failed to catch the UFO altogether, Barauna later discovered, as he had been jostled by excited bystanders. It was said that many of the crew members on deck watched the spectacle. Cdr Bacellar, who had been below decks during the sighting, wanted the pictures developed immediately. Barauna, shaken by the sighting, waited an hour to calm down before using an improvised darkroom to process the film. He was helped by Viegas, while Cdr Bacellar waited outside.

The still-damp negatives were shown to the crew, who agreed that they showed the UFO they had seen. The pictures were published in the Brazilian press on 21 February. A United Press International report of 25 February stated that the Brazilian Navy had analyzed them and that Brazil's president, Sr Juscelino Kubitschek, personally vouched for their authenticity.

The Scottish skeptic Steuart Campbell argued that those on board the Almirante Saldanha actually saw a mirage of the planet Jupiter, which was setting at the point the UFO disappeared, a few degrees south of due west.[6] He proposed that the 'double merged and magnified image' was 'seen via mirage':

The movement of the image indicates that a temperature inversion had folded down to the south-west so that its surface was nearly vertical... the vertical component of the thermocline could contain a wave which drifted first one way and then another... The concave part of the thermocline could duct the image around until the change in curvature allowed it to be seen by anyone in the line of sight... The thermocline would have been curved in two directions, like a shallow bubble... The batlike movement of the image indicates there were ripples in the inversion layer...

The explanation is quite ingenious, but it hardly conforms to the principle known as Occam's razor – that any explanation ought to depend on as few hypotheses ('if... would... could...') as possible.

Campbell had not only proposed a highly specialized set of circumstances, but according to Robert Shaeffer (another UFO skeptic), he had ignored three crucial facts: 'Jupiter can be just marginally visible when the sun is low in the sky,' Shaeffer wrote; whereas the Trindade sighting took place almost at noon.

Even if Jupiter could produce a mirage in daylight, Campbell:

fails to understand that... the surface brightness of the mirage would be far less than that of the object causing it because the light is diffused outward, rendering the object even less visible in daylight than it would be before...

In any case, one vital piece of information missing from... Campbell's hypothesising, is that mirages are never seen more than half a degree above the horizon, even under the most unusual circumstances.[7]

Case #27

The UFO and the Nuclear Alert

NORTH WEST CAPE, WESTERN AUSTRALIA
25 October 1973

The following report was among RAAF UFO sightings files first examined by Bill Chalker in 1975. Two US servicemen stationed at the US Navy's Communications Station at North West Cape independently observed a mysterious object. The base incorporates an NSA facility within the Naval Security Group. Area 'B' within the base contains a high-frequency transmitter.

At about 7.15 p.m., Lt Commander M[censored], USN, was driving south from the Communications Station to nearby Exmouth when he saw a 'large black airborne object' in the west at a distance of about 5 miles (8km). He watched it hover, at an estimated altitude of 2000ft (600m), for about 20–25seconds. It then flew off to the north, 'accelerating beyond belief'. Lt Cdr M said he had 'never experienced anything like it.' The UFO made no noise and left no exhaust or contrail.

At much the same time, Fire Captain (USN) Bill L[censored] was on the base itself when he was called to close the officer's club. In his own words:

'I proceeded towards the Club in the Fire Department pick-up 488, when my attention was drawn to a large black object, which at first I took to be a small cloud formation, due west of Area "B". Whilst traveling towards the Officers' Club I couldn't help but be attracted by this object's appearance.

'On alighting from pick-up 488, I stood for several minutes and watched this black sphere hovering. The sky was clear and pale green-blue. No clouds were about whatsoever. The object was completely stationary except for a halo round the center, which appeared to be either revolving or pulsating. After I had stood watching it for approx. 4 minutes, it suddenly took off at tremendous speed and disappeared in a northerly direction, in a few seconds.

'I consider this object to have been approx. 10 metres [30ft] in diameter, hovering at 300 metres [985ft] over the hills [Mt Athol] due west of the base. It was black, maybe due to my looking in the direction of the setting sun. No lights appeared on it at any time.'

Campbell had noted that Jupiter was one degree above the horizon at noon on 16 January 1958. If they were not of a mirage, were the Trindade pictures a hoax? There is plenty of reason to think so. Barauna was no doubt aware that several UFOs had been seen from Trindade in the weeks before he arrived: they were, so to speak, 'in the air'.

He had no need to doctor his film beforehand: on the 2.25in (55mm)-square frame his Rolleiflex used, the UFO would have been a barely visible 0.0625in (1.5mm) long. Possibly, a seagull was flying past the ship at the time – making a tiny speck on the negatives. This would have been sufficient to convince the already excited witnesses who saw the negatives on board the ship.

Not only did the film stay with Barauna for the rest of the voyage, and not only was he at home in Rio de Janeiro for two days before Cdr Bacellar called to take it for the Navy to analyze, but Barauna had already cut the UFO pictures away from the rest of the film while on the boat, ostensibly to intensify the images with silver salts. There is thus no certainty that the negatives he handed to the Navy were actually from the same film shot on the boat. It is also interesting that when James Wadsworth of the Condon Committee wrote to Barauna at his known current address in 1968, asking him to discuss the pictures, he received no response.[8]

But as Steuart Campbell remarks, it does not follow that 'because Barauna might have faked the pictures he must have done so'. Consider, on the other hand, that Viegas described the UFO as 'brighter than the moon' while Barauna called it 'dark gray' (as he might if he knew how the images were to appear on the film).

Barauna also told newsmen that the Brazilian Navy had calculated the speed of the UFO to be about 600mph (1000km/h) and its size as 120ft (36m) in diameter and 24ft (7m) high. The Navy's report on the Trindade sightings, written on 2 March 1958 for Fleet Admiral Antonio Maria de Carvalho, chief of the Navy high command, mentions no such figures, and says that the photographic evidence 'somehow loses its convincing quality due to the impossibility of proving if there was or was not a previous photomontage'. It also notes that 'no officer or sailor of the Fleet saw the phenomena'. This also contradicts Barauna's testimony, but is consistent with the whole event being over in less than half a minute.

The Brazilian Navy's lack of enthusiasm for the pictures – demonstrated from start to finish of the affair – paradoxically explains their order to sailors not to speak to the press about the sighting. Against the Navy's advice, the President of Brazil, Snr Juscelino Kubitschek, had released the photos to the press on 20 February. In a country where the military was also a political faction, the Navy naturally wanted to maintain a united front. Barauna may have been embarrassed, in the end, by a 'hoax' that got horribly out of hand, until he was ensnared by it.

Australia and the NSA

In 1973, Australia hosted a quite different multiply-witnessed UFO event (see Case #27). Bill Chalker, who discovered the sighting report, put an intriguing spin on the mysterious black object, seen by two American witnesses a considerable distance apart, that hovered near the US Navy's top-security Communications Station at North West Cape, Western Australia.

Chalker saw the event in the context of the Yom Kippur war. Hostilities began on 6 October 1973 with a simultaneous attack by Egypt, Jordan and Syria on Israel, whose general staff had misread the military situation and were caught unprepared. On all fronts a desperate fighting withdrawal began as Israel's citizen army frantically mobilized; the battlefields saw scenes of unbelievable heroism, especially in the hard-won tank battles on the Golan Heights. Then, on 11 October, North West Cape and the other US bases in Australia went to a high alert.

The reason for this (not elucidated by Chalker) was that, having begun a successful counter-attack against Egyptian forces on 8 October, the Israelis launched another against Syria at 11.00 a.m. local time on 11 October. Within six hours they had knocked the Syrian forces back by 10

Case #28

Valentich Vanishes

BASS STRAIT, AUSTRALIA

21 October 1978

Frederick Valentich, aged 20, took off in a rented Cessna 182 from Moorabbin Airport, Melbourne, at 6.19 p.m. to make a 300-mile (500-km) round trip to King Island in Bass Strait. He was to collect crayfish for the officers of the local Air Training Corps, and expected to be back by 10.00 p.m.

At 7.06 p.m., Melbourne ground control had Valentich on the radio asking if there were any aircraft in his vicinity below 5000ft (1500m). Negative, said Melbourne. Valentich said an aircraft with four bright lights had just passed over, 1000ft (300m) above him. He couldn't tell the type. Then he said it was approaching him from the east, and: 'It's not an aircraft... It has a long shape... coming for me right now...' Then the thing vanished. But Valentich's engine was rough-idling and coughing, and suddenly he said: 'Unknown aircraft now on top of me.' 'Acknowledge,' said Melbourne. There was a 17-second burst of 'metallic' noise, and no further messages from the Cessna. A search began at 7.28 p.m. and went on for a week. No trace of Valentich or the aircraft was ever found.

The Valentich disappearance is a genuine mystery, from any angle. This was his first solo night flight. Just possibly, inexperience led him to turn the aircraft on its back, causing the engine to die. Valentich also filed only a one-way flight plan, despite his stated intention to be back on the mainland that night. This has led some to suspect a hoax and a deliberate disappearance, or possibly a suicide, although Valentich appears to have had no motive for either.

On the same day, and in the same area, that pilot Frederick Valentich vanished, plumber Roy Manifold took six pictures of the sunset over Crayfish Bay, Bass Strait, Australia. Looking straight into the sun, Manifold saw nothing unusual, but the fifth shot showed something apparently rising from the sea, and the sixth showed the curious object seen here. It is backlit by the sun, and the film showed no defects. Military and academic skeptics suggested the object was a small, 'dying' cumulus cloud. If so, where is it in the previous frames, all exposed within 30 seconds of this one?

miles (15km), and in places twice that. Looming behind the contestants were the Soviet Union, standing by the Arab nations, and the USA, backing Israel. The Americans believed that the Soviet Union might support its clients directly if Israel decisively turned the tide of the war. Israel did so, but intense diplomacy averted an escalation and a UN resolution called for a

ceasefire at 6.52 p.m. on 22 October. The combatants accepted the deadline, but bitter fighting continued on the southern Egyptian front until late on 24 October.[9]

At this point, as Chalker notes, the NSA's misreading of a signal from Syria to the USSR in turn misled the US government into thinking the Soviets were preparing airborne divisions to move into the Middle East. On 25 October came the reaction. The North West Cape station signaled US forces in the region, putting them on nuclear alert – without telling the Australian government. And on the same day a mysterious black UFO visited the NSA/US Navy station at North West Cape.

Chalker wonders if this UFO event is the one glimpsed at paragraph 9 of NSA's top-secret affidavit of 1980 to the US Federal court, which discusses NSA SIGINT (signals intelligence). Chalker does not pretend to know if the strange black object was a remote-

controled drone of either a friendly or hostile power, or a *bona-fide* UFO. But he does conclude that the case shows that UFO sightings may harbor implications for national security.

Chalker is undoubtedly correct, if the object was indeed a piece of airborne hardware. But the fact that the witnesses may both have been in possession of a terrible secret that, for all they knew, was the first step toward Armageddon, may also be the key to their experiences. Several ufologists have observed how UFO sightings increase in times of national (which is also personal) stress, shock, or unease about the future.

American UFO flaps, in the days when they used to happen, bloomed regularly in the late summer of presidential election years. The flap of 1973 – in which this sighting may reasonably be counted – began amid far greater uncertainty, with the first Congressional hearings on Watergate, chaos in the Nixon administration, and the scandal-ridden resignation of vice-president Spiro Agnew; it peaked against the background of the Yom Kippur war and the ensuing crisis in which oil prices tripled overnight. While it seems altogether likely that a physical object of some kind triggered the sighting, this UFO is strikingly symbolic. Like a mocking negation of the antipodean sun, black and foreboding, it hangs in the west, the traditional direction of death, and disappears into the war-torn wasteland of the north. A psycho-social interpretation of this case at least deserves some consideration.

The Atlantic shore

On the other side of the world, in Spain, the process of liberating UFO files into public view took a good deal longer than in Australia, but from 1968 the process of investigating reports was no secret and was admirably thorough. Once a written UFO report was received, a military judge (commonly a lieutenant colonel) was appointed to delve into the case. 'Observation conditions', the weather, instruments used, noise, and the dynamics of the object were all examined. Any explanation was passed on to witnesses 'for their peace of mind'. There were, nevertheless, occasional bungles: a UFO visible from central and eastern Spain at 10.15 p.m. on 12 July 1983 was accounted for as either a meteorite or the re-entry of space debris. It was in fact, as the French Navy later confirmed, a test-firing of an M-4 ballistic missile from the submarine Gymnote, in the Atlantic off the coast of Britanny.

Vincente-Juan Ballester Olmos's analysis of the 1400 pages of documents released to him show the proportion of 'unknowns' to solved cases is similar to that found in the USA: 64 out of 71 sightings, from 1962-1979, are accounted for. Of these, a startling 16 (22.5 per cent) were hoaxes – 14 of them from just three people.

Of the officially solved cases, Ballester Olmos found two from January 1975 whose explanation he felt was too facile (see Case #29). In one, four soldiers patroling the Air Force Firing Range at Las Bardenas Reales at 11.00 p.m. on 2 January saw some lights in the northeast moving 80ft (25m) above the ground, rounding the main tower of the range, increasing altitude and disappearing to the south. Another light flew slowly toward the tower, then sped off to the north. Invited to witness the phenomena, the lieutenant colonel in command of the range looked at the lights through binoculars and discovered the Moon on the rise.

No ground traces were found. As with other cases, it's useful to recall the circumstances at the time: General Francisco Franco, the ruler of Spain for 35 years, was on his deathbed. Radical changes, possibly massive upheaval, threatened Spanish society.

Most of the released material was gathered under a ruthless dictatorship

---

Case #29

A New Year's UFO In Spain

BURGOS-SANTANDER, CASTILLA LA VIEJA, SPAIN

1 January 1975

After the Christmas leave, four soldiers were returning in the early morning from Santander to the Army Engineer Academy at Burgos. At 6.30 a.m., the driver noticed a particularly bright star and pointed it out to his companions. Later, all four saw a 'luminous object' descend in an arc to the ground nearby at high speed. The soldiers got out of the car and saw an 'object shaped like a truncated cone, 2m [6ft] tall and 3m [10ft] wide [which] stood and irradiated bright white-yellow light.

'The light was extinguished but the dark soon became light again when four identical objects appeared.' The four UFOs formed a row, 'emitting jets of white light downward'. After 10 minutes, the soldiers decided to carry on with their journey lest they be late on parade.

The military judge appointed to investigate the sighting concluded that 'the car's occupants were predisposed, tired and drowsy' and in a state of suggestibility had shared some kind of hallucination. 'An opinion I do not share at all,' declared Sr Ballester Olmos, Spain's leading ufologist.

A UFO seen from the Canary Islands at night on 5 March 1979. The Spanish Air Force investigated and offered a number of explanations for this and several similar sightings, including the possibility of 'visiting spacecraft'. In fact all were caused by missiles launched from NATO submarines in the Atlantic Ocean.

that was in the habit of telling people as little as it possibly could. In light of that, Ballester Olmos's words on the matter of a possible cover-up bear repeating (often):

The knowledge I have acquired through many sincere and straightforward discussions with the officers in charge allows me to guarantee the objectivity and crystal-clear attitude of the Spanish Air Force...

My investigation has found no trace of smoke-screens or any deliberate deceptions of the sort 'society is not prepared to accept the great truth about UFOs'. All this is part of stories fabricated by those who love paranoid theses and who are misery sellers.[10]

We would describe such individuals as doom merchants.

The Belgian triangles

Beginning on 29 November 1989, one of the biggest flaps of recent years overtook Belgium (see Case #32) and reached its peak in April 1990. Professor of physics Auguste Meessen managed to secure the radar tapes of several of these incidents. His analysis revealed a previously unrecognized atmospheric phenomenon that he called 'flying angels', but much data remained unexplained.

While Meessen found that none of the radar traces corresponded to any of the visual reports, his report of November 1990[11] spent many words satirising the press treatment of the wave, wondered 'if UFOs are extra-terrestrial, why are their shapes now different from previously reported objects?' and asserted that the collective unconscious 'does not, for the most part, desire extra-terrestrials'.

In October 1991, SOBEPS, the main UFO group involved in the flap, published a 500-page dossier on the events. It had an introduction by Dr J.-P. Petit of the French National Center of Scientific Research (CNRS) and included papers by Meessen advocating the ETH as the best explanation for the sightings. The book sold out rapidly, but was not universally admired. Ten Belgian scientists denounced Petit and Meessen for their 'rash statements and pseudo-scientific approach'.

Meessen had already speculated about UFO propulsion systems on the basis of a tape-recording that turned out to be of radio interference from an over-the-horizon radar. Petit was soon to publish a book in which he revealed that his research at CNRS had been dictated to him by aliens from Ummo! (The Ummo affair was an elaborate hoax that started in Spain in 1965 and continued for years.)

In a long analysis in 1992[12] Belgian skeptic Wim van Utrecht disposed of several items of would-be photographic evidence, including one whose lights, he drily remarked, showed that Belgian UFOs 'strictly abide by European safety regulations for air traffic'. As Meessen had found but ignored, van Utrecht noted a

Case #30

Lumière Dans Le Jardin

TRANS-EN-PROVENCE, FRANCE
8 February 1981

At about 5.00 p.m., M. Collini, in the words of the French government's UFO study group GEPAN, 'was working quietly in his garden at Trans-en-Provence. Suddenly his attention was attracted by a low whistling sound that appeared to come from the far end of his property.'

The report continues: 'Turning around, [M. Collini] saw in the sky above the trees something approaching a terrace at the bottom of the garden. The ovoid object suddenly landed. The witness moved forward and observed the strange phenomenon behind a small building.

'Less than a minute later, the phenomenon suddenly rose and moved away in a direction similar to that of its arrival, still continuing to emit a low whistle. M. Collini immediately went to the apparent scene of the landing and observed circular marks and a clear crown-shaped imprint on the ground.'

Gendarmes arrived the next day to take soil and vegetation samples. On 20 March, GEPAN investigators took further samples and interviewed M. Collini. The tests showed that the witness 'had no psychological problems and that his testimony was internally and externally consistent' – in other words, he did not contradict himself, and there was evidence that something had landed at the spot he described. The soil at the landing site showed signs of having been been heated to between 300 C and 600 C, while the plants there were prematurely aged and had lost up to 50 per cent of their chlorophyll. No residual radioactivity was evident.

Clearly, something physically real did land on M. Collini's property that evening. Was it an unusual natural phenomenon – perhaps an 'earthlight' – that scorched the earth, or was it an unknown kind of flying machine?

complete lack of correlation between ground reports and radar traces from the 30/31 March sightings; sky maps showed many visual reports were probably bright stars and planets.

In addition, the SOBEPS book showed that witnesses reported not just triangles that night, but 'rectangle, trapezoid, diamond and boomerang shapes', while 'protrusions, windows, domes and hatches always appear to be positioned at different sides of the objects'. Which scarcely makes sense if the same group of identical triangular UFOs was traversing eastern Belgium, as has been claimed.

On that point, van Utrecht observed that almost all of the reports originated from south of the language border between the northern, Flemish-speaking part of Belgium and the French-speaking south. He suggested that this could be explained 'either by postulating that the intelligences behind the UFOs adapt their flight-paths to culturally defined borders, or by accepting that cultural factors had a strong influence on the reporting process'.

In 1993, a confidential study by a civilian engineer from the Belgian Electronic War Center and a major of sappers 'revealed that the unidentified F-16 radar returns captured on video on 30-31 March 1990, were partly due to unusual atmospheric conditions on that night and partly to the fact that the F-16 radar in question had mistakenly locked onto the second F-16 that was taking part in the UFO chase!' Van Utrecht speculated that, among several other reasons, the report may not have been released to the public because 'the military wanted to conceal a malfunction of newly acquired expensive radar equipment'.[13]

That is about the extent of a UFO cover-up in Belgium.

The Rendlesham mystery

An event that certainly has involved a cover-up of sorts, and that is altogether more mysterious, is the 'landing' of a UFO, allegedly twice, over two nights sometime between 26 and 31 December 1980 in a forest next to the USAF base at RAF Woodbridge in Suffolk, England.

The most detailed reconstruction of the events (see Case #31),[14] by long-serving British ufologist Jenny Randles, places them in the wee small hours of 26 and 27 December, a day earlier than the only official document yet to surface on the affair, a report to the Royal Air Force (RAF) by the USAF deputy base commander, Lt Col Charles I. Halt. Apart from that one-page note, a mass of testimony has been proffered by other alleged witnesses to the events, both military and civilian, including a tape made during one sighting by Lt Col Halt.

Randles, who has expended an enormous amount of energy investigating the case, is not convinced that if anything actually came to earth in Rendlesham Forest that it was necessarily extra-terrestrial. But hers is a lone voice among ufologists, most of whom are determined to select from the conflicting evidence available what they need to support their belief that a *bona-fide* 'flying saucer' visited England that midwinter.

Because the testimony is voluminous, various and conflicting, only a select few items can be considered here. Skeptics have ascribed the reports of aliens and apparent spacecraft to exaggeration, misperception, dreams and off-base attention-seeking by immature servicemen. They have proposed various mundane sources for the lights, including mirages of stars. Most suggest that the pulsing beam from nearby Orford Ness lighthouse inspired the 'basic' UFO sightings (the 5-second flashes do coincide with part of the narrative on Halt's tape), while

DEPARTMENT OF THE AIR FORCE
HEADQUARTERS 81ST COMBAT SUPPORT GROUP (USAFE)
APO NEW YORK 09755

REPLY TO
ATTN OF.   CD   13 Jan 81

SUBJECT: Unexplained Lights

TO: RAF/CC

1. Early in the morning of 27 Dec 80 (approximately 0300L), two USAF security police patrolmen saw unusual lights outside the back gate at RAF Woodbridge. Thinking an aircraft might have crashed or been forced down, they called for permission to go outside the gate to investigate. The on-duty flight chief responded and allowed three patrolmen to proceed on foot. The individuals reported seeing a strange glowing object in the forest. The object was described as being metalic in appearance and triangular in shape, approximately two to three meters across the base and approximately two meters high. It illuminated the entire forest with a white light. The object itself had a pulsing red light on top and a bank(s) of blue lights underneath. The object was hovering or on legs. As the patrolmen approached the object, it maneuvered through the trees and disappeared. At this time the animals on a nearby farm went into a frenzy. The object was briefly sighted approximately an hour later near the back gate.

2. The next day, three depressions 1 1/2" deep and 7" in diameter were found where the object had been sighted on the ground. The following night (29 Dec 80) the area was checked for radiation. Beta/gamma readings of 0.1 milliroentgens were recorded with peak readings in the three depressions and near the center of the triangle formed by the depressions. A nearby tree had moderate (.05-.07) readings on the side of the tree toward the depressions.

3. Later in the night a red sun-like light was seen through the trees. It moved about and pulsed. At one point it appeared to throw off glowing particles and then broke into five separate white objects and then disappeared. Immediately thereafter, three star-like objects were noticed in the sky, two objects to the north and one to the south, all of which were about 10° off the horizon. The objects moved rapidly in sharp angular movements and displayed red, green and blue lights. The objects to the north appeared to be elliptical through an 8-12 power lens. They then turned to full circles. The objects to the north remained in the sky for an hour or more. The object to the south was visible for two or three hours and beamed down a stream of light from time to time. Numerous individuals, including the undersigned, witnessed the activities in paragraphs 2 and 3.

CHARLES I. HALT, Lt Col, USAF
Deputy Base Commander

Steuart Campbell, with characteristic individualism, prefers the Shipwash lightship off the Suffolk coast as a source. None of these reductive accounts in my estimation properly addresses the stories of alien contact or even the reports of a saucer-like craft seen in the woods.

Jacques Vallée, who in this instance hovers between skepticism and belief, has taken the most elaborate accounts as genuine, and proposed two solutions. The first is that the US military has developed UFO-like weapons, and one touched down in the forest, possibly accidentally. The second is that the object and the aliens were deliberate fabrications designed to discover servicemen's reactions to an apparent UFO – perhaps to gauge how enemy

soldiers might react to UFO-like military craft. He appears to be alone in this diagnosis.[15]

Yet another skeptical interpretation takes a slightly Machiavellian view of the reports, and takes its cue from the airmen's tales of aliens floating in light beams and the story that USAF intelligence agents casually mentioned aliens while extracting the radar tape from the operators at RAF Watton (an episode that also bothers Randles). Indeed it is curious, and perhaps significant, that the first stories about the case were among the most extravagant, and they were told, in pubs, to people known to be interested in paranormal or anomalous events.

Here is the scenario. It is known that a large, very bright meteor fell

Case #31

Down In The Woods

RAF WOODBRIDGE, SUFFOLK, UNITED KINGDOM
26 and 27 December 1980

According to the most detailed reconstruction of the events, at about 1.00 a.m. on Friday 26 December radars at RAF Watton in Norfolk registered an 'unknown' flying toward the coast over the North Sea. It disappeared from the scopes in the vicinity of Rendlesham Forest; the radar operators wondered if it had come to ground. At about this same time, next to the forest, security police at the eastern ('back') gate of the USAF activity on RAF Woodbridge saw lights coming down from the sky into the trees. They were granted permission to investigate, and according to them, but not the official report on the event, left in a jeep and entered the forest.

The forest track became impassable, and the patrolmen abandoned their vehicle and continued on foot. At some point, it is said, their radios failed. They then came across a conical or triangular object 6–10ft (2–3m) across the base and 6ft (2m) high. The base's deputy commander, Lt Col Charles Halt, described it in an official report as 'metallic in appearance'. It 'illuminated the entire forest with a white light' and 'had a pulsing red light on top and a bank of blue lights underneath. The object was hovering or on legs.' As the patrolmen approached, the UFO 'maneuvered through the trees and disappeared.' Nearby farm animals 'went into a frenzy.' The object, Halt continued, 'was briefly sighted approximately an hour later near the back gate.'

There are also reports that on this night aliens floated in a beam of light beneath the UFO, apparently repairing it, and even a claim that the base commander, Col (now General) Gordon Williams, communicated with the aliens. When daylight came, various indentations were found on the ground where the UFO had been and the area was checked for radioactivity.

The next night, the UFO was seen again; in 1994 Lt Col Halt described being called from a formal dinner to investigate. He took Lt Bruce Englund, Sgt Bobby Ball (the senior Air Force Security Police NCO), and a Sgt Neviles in a jeep into the wood. Halt tape-recorded his own comments as he and the others watched strange lights darting about the sky. By his later account and according to the tape made at the time, there were only the four of them present. One light (he said in 1994) was red 'like the sun coming up in the morning' and about 400–600ft (120–180m) away. It had a black center 'like an eye' that opened and closed. The object appeared to move into a field, and Halt and his party went after it.

They then saw two elliptical objects in the north showing green, red and blue lights. Next they noticed another object in the south, shining beams down to the ground on the base, lighting up aircraft on the flight line. They did not diffuse light like normal searchlights. Halt wondered if the object was a probe. 'Then, just as fast as it came, sshht, it was gone.' The objects seemed to search the area until 4.00 a.m.

Some days later, USAF intelligence agents arrived at RAF Watton and 'borrowed' the radar tapes, saying that a UFO and an alien crew had crashed near Woodbridge.

Many of the alleged witnesses' accounts conflict, particularly concerning what was seen and how many people saw it. There are accounts of the airmen seeing the UFO on the first night becoming disoriented and having to be retrieved by search parties. One witness maintains that before the second sighting a large number of personnel, including British police officers, gathered to await the UFO's arrival in a pre-arranged spot. Animals were seen fleeing the forest, and gas-powered light-alls were set up in a clearing. While some 30 airmen were involved in the search for evidence of the previous night's landing, the UFO landed again nearby. Halt's memo, his tape-recording, and his later account all fail to bear this out, and it is bizarre that Halt and his party failed to notice it.

There are several mysteries involved in the Rendlesham Forest events. Whether they have to do with 'disinformation' spread by USAF intelligence, the effects of the festive season, the vagaries of human perception, the crash of an actual object of some kind, or a combination of all of these things, is not clear – and may never be.

Case #32

Falcons Hunt Triangles

BRUSSELS-TIENEN-LIEGE-EUPEN AXIS, BELGIUM
30–31 March, 1990

The Belgian UFO flap opened on 29 November 1989, when hundreds of people in and around Eupen, near the German border, saw a huge triangular UFO, showing bright spotlights, pass over the town. The prime witesses were two gendarmes. In the following months, similar craft were reported from around the country. Many skywatches were organized, and many photographs and some 30 videotapes were taken of the UFOs.

By March 1990 the Belgian authorities had received over 2500 reports of triangular UFOs, mostly around Eupen and Liège, since November 1989. The Royal Belgian Air Force (RBAF) agreed that if a Brussels-based UFO research group, SOBEPS, would co-ordinate reports at ground level, the RBAF would handle tracking and interception.

During the night of 30–31 March, police patrols and some civilian witnesses linked to SOBEPS reported from 11.00 p.m. that a UFO – the first report, from a gendarme at Ramillies, mentioned three, showing red, green and yellow lights – appeared to be flying on a consistent course across Belgium. RBAF radars at Glons and Semmerzake confirmed the sightings and, at 00.05 a.m., two F-16 Fighting Falcons were scrambled to intercept. The UFO had been flying slowly at 150mph (280km/h) at 9000ft (2750m) until the F-16s' radar locked on to it, when it accelerated at an extraordinary rate to 970mph (1800km/h) and then dived to below 5000ft (1500m). Next it flashed up to 11,000ft (3350m) and then suddenly dived again, and in a few seconds it became entirely lost to radar amid 'ground clutter'. The chase continued, with several brief lock-ons, until 1.02 a.m., when the F-16s headed for their base, landing a few minutes later. Ground observers reported that at around 1.30 a.m. four UFOs 'lost their luminosity' and 'seemed to disappear in four different directions'. Video tapes of the airborne radar read-outs were later released to the press.

The RBAF at first suspected that the USAF was testing the effectiveness of their 'stealth' aircraft – in particular the F117A fighter, which has an unusual triangular configuration. The USAF denied the charge twice, in December 1989 and again in June 1990, saying the plane had 'never flown in the European theater'. This may have been disingenuous: there were persistent rumors in aviation circles in the late 1980s that the F117A was occasionally operating at night from USAF bases in eastern England, while the equally unorthodox-looking B-2 stealth bomber openly visited the UK not long after its unveiling in November 1988.

Belgian skeptic Wim van Utrecht demolished many of the claims surrounding the events of 30–31 March 1990 (see text) but conceded that 'some kind of unusual flying machine did manifest itself over our country on two or three occasions' in November and December 1989. The object 'may have been an experimental, self-propelled balloon of triangular configuration. This would explain not only the slow and almost silent overflight... but also its reason to carry [lights] attuned to standard safety regulations... Blimps and new generation airships are now advertised in military circles as the best possible solution for covert reconnaissance duties.'

over the North Sea to the east of Woodbridge at 2.50 a.m. on 26 December. The patrolmen at the east gate of the base saw this, misjudged its distance, and thought it was something crashing into the wood. They actually found nothing there, but jokes about 'little green men' and flying saucers were inevitably made.

These may have turned, like Chinese whispers, into tales and rumors that aliens and UFOs were really seen in Rendlesham Forest. The following night, bright stars or light-house flashes seemed significant to other patrolmen, who were already primed for strange events by these stories. Col Halt would seem to be one who gave some credit to the tales of a UFO landing, and decided to investigate and take measurements in

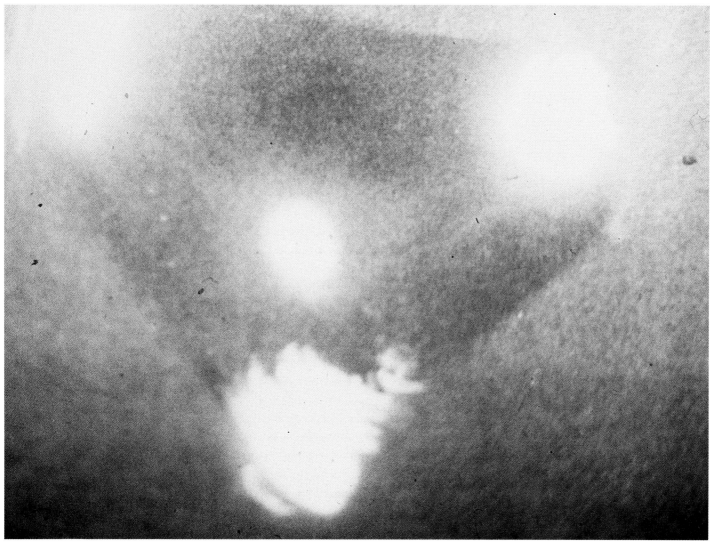

The sole photograph of decent quality taken during the wave of triangular UFOs seen over Belgium in 1990. A factory worker took it at Petit-Rechain, just east of Liège, on the night of 31 March. Belgian skeptic Wim van Utrecht and members of the Belgian Royal Military School have shredded technical aspects of the image and the supporting testimony of witnesses and strongly suspect the picture is a fabrication.

the woods, in the middle of the night. His brilliant light-all may have been taken by some to be a landed UFO, and his invasion of the forest undoubtedly disturbed animals nearby.

It is apparent from the tape-recording he made that his party had little idea of what they were measuring with their Geiger counter. As Steuart Campbell comments, they seemed to be excited that it clicked at all. There is some doubt that they understood the starlite scope they were also carrying. This gathers available light and intensifies it – nothing more. The airmen seemed to think it detected infra-red (IR) radiation (if it did, it was not a starlite scope, but a thermal imager; but they never called it that). They pointed it at incisions on pine trees in a clearing and thought the cuts were giving out unusual amounts of heat. They found the same thing on the sides of all the trees facing into the clearing.

This tends to confirm that they were misusing a light-intensifier, as the cuts, exposing white wood, would obviously be far brighter than the surrounding bark of the pines and there would be more light in a clearing than inside the closely planted wood. If the airmen were mistaking intensified visible light for IR radiation, they would have the wrong impression: that greater heat was exuding from the trees within the clearing.

This *pot-pourri* of rumor and blunders would have added fuel to the tall tales circulating on the base. At this point, USAF intelligence enters the picture. All USAF bases in the UK were sensitive to potential security leaks at this time: a lively national debate about their harboring cruise missiles was well under way.

Here was a fine opportunity to test the discretion of those stationed at Woodbridge and its twin base at neighboring Bentwaters. Agents were dispatched to RAF Watton to pick up the radar tapes of 26 December, which were known to show an unknown target (probably the ionized trail of the fireball falling to Earth), and were told to spin a yarn about flying saucers

Case #33

A Flying Catamaran?

WESTERN ENGLAND and WALES, UNITED KINGDOM

30–31 March 1993

Numerous witnesses from western and south Wales and western England reported that between 1.05 and 1.10 a.m. on 31 March, against a clear sky, they saw two brilliant globular objects traveling at speed in a north-west to south-easterly direction. The UFOs left long vapor trails and made no sound. Estimates of height varied from 2000ft (600m) to 30,000ft (9000m). Local air traffic control radars had no unidentifieds on their screens at this time.

Between 1.10 and 2.40 a.m., a UFO of 'some considerable size' was seen first over North Devon, then at 2.00 a.m. over Bridgewater, Somerset, next over Shropshire and finally over South Yorkshire – thus following first an easterly and then a north-easterly route. The most detailed report came from Bridgewater, where at 2.00 a.m. a number of fishermen (known locally as 'elvers', as they were fishing for eels) on the River Parrot saw a 'very large catamaran-shaped object' fly toward them, before passing overhead in complete silence at about 800ft (250m) altitude. Two very bright white lights showed at its rear, and two orange lights at its center. A similar UFO was reported at earlier times from 8.00 to 11.00 p.m. the previous evening (30 March) from locations in Cornwall, Somerset and North Devon.

At about 1.05 a.m. on 31 March the casing of a Russian Tsyklon rocket, which had put the Cosmos 2238 radio satellite into orbit, re-entered the Earth's atmosphere over Ireland, broke in two, and went in a south-easterly direction over the western UK at a height of about 55 miles (90km). It passed over Land's End at about 1.10 a.m. This undoubtedly accounts for the Welsh and western English sightings at about that time. However, the Ministry of Defence had no explanation for the earlier or later sightings, and officially classified the UFO as an 'unknown'.

It's possible to absorb some, but not all, of these sightings into the 'known' category. The elvers' report is almost certainly of the Tsyklon debris, with a mistaken estimate of the time. In Cornwall a patroling police sergeant saw what he described as 'two very bright lights... hovering at about 2000ft (600m)', which suddenly started to ascend 'at a fairly fast rate of knots.' Despite the 'vapor trails' and the direction of flight being exactly the same as the Tsyklon debris, the local UFO investigator classed this set of aerial lights among the unknowns because of the etimated height and the appearance of two other lights that gave the 'UFO' the appearance of a single structured craft. Other reports with anomalous details but logged at about 1.10 a.m. can likewise safely be attributed to the re-entry, despite claims of seeing a structure in the sky.

If this seems a sweeping claim, I have good reason to make it. I witnessed the Tsyklon debris re-entry, in the company of one other person. Comparing memories of the experience later, it transpired that where I saw two separate, yellowish lights, she saw red lights, but was not sure whether they were separate, or attached to one large craft. I thought we were standing in a back field on her property; we were actually in a front field. Also wrongly, if not surprisingly, being familiar with innumerable military aircraft at all altitudes during daylight, I thought the lights were at about 2000ft (600m); she made no estimate. We both thought they were fast-moving jets until we realized they were absolutely silent. And we both agreed on the (correct) time. Both of us do jobs in which minute attention to detail is critical – but our long training and experience as observers of particular kinds of material did not transfer to this unprecedented, although not even slightly alarming, circumstance. How reliable are UFO witnesses – even those legendary 'trained observers'?

Dear Mr Cooper,

Thank you for sending me a copy of your Interim Report on the wave of UFO sightings that occurred in the early hours of Wednesday 31 March.

I have attached a copy of a map that I have produced, setting out the locations of sightings, together with a time and heading, if known. I have included the sightings described in your report (some of which we already had details of), together with some other reports that you may not have heard about. Our policy of witness confidentiality means that I am unable to give out names and addresses, but the following locations correspond to the crosses on the map:

Penistone, S Yorks.
Bradway, S Yorks.
Cosford, Staffs.
Rugeley, Staffs.
Shawbury, Salop.
Grateley, Hants.
Merthyr Tydfil, Mid Glamorgan.
Haverfordwest, Dyfed.
Crymych, Dyfed.
Bristol, Avon.
Bridgewater, Somerset.
Quantock Hills, Somerset.
Bishop's Lydeard, Somerset.
Taunton, Somerset.
Minehead, Somerset.
Braunton, Devon.
Ilfracombe, Devon.
Plymouth, Devon.
Exeter, Devon.
Liskeard, Cornwall.
Wadebridge, Cornwall.
St Ives, Cornwall.

I hope this will be useful to you in your investigation; I will keep you informed of developments.

UFO sightings late 30th/early 31st March '93

Notes: All times are local
Pencil arrows show estimated heading of UF

Signs of unwonted openness at the British Ministry of Defence: documents revealing some sparse details of UFO reports over the UK from the night of 31 March 1993, sent to a civilian investigator. The official who provided the information has since said he is convinced there is no deliberate cover-up or secret knowledge of UFO activity in the UK government machine.

and aliens. An impressionable young airman was told a similar story, or already believed it, and promoted himself to a leading role in it. (There are three claimants to the parts played by only two actual security policemen on the first night, after all.)

A waiting game

Air Force Intelligence then waited to see how long the story would take, and from where, to come back to them or into the public domain. Col Halt may or may not have played a witting part in this experiment: if witting, his memo to the RAF can be seen as a cover story for startling stories emanating from men under his command. In the event, the impressionable young airman was shipped back to the USA and gently discharged from the service. The rest is history – and legend.

Like every other attempt to make sense of all the claims, contradictions and bizarre aspects of the Rendlesham incident, this one has holes in it. But some such scenario would account for a very high proportion of the most puzzling aspects of the affair, including the lack of documentation held by the UK government and their otherwise eccentric lack of interest in it. Perhaps one day the truth will out.

Meanwhile, the story of a 'sky crash' in southern England will doubtless continue to flourish and feed the myth of a worldwide cover-up of UFO and alien reality.

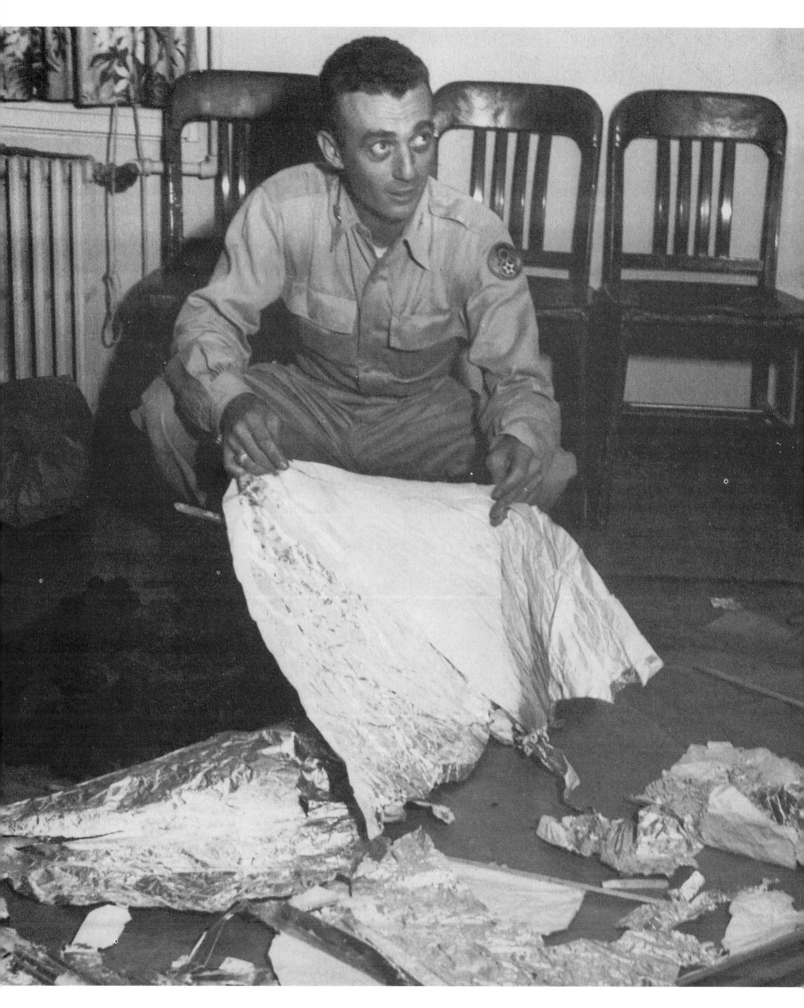

Chapter Eight

BURSTING THE ROSWELL BALLOON

AN INCIDENT BECOMES AN EPIC

NO UFO EVENT has attracted as much attention or caused as much controversy as the 'Roswell Incident' of 1947. The proponents' case is that at least one, possibly two, flying disks crashed in New Mexico during July of that year and that a rancher named Mac Brazel found some of the debris from the crash. They believe that the US Air Force retrieved that, the disk(s), and a number of alien bodies from the desert. The cover-up of the truth is said to have been in place within hours of the wreckage being recovered and to have remained in place ever since.

Thousands of dollars have been spent by individual researchers and

Major Jesse Marcel, intelligence officer at Roswell Army Air Field in July 1947, holds the tattered remains of a 'flying disk' found that summer on a sheep ranch some 75 miles (120km) from Roswell. Marcel maintained that the material seemed 'not of this Earth', but newly revealed evidence suggests he may not have been the most reliable of witnesses.

UFO organizations in attempts to uncover what actually happened. By the end of 1995, five full-length books had been written on the case, and it had been mentioned, supported, dissected or scorned in dozens more and in a deluge of conference papers.

The US Air Force had scoured its files, and the US Government Accounting Office (GAO) had sought a 'paper trail' that would reveal evidence of a top-secret operation to recover a crashed UFO – to no avail.

Those who have spent a considerable number of years tracking down leads, witnesses, and circumstantial evidence that something truly extraordinary fell out of the sky that summer view the official verdict with a certain cynicism. One has baldly called it 'garbage'. As far as they are concerned, the failure of the USAF and the GAO to rip the lid off the case is merely evidence that the secret of Roswell is so huge and so momentous that the cover-up has to be maintained.

While the advocates of a UFO crash near Roswell concur on this point, the other matters on which

they agree form a very short list indeed. This makes the Roswell case peculiarly difficult to assess. The two major teams of pro-crash researchers have produced quite distinct reconstructions of the events leading up to the crash, differ over how many UFOs crashed and where, disagree on the number of aliens found, and have their own prized 'star' witnesses to the events. Over time, they – along with many key witnesses – have also changed their minds about all of these things. On top of all that, the two groups have derided each other in terms that are strong even by the muscular standards of ufological polemics.

Whichever chronicle one reads, the sequence of alleged events in the Roswell case is extremely complex and detailed. And narratives have altered, grown and been disputed over time. The accounts and assessments of the Roswell episode that follow are thus inevitably broad and selective. Partisans of the case may call this treatment sweeping, and both they and skeptics will doubtless miss mention of favorite elements in the

Leased Wire
Associated Press

Roswell Daily Record

RECORD PHONES
Business Office 2288
News Department 2287

VOL. 47. NUMBER 99   ESTABLISHED 1888   ROSWELL, NEW MEXICO, TUESDAY, JULY 8, 1947   6c PER COPY.

Movies as Usual

GRAND

Levees broke and flood waters rolled into the town of Grand Tower, Ill., but while the manager of the movie theater sweeps out the water that has entered the lobby these youngsters are standing in line for tickets for the night's performance. (AP Wirephoto)

Some of Soviet Satellites May Attend Paris Meeting

Paris, July 8 — Indications mounted today that at least some of the nations within the Soviet orbit would attend the Paris conference on the Marshall aid-to...

Roswellians Have Differing Opinions On Flying Saucers

Roswell is a bit uncertain about these flying disks, it would appear from interviews today with a number of local citizens, with about as many ideas concerning them as there are people interviewed.

The reactions ran the gamut from...

Claims Army Is Stacking Courts Martial

Indiana Senator Lays Protest Before Patterson

Washington, July 8 — Senator Jenner (R-Ind.) contended today that "the high command in the European theatre is stacking courts martial against defendants in court martial."

House Passes Tax Slash by Large Margin

Defeat Amendment By Demos to Remove Many from Rolls

Washington, July 8 — The house passed today the Republican-backed bill to cut income taxes by $4,000,000,000 annually for 49,000,000 taxpayers, beginning Jan. 1.

American League Wins All-Star Game

Chicago, July 8 — The American league, peeking away with an eight-hit attack and ringing the bell with its pinchhitters, continued its all-star mastery over the National league by coming from...

Security Council Paves Way to Talks On Arms Reductions

Lake Success, July 8 — The United Nations security council today approved an American blueprint for arms reduction discussions despite a Russian warning that the plan would bring about a collapse of arms regulation efforts

RAAF Captures Flying Saucer On Ranch in Roswell Region

No Details of Flying Disk Are Revealed

Roswell Hardware Man and Wife Report Disk Seen

The intelligence office of the 509th Bombardment group at Roswell Army Air Field announced at noon today, that the field has come into possession of a flying saucer.

Ex-King Carol Weds Mme. Lupescu

Former King Carol of Romania and Mme. Elena Lupescu relax aboard the S. S. America bound for Cuba and Mexico in May, 1941. A member of Carol's household in Rio de Janeiro said the ex-king and his companion for 23 years in reign and exile were recently married at their hotel Copacabana Palace suite. (AP Wirephoto)

Miners and Operators Sign Highest Wage Pact in History

Washington, July 8 — An agreement averting a nationwide soft coal strike was signed today by John L. Lewis and a majority of the bituminous operators.

---

story (for example: as an occasional shepherd myself, I remain underwhelmed by one published claim that sheep, stupid as they are, will eat fragments of weather balloons or flying saucers). But this is a chapter, not a book, about Roswell: the discussion has to be relatively brief. But it is, I believe, both representative and fair.[1]

The first reports

The first the public knew of the Roswell incident was an astonishing headline in Roswell's evening paper, the *Daily Record*, of 8 July 1947, which trumpeted: RAAF CAPTURES FLYING SAUCER ON RANCH IN ROSWELL REGION. The column began:

The Intelligence Office of the 509th Bombardment group at Roswell Army Air Field announced at noon today that the field has come into possession of a flying saucer.

According to information released by the department, over authority of Major J.A. Marcel, intelligence officer, the disk was recovered on a ranch in the Roswell vicinity, after an unidentified rancher had notified Sheriff Geo. Wilcox, here, that he had found the instrument on his premises.

Major Marcel and a detail from his department went to the ranch and recovered the disk, it was stated.

After the intelligence office here had inspected the instrument it was flown to 'higher headquarters.'

The intelligence office stated that no details of the saucer's construction or its appearance had been revealed.

And it continued, in part:

Mr and Mrs Dan Wilmot apparently were [sic] *the only persons in Roswell who have seen what they thought was a flying disk.*

They were sitting on their porch at 105 South Penn last Wednesday night [2 July] *at about ten minutes before ten o'clock when a large glowing object zoomed out of the sky from the southeast, going in a*

Roswell's evening paper of 8 July 1947 announces the discovery of wreckage of a 'flying disk' on Mac Brazel's ranch. The report refers to the downed UFO as an 'instrument' - a curious description if the material came from an extra-terrestrial craft.

---

northwesterly direction at a high rate of speed...

Wilmot said it appeared to him to be about 1,500 feet [450m] *high and going fast. He estimated between 400 and 500 miles per hour* [640 and 800 km/h].

In appearance it looked oval in shape like two inverted saucers, faced mouth to mouth, or like two old type washbowls places together in the same fashion.

Of several stories about the find that went out on the Associated Press wire, one transmitted at 4.30 p.m. the same day elaborated:

The many rumors regarding the flying disc became a reality yesterday when the

Intelligence Office of the 509th Bomb Group of the Eighth Air Force, Roswell Army Air Field, was fortunate enough to gain possession of a disc through the co-operation of one of the local ranchers and the sheriff's office of Chaves County.

The flying object landed on a ranch near Roswell some time last week. Not having phone facilities, the rancher stored the disc until such time as he was able to contact the sheriff's office, who in turn notified Major Jesse A. Marcel, of the 509th Bomb Group Intelligence Office.

Action was immediately taken and the disc was picked up at the rancher's home. It was inspected by the Roswell Army Air Field and subsequently loaned by Major Marcel to higher headquarters.

The unnamed rancher in these reports was W.W. 'Mac' Brazel, whose rough, isolated sheep ranch lay in Lincoln County, 30 miles (48km) or so southeast of Corona, and some 75 miles (120km) northwest of Roswell. The following day, the *Record* published an interview with Brazel in which he described how he had found the wreckage on 14 June. It was scattered over an area about 600ft (180m) in diameter. On 4 July he gathered it up. 'The tinfoil, paper, tape, and sticks made a bundle about three feet (1m) long and 7 or 8 inches (180-200mm) thick... the entire lot would have weighed maybe five pounds (2.3kg)... Considerable scotch tape and some tape with flowers printed upon it had been used in the construction.' Brazel's parting shot was:

'I am sure what I found was not any weather observation balloon,' he said. 'But

if I find anything else besides a bomb they are going to have a hard time getting me to say anything about it.'

Much would be made of that remark. Years later people would recall that Brazel was held *incommunicado* – some say in jail, others at the air base – for between two days and a week after the interview, and that what he said to the newspaper was significantly different from the story he had told before.

After finding the wreckage, Brazel went in to Corona where, for the first time (as well as no phone, he had no radio), he heard about the rash of flying saucers that had been reported all over the USA since 24 June. Wondering if the debris on his land was somehow connected – and, some say, interested in the rewards on offer to anyone who found a downed disk – he told the Roswell sheriff of his find on Monday 7 July, while he was in town to sell some wool.

Brazel took Marcel and Sheridan Cavitt, of the Counter-Intelligence Corps, out to the ranch to view the material, and they brought it back to Roswell. After that, according to Brazel's son years later, troops descended on the ranch, keeping everyone off the land until they had cleared it of all the debris.

By the afternoon of 8 July, Marcel and the wreckage had been flown to the Fort Worth headquarters of 8th Air Force. Warrant Officer Irving Newton was called in to the office of Brig. General Roger Ramey, the commanding general, to identify it. He immediately recognized the remains of a weather balloon and RAWIN radar reflector.

General Ramey went on the radio to deny any connexion with flying saucers. 'There is no such gadget known to the Army,' he said bluntly. In Roswell the following day, the *Daily Record's* lead headline ran across eight columns: GENERAL RAMEY EMPTIES ROSWELL SAUCER.

And that, for more than three decades, was that. The story, along with others of the same kind, lay dormant after Frank Scully's 1950 book *Behind the Flying Saucers* had been discredited (see Chapter One). Interest in the subject revived in the 1970s after one Robert Carr issued a spruced-up claim that a saucer had crashed near Aztec, New Mexico, and Leonard Stringfield published a sworn statement by a 'former engineer at Wright-Patterson AFB' who had personally examined a crashed UFO near Kingman, Arizona, on 21 May 1953. That almost every

On 9 July 1947, the Roswell paper told its readers of the Eighth Air Force's commanding general's assessment of the 'flying saucer' wreckage found locally. Those who believe the debris came from an alien spaceship are convinced that a cover-up of the truth began with this high-level debunking, and has continued to this day.

detail in both stories was lifted straight from Scully's book did not deter a number of ufologists from starting to burrow once more into the whole field of crashed UFOs. It was even cautiously suggested that Scully's tale was really true, and had been suppressed by the authorities.

The case re-opens

By 1978 Stanton Friedman and William L. Moore had rediscovered the Roswell reports, tracked down Jesse Marcel, and, they believed, had evidence that Brazel had found parts of an alien craft. The results of their research were published in 1980 in *The Roswell Incident*. The book cited Charles Berlitz and Moore as authors; Friedman was hurt at receiving less than due credit for his contribution.

The Roswell Incident proposed that Brazel had been told to mislead the press about the true date of his discovery. The authors believed that on 2 July Dan Wilmot and his wife had

seen the object whose debris Brazel found near Corona. According to hearsay, civil engineer Grady L. Barnett of Socorro was working on the Plains of St Agustin some 50 miles (80km) due west of Socorro and over 180 miles (290km) west of Roswell – on 3 July, the authors assumed – when he saw light glinting off a metallic object on the ground. He thought it might be a crashed aircraft.

He found no aircraft, but 'some sort of metallic, disk-shaped object', about 30ft (9m) in diameter, split open. Inside it, and scattered beside it on the ground as well, were a number of bodies. They were small, hairless humanoids with large heads, wearing gray, one-piece suits without any visible fasteners. While gazing at this astonishing scene, Barnett was joined by a group of archeology students from the University of Pennsylvania. Shortly after that, a US Army jeep roared up. The officer on board at once declared the area off limits and under military control. The area was

A reconstruction of the Roswell UFO's crash site – its exact location, and even the number of craft involved, is a matter of dispute among various alleged witnesses – at the UFO Enigma Museum, near the old Roswell Army Air Field.

cordoned off, the civilians told to leave – and informed sternly that it was 'their patriotic duty' to say nothing of what they had seen – and troops began to move in to take charge of the crash.

From these scanty details Moore and Friedman pieced together a flight path for the UFO: that it came from somewhere south-east of Roswell, suffered some kind of damage or accident over Brazel's ranch, where it shed some debris, then veered west to crash in the desert on the Plains of St Agustin. It was also clear to them that the US military was very keen to keep the precise details of what had happened under wraps.

For example, Jesse Marcel maintained that the Army called two press conferences to proclaim the debris found on Brazel's ranch was nothing more exciting than the remains of a weather balloon. At the first he was photographed holding the wreckage he had retrieved. This was removed, and different debris was displayed for reporters to see and photograph.

Unlike the material Marcel had handled, however, this was flimsy, fragile stuff. He said what he had found was like 'nothing made on Earth': it resisted prolonged attack by cigarette lighter, blowtorch and a 16lb (7.25kg) sledgehammer and, despite its thinness, could not be cut or torn. And of course the Army pointedly said nothing about Barnett's find out in the desert west of Socorro.

There is one more curious event to note. Lydia Sleppy, a teletype operator in Albuquerque, was putting reports of the 'crashed disk' story on the wire, relayed to her by phone from radio reporter Johnny McBoyle in Roswell, when her machine ground to a halt. Then, says The Roswell Incident, it chattered out this curt message: ATTENTION ALBUQUERQUE: DO NOT TRANSMIT. REPEAT DO NOT TRANSMIT THIS MESSAGE. STOP COMMUNICATION IMMEDIATELY. The sender was not identified.

Roswell revisited: the 1990s

Thus the story stood until 1991, when Kevin D. Randle and Donald R. Schmitt published the results of their own lengthy research, UFO Crash at Roswell. The Center for UFO Studies in Chicago also put out an 'historical survey' that included a comprehensive shredding of the MJ-12 papers by Joe Nickell and John F. Fischer.

Randle and Schmitt dismissed the story that Barney Barnett had found a crashed saucer on the Plains of St Agustin. The Roswell UFO had crashed only a few miles from where it had shed debris onto the Brazel ranch, and was spotted from the air. Before the military could reach it overland, Barnett and the archeology students stumbled on it. There were only three decaying bodies.

The awkward detail that Barnett's wife's diary put him near Pie Town, over 200 miles (320km) to the west, they ascribed to Barnett's obedience to the military. He was covering his tracks. They accepted Marcel's version of events. One of the 'star' witnesses in the book was former Brig. General Arthur E. Exon USAF, who had heard of the research into the remains of the UFO and its alien crew while he was serving at Wright Field as a light colonel in July 1947.

In 1992, Stanton Friedman and his new co-author Don Berliner published Crash at Corona, which reasserted the authenticity of the MJ-12 papers and restated the argument that a UFO had fallen on the Plains of St Agustin on 2 July. The invention of the transistor, it was hinted, might have been one fruit of studying the wreckage. The authors produced a star witness who, with his family, had actually seen the downed saucer, the alien bodies, and the arrival of both the archeologists and the military.

Gerald Anderson, who was aged just five when the crash occurred, particularly recalled a flame-haired officer and a black sergeant being among the military, and he put together an identikit picture of the leader of the archeological team that matched the features of the New Mexico anthropologist Dr Winfred Buskirk. Anderson's powers of recall were acknowledged to be phenomenal.

In a further twist, Friedman and Berliner concluded that two saucers had crashed – after colliding in the sky. Altogether eight alien bodies were recovered; one or two may have been alive. Lydia Sleppy's interrupted tele-type transmission, it was revealed for the first time, was the work of the FBI, who were allegedly monitoring the wires. And Glenn Dennis, who was a mortician and Roswell's part-time ambulance driver, remembered how the air base had requested child-sized, hermetically sealed caskets, how he had seen some of the wreckage in the back of an Army ambulance, and had later been told much about the alien bodies by an unnamed nurse from the base hospital.

Randle and Schmitt returned to the fray in 1994 with their book The Truth About the UFO Crash at Roswell. By then the writers were known to be on less than cordial terms with Friedman and Berliner. Meanwhile, Karl T. Pflock had produced a revisionist history, titled Roswell in Perspective, which suggested that a then top-secret Mogul balloon array had landed on Brazel's field. The Truth… gave their 'rivals' short shrift. Randle and Schmitt now informed their readers that the UFO (just one) had crashed some 35 miles (55km) north of Roswell on 5 July, not on 2 July.

They dismissed the Barnett story as hearsay (it had always been that), and listed the forgeries, lies and evasions which, they claimed, made up Gerald Anderson's testimony. These included a fake diary, a doctored phone bill and shifts in his story that moved the site of his encounter with the UFO and the recovery team to at least three different locations.

His identikit picture of Dr Buskirk was the product of having been taught by Buskirk at high school, 10 years after the Roswell incident. Anderson at first denied having been to the school in question, but he mysteriously appears in class photographs at the time Buskirk taught there.

However, Randle and Schmitt had found a new archeological team, this one led by Dr Currey Holden. They wrote that 'there is no reason not to believe he had been there' at the crash

In downtown Roswell, the UFO Museum and Research Center invites the curious to consider the evidence for UFOs. One of the Center's directors, Glenn Dennis - a star witness for Roswell believers - is no stranger to the tourist trade: he also runs a museum in nearby Lincoln, the former county town where outlaw Billy the Kid made a spectacular jailbreak in 1882.

site, although Holden's diaries power-fully suggested he had been in Lubbock, Texas, the whole time, doing anything – such as attending a wedding – but archeological work.

The British critic Christopher D. Allan thoroughly demolished all of the new 'archeological' claims that were in the book, pointing out in particular that 'at no point have Randle and Schmitt tried to establish whether the location they claim to be the "crash" site was even known to be... of archaeological interest.'

A chapter of singular obscurity was devoted to General Nathan Twining's 1947 summary of his command's opinions on UFOs (see Chapter One) and Projects Moon Dust and Blue Fly (see Chapter Five). Some paragraphs of this section, and all the reasoning, defy this reader's understanding. The gist seems to be that Twining knew about the Roswell incident but pro-posed a classified investigation because the Air Force wanted to know more about UFOs in general; and that (as is obvious) Moon Dust would have been used to retrieve crashed UFOs, were any UFOs to crash.

The 'star witness' in *The Truth...* was one Jim Ragsdale, who with his girlfriend 'Trudy Truelove' had actual-ly seen the UFO crash on the night of 4 July. Like Gerald Anderson, he soon began to alter and embellish his story, and by the end of 1995 Randle had repudiated him. Randle had also fallen out with his co-author Don Schmitt, who had lied about his occupation and qualifications.

Deconstructing the Roswell incident

One of the striking features of the voluminous writings (which extend far beyond the printed books) that present the Roswell incident as the crash of an alien spacecraft is that their interpretations of events has (unlike the results of most historical research) become more, not less, ambiguous and uncertain as to what actually hap-pened. Only two of the five books mentioned here agree on where, or even when, the UFO, or UFOs, 'really' crashed and spilled aliens on to the desert floor. There are no reliable claimants to first-hand experience of the crashlanding itself.

Yet all the proponents insist it must have happened – if only because Brazel's bits and pieces, unEarthly as they seemed to Jesse Marcel, plainly a spacecraft do not make. No more do

some nuts and bolts, a broken light-bulb and a burst airbag amount to an automobile. There were no guts to the thing whose tattered remains Brazel found: no engine, no doors, no con-trols, no instruments, seats, food, drink or lavatory, and certainly no crew. If that indubitably real wreckage was to be shown to be extra-terrestrial, something bigger and better had to be found elsewhere to provide the neces-sary exhibit.

The crashed-saucer advocates have massaged the few facts at their disposal so that this vital, if eternally elusive, additional element was always present. For their reasoning to succeed, they had to revise what they often call the 'timeline' of the incident – that is, what happened when. The Wilmots' sighting of a UFO on 2 July was, ini-tially, duly chosen as the true date of the crash. There is no other reason to question Brazel's statement that he found the debris on the Foster ranch on 14 June (it may, of course, have dropped out of the sky a good deal earlier). Even if Brazel did parrot an Air Force line about what he found, there was no need to make him change the date.

The stories about Brazel's incarcer-ation and pressuring by the Air Force are what one might expect from decades-old recollections of exciting, faintly 'secret' events at which people have been no more than spectators. The memories are most likely of rumor and gossip: the best anyone can actually remember is Brazel walking

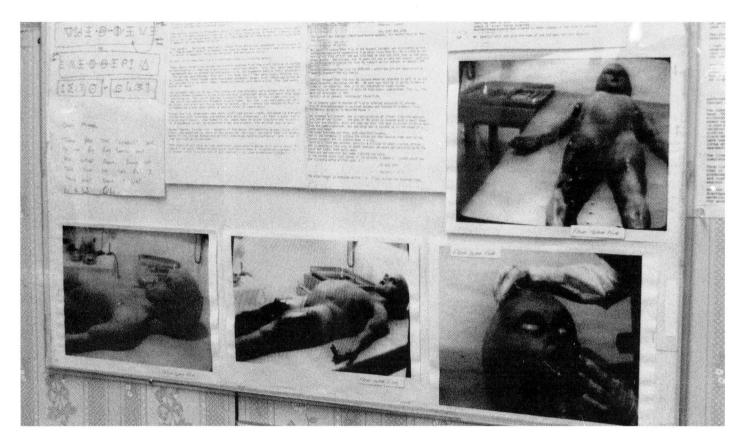

around town with some military types on or around 9 July. The one individual who claimed to have heard Brazel's 'original' account inconveniently refused to reveal any details. It will become apparent why there is no good reason to believe Brazel did change his story.

All the allegedly first-hand accounts of a second (or third) crash site have crumbled to nothing under scrutiny; only the faith and determination of the Roswell researchers keeps the legend of more wreckage and alien corpses alive. Brazel, CIC agent Sheridan W. Cavitt, and even Jesse Marcel never at any time claimed to have seen alien bodies. The nature of the wreckage that Brazel found thus becomes central to deciding whether anything 'not of this Earth' landed anywhere near Roswell in 1947. Even if it did, we still have only a very incomplete and insubstantial saucer. By way of evidence either way, we are left today with the testimony of five people who, we can be certain, saw or handled the debris. They are Jesse Marcel and his son Jesse Jr, Sheridan

Cavitt, Irving Newton, and Mac Brazel's son Bill.

Sheridan Cavitt, interviewed by the USAF on 24 May 1994, said the debris was 'too flimsy to carry people or anything of that sort. It never crossed my mind it could be anything but a radio sonde.' The wreckage covered an area about 20ft (6m) square, and there was no gouge or 'other obvious sign of impact'.

Cavitt, whose chain of command bypassed the base commander, thought the matter so trifling he did not even bother to report it: 'It looked to me, somebody lost a weather balloon. I couldn't care less... tough luck.' No one from the Pentagon enquired about it. And Cavitt was not sworn to secrecy about it, as Randle and Schmitt – whom he called 'clowns' – had insisted to his face; despite his denials.

Point by point, with a richly mordant wit, Cavitt repudiated details of the crash material, its recovery and later events that the UFO advocates had made vital to the Roswell legend. 'They don't believe you when you tell

Stills from a movie, released in 1995, that purportedly show the autopsy of one of the aliens retrieved from the Roswell UFO. The film was greeted with almost universal derision by ufologists. Among a plethora of objections to its likely authenticity were: the failure of British entrepreneur Ray Santilli, who acquired the footage, to release any of it for scientific testing, despite numerous promises to do so; the absence of any X-rays that the pathologists would normally use as reference; potential health hazards in the operating room such as a telephone (itself proven to be made later than 1947) and a mysterious safe; the use of a lone, hand-held camera to make this historic record, with no sign of additional still cameras, fixed movie cameras or – a virtual certainty at the time – the presence of a surgical artist; the speed and carelessness of the autopsy – one pathologist said that, given such an extraordinary subject, he might take days over the dissection; the bizarre fashion in which the creature's brain is removed, as if it had no connexion to the optical nerves or spinal cord; and the implausible story of the alleged cameraman, who claimed the film was 'overlooked' by the Pentagon for 48 years.

the truth,' he said wryly, and offered to 'prick my finger and sign it in blood' that he knew nothing about crashed spaceships or 'little men'. But he did recall an in-flight refueling exercise in 1947 in which two B-29s crashed. Some witnesses, he thought, might later have confused the bodies from that with 'aliens'.

Irving Newton, on being interviewed by the USAF on 21 July 1994, said that he 'walked into the General's office where this supposed flying saucer was lying all over the floor. As soon as I saw it, I giggled... I told them that this was a balloon and a RAWIN [Radar Wind] target.' Newton also recalled General Ramey canceling the planned shipment of the wreckage to Wright Patterson. And he shed an interesting light on Jesse Marcel's behavior when the two met at Fort Worth:

While I was examining the debris, Major Marcel was picking up pieces of the target sticks and trying to convince me that some notations on the sticks were alien writings. There were figures on the sticks lavender or pink in color, [they] appeared to be weather-faded markings, with no rhyme or reason. He did not convince me these were alien writings.

Marcel, even then, it seems, may have been entranced by the idea that he had collected an extra-terrestrial spacecraft. Newton said he 'chased me all around that room' trying to convince Fort Worth's resident weather expert that the material was unusually tough, the markings strange, and the whole thing extra-terrestrial.

There is circumstantial evidence that Marcel had been caught up by the 1947 flying-saucer flap and was an early ETHer. I believe he never lost that enthusiasm, and by the time Stanton Friedman unearthed him in 1978 his specific memories of the Roswell incident had, like those of many others, been indelibly stained and entangled with other stories of saucer crashes. I submit that the story he told Friedman, and repeated many times thereafter, was an amalgam of the truth, wishful thinking, outright fantasy – and, sadly, plain lies.

The legend of Jesse Marcel

In presenting this argument, let's look first at Marcel's claims and his role in the development of the Roswell saga.

Lieutenant Walter Haut, the 509th Bomb Group's public information officer, could not remember in 1995 exactly who had suggested using the terms 'flying disk' or 'saucer' in his press release of 8 July 1947, or whether he had even written the release himself. However, a thoughtful reader of the *Record's* lead story cannot help noticing that the human star of this sensational piece is none other

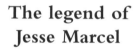

The official culprit in the Roswell Incident: a test launch of a balloon in the top-secret Project Mogul. According to surviving project members, a large array of these balloons could certainly have come to ground on Brazel's ranch, and their debris would fit his description of what he found.

than Jesse Marcel – who was the first to hear of the 'saucer' story from Sheriff Wilcox. Did he write, or dictate, the press release? It was certainly issued 'over authority of Major J.A. Marcel'. His looming presence and the bit-part alotted to Cavitt ('a detail') in the printed report point to him as the source of the flying-saucer phrases, especially in light of Newton's account of the scene at Fort Worth.

Marcel's next documented appearance in the narrative is with the debris in General Ramey's office. The uncropped photographs taken at the time reveal clearly enough that the debris displayed by Marcel is exactly the same as that shown in the pictures with Irving Newton, General Ramey

and his chief of staff, Col Thomas Dubose – contrary to Marcel's claim that the 'real' wreckage was switched for something innocuous after his picture was taken.

When Stanton Friedman tracked him down in 1978, and ever after, Marcel maintained that the wreckage that he found had proved to be inexplicably tough, resisting both fire and sledgehammer. It was not, he said, 'of this Earth'. If there was no switch of debris at Fort Worth, how can one explain Marcel's statement? How, in any case, does anyone reconcile the ineffable strength of the material in Marcel's account with the fact that he found it shattered in tiny pieces on Brazel's ranch?

That he took some home and let his son handle pieces of it (as Bill Brazel did, too) powerfully argues that the material was neither extra-terrestrial nor classified. Marcel was an intelligence officer. He would not have been that indiscreet – then, or three decades afterward, if Stanton Friedman is right in his oft-repeated insistence that 'secrets can be kept'.

In the Roswell legend, Marcel said nothing about the alien bodies that had been allegedly scattered in any one of five or six shifting sites, but still supposedly passing through the Roswell air base. It is curious that he failed to mention them, while having no qualms about broadcasting his other allegedly secret knowledge.

Major Jesse A. Marcel could, in fact, keep secrets, and the biggest one he kept from the pro-UFO investigators was the truth about his own life. Marcel told ufologists that he had flown in bombers on combat missions during World War II as a waist gunner, a bombardier and a pilot. He had shot down five enemy aircraft, was awarded five Air Medals in consequence, and was shot down once himself. He said he had a bachelor's degree in physics from George Washington University, Washington, DC.

His certainty about the high strangeness of the Roswell debris was based on his being 'acquainted with virtually every type of weather-observation or radar tracking device being used by either the civilians or the military'. Shortly after playing his part in the affair at Roswell, he was promoted Lieutenant Colonel, and in August 1949 was so highly regarded in intelligence circles that he 'wrote the very report President Truman read on the air declaring that Russia had exploded an atomic device.'

In December 1995 Robert Todd published the results of an elementary piece of detective work that no other Roswell researcher had thought to undertake: he had examined Marcel's official service record. None of Marcel's claims stood up under scrutiny. His combat flying was limited to a passenger's job, as an observer for intelligence; and as such, for flying the required number of missions, he was awarded two Air Medals. He had no air crew training or experience. Five kills as a gunner would have made him an official 'ace'. He was nothing of the sort; even his rating with small arms was dismal. He had no degree of any kind. He had no knowledge of radar tracking or weather balloons.

As Todd points out, 'radar targets were a highly specialized piece of equipment unknown to most people except the relative handful... who used them'. (This would also explain Brazel's famous public denial that he had found a weather balloon.) Marcel's promotion to light colonel was in the reserve: it was never his active-service rank.

There is absolutely no evidence that he was shot down in combat (like many other fantasists he claimed to be the sole survivor of the incident), and none that he was even remotely involved in Truman's announcement of Soviet nuclear capability – which was not made on the radio.

'Clearly Marcel had a problem with the truth,' Todd remarked with masterful self-control. This catalogue of Marcel's lies and grossly misleading statements amounts to rather more than a common vice among veterans, which is to elevate one or two wartime incidents to heroic proportions. It is different in kind, because it is consistent and comprehensive in its distortions and untruths. It is a very long way from the tendency of many other combat veterans – to say little or nothing at all about their experiences, except among their peers.

The key man

To a large extent, from initial involvement and press release to his statements many years later, Marcel is the foundation stone of the Roswell incident. His reliability is crucial to the extra-terrestrialists' case. Yet he aggrandized most aspects of his life, not just his war record, to the point of losing touch with reality. If he acted true to that form and exaggerated about the Roswell wreckage, what substance is left to the notion that something extraordinary fell to Earth in New Mexico in 1947?

We now need to examine the testimony of some secondary witnesses of events at Roswell to see if they can compensate for the collapse of Marcel's credibility.

Brigadier General Roger M. Ramey, commander of Eighth Air Force, which included the units at Roswell AAF, with the remains of the 'flying disk' at his heaquarters at Fort Worth, Texas. Jesse Marcel said that he was pictured with the real wreckage from the Roswell UFO, then Ramey switched it for the innocuous debris of a weather balloon. Comparison of the pictures shows the material is the same in both.

The USAF's final words on the matter of Roswell. The investigation turned up only two official documents referring to the case, and its solution to the mystery was, by its own admission, something of a guess. Predictably, the Air Force report has only served to reinforce the idea of a cover-up for those who think an alien craft crashed near Roswell in 1947.

Mortician Glenn Dennis was 22 years old when 'Nurse X' told him about the alien bodies that had been brought into the Roswell Army Air Field hospital. Sometime around 8 July he had driven an airman, injured in a motorcycle accident, to the base. In a couple of old Army field ambulances outside the base hospital he caught sight of some strange wreckage with marks that reminded him of Egyptian hieroglyphics.

Stepping inside the hospital, he was confronted by a red-headed captain and black sergeant whom he'd never seen before. They warned him to say nothing about a crash or, threatened the captain: 'Somebody will be picking your bones out of the desert.' The sergeant responded: 'Sir, he would make better dog food.' At this point Dennis's friend Nurse X – whom he later named as Naomi Maria Selff – came on the scene and saw Dennis hustled out of the hospital.

Next day, Lieutenant Selff met Dennis for lunch. She described the dead aliens she had seen. Two were hideously mangled, and stank with 'the most horrible, most gruesome smell'. A third, less mutilated, lay nearby. Two doctors, not from Roswell, asked her to take notes as they examined the remains. The creatures were small, had dispropor- tionately large heads, 'very, very large' eyes 'set so far back you couldn't tell what they looked like'. There were four fingers on each hand and two canals in each ear. Their bones were 'flexible'.

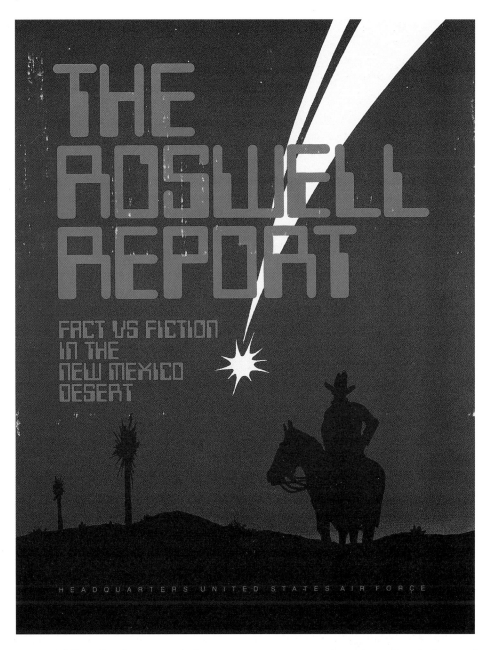

THE ROSWELL REPORT

FACT VS FICTION IN THE NEW MEXICO DESERT

HEADQUARTERS UNITED STATES AIR FORCE

Lt Selff made drawings and notes for Dennis, which he kept at the funeral home where he worked. Unfortunately, he left them behind when he left there in 1962, and they were thrown away. In the days after they met, Dennis tried to contact Lt Selff, but was told she had been transferred elsewhere. A few months later a letter he sent her was returned marked 'Deceased'. Dennis discussed none of this with anyone except his father.

Randle and Schmitt claimed that they had tried to track down both 'Nurse X' and the five nurses who appeared in the base's 1947 yearbook. Schmitt informed the journalist Paul McCarthy that:

Since 1989 he and Randle... had scoured the planet up, down, and sideways for those nurses... to no avail. The suggestion: The government had wilfully purged the nurses from the record, and, possibly, the earth, in its effort to hide the alien crash at Roswell. After all, the assumption went, dead women tell no tales.

McCarthy was given a name for Dennis's nurse by Randle, and then checked Randle's and Schmitt's research. He found that Randle had delegated the quest to Schmitt, who delegated it to two assistants; neither of whom had taken the elementary step of contacting the National Personnel Records Center in St Louis, Missouri. McCarthy did approach St

The 'alien hieroglyphs' that were seen on the Roswell debris – above, as recalled by Jesse Marcel's son and, below, as remembered by Project Mogul member Prof. Charles B. Moore. The latter is nearer to the patterns described by Mac Brazel, who found the wreckage.

Louis, and found 'in three days flat' what Randle and Schmitt had allegedly spent five years trying to unearth: the histories of the five nurses in the RAAF 1947 year book. Only one – Lt Col Rosemary J. Brown – was still alive, and she told McCarthy that she had 'no sense of anything weird happening at all' in the summer of 1947. Of Dennis's 'Nurse X' there was no sign in the records, and Col Brown remembered nothing of her, although she did remember the other four 'year book' nurses.

'Nurse X', Lt Naomi Selff or whatever other name Glenn Dennis gave

her very likely does not exist. That she does not appear in the base yearbook provides only 85-90 per cent of a good reason to say this: between 10 and 15 per cent of the Roswell personnel also did not. But Col Brown did not recall her. We have only Dennis's word that she ever existed, and there are other reasons to doubt his story besides the inconvenient, or unfortunate, absence of his friend from the records.

It is unlikely, for example, that in 1947 the military would have threatened him, or any of the other self-proclaimed civilian witnesses to events surrounding the alleged saucer

crash. It is much more probable that they would have appealed politely but firmly to the witnesses' patriotism in requesting silence. It stretches belief that over the years none of these peripheral 'witnesses' spoke to each other about what had happened, even

*In the same edition in which it announced the Air Force had 'emptied' the Roswell saucer, the local **Daily Record** published this interview with the man who found it. Key points in his testimony to support the legend that he came upon the remains of an alien spacecraft have since been denied.*

Harassed Rancher who Located 'Saucer' Sorry He Told About It

W. W. Brazel, 48, Lincoln county rancher living 30 miles south east of Corona, today told his story of finding what the army at first described as a flying disk, but the publicity which attended his find caused him to add that if he ever found anything else short of a bomb he sure wasn't going to say anything about it.

Brazel was brought here late yesterday by W. E. Whitmore, of radio station KGFL, had his picture taken and gave an interview to the Record and Jason Kellahin, sent here from the Albuquerque bureau of the Associated Press to cover the story. The picture he posed for was sent out over AP telephoto wire sending machine specially set up in the Record office by R. D. Adair, AP wire chief sent here from Albuquerque for the sole purpose of getting out his picture and that of sheriff George Wilcox, to whom Brazel originally gave the information of his find.

Brazel related that on June 14 he and an 8-year old son, Vernon were about 7 or 8 miles from the ranch house of the J. B. Foster ranch, which he operates, when they came upon a large area of bright wreckage made up on rubber strips, tinfoil, a rather tough paper and sticks.

At the time Brazel was in a hurry to get his round made and he did not pay much attention to it. But he did remark about what he had seen and on July 4 he, his wife, Vernon and a daughter Betty, age 14, went back to the spot and gathered up quite a bit of the debris.

The next day he first heard about the flying disks, and he wondered if what he had found might be the remnants of one of these.

Monday he came to town to sell some wool and while here he went to see sheriff George Wilcox and "whispered kinda confidential like" that he might have found a flying disk.

Wilcox got in touch with the Roswell Army Air Field and Maj. Jesse A. Marcel and a man in plain clothes accompanied him home, where they picked up the rest of the pieces of the "disk" and went to his home to try to reconstruct it.

According to Brazel they simply could not reconstruct it at all. They tried to make a kite out of it, but could not do that and could not find any way to put it back together so that it would fit.

Then Major Marcel brought it to Roswell and that was the last he heard of it until the story broke that he had found a flying disk.

Brazel said that he did not see it fall from the sky and did not see it before it was torn up, so he did not know the size or shape it might have been, but he thought it might have been about as large as a table top. The balloon which held it up, if that was how it worked, must have been about 12 feet long, he felt, measuring the distance by the size of the room in which he sat. The rubber was smoky gray in color and scattered over an area about 200 yards in diameter.

When the debris was gathered up the tinfoil, paper, tape, and sticks made a bundle about three feet long and 7 or 8 inches thick, while the rubber made a bundle about 18 or 20 inches long and about 8 inches thick. In all, he estimated, the entire lot would have weighed maybe five pounds.

There was no sign of any metal in the area which might have been used for an engine and no sign of any propellers of any kind, although at least one paper fin had been glued onto some of the tinfoil.

There were no words to be found anywhere on the instrument, although there were letters on some of the parts. Considerable scotch tape and some tape with flowers printed upon it had been used in the construction.

No strings or wire were to be found but there were some eyelets in the paper to indicate that some sort of attachment may have been used.

Brazel said that he had previously found two weather observation balloons on the ranch, but that what he found this time did not in any way resemble either of these.

"I am sure what I found was not any weather observation balloon," he said. "But if I find anything else, besides a bomb they are going to have a hard time getting me to say anything about it."

if they never revealed anything to anyone else. It is quite implausible that in 1947 a black soldier would have spoken to any white man, about another, in the language Dennis reports. It is incredible that Dennis would have left potentially priceless documentation of an alien visitation at his workplace, and for so long that it was taken 'to the town dump'.

Back to the future

How did the Roswell 'witnesses' come to produce testimony that is illogical and unbelievable and yet consistent in certain details?

Readers with long memories will recall Silas Newton and Leo GeBauer, the originators of the story of a saucer that crashlanded in Aztec, New Mexico in 1949. Hollywood columnist Frank Scully turned the tale into a bestseller, *Behind the Flying Saucers*, in 1950. In 1985, William L. Moore, one of the chief exhumers of the Roswell incident, presented a brilliantly researched and argued paper to the MUFON UFO Symposium in St Louis, Missouri. It gave chapter and verse on Newton and GeBauer and the scam they were running.

Newton had been a rabid saucer buff since seeing a UFO in Wyoming in 1947. He met GeBauer in June or July 1949. On 19 August, Newton saw news reports of two desert prospectors, identified only as 'Fitzgerald and Garney', who saw a saucer spin out of control and plow into a sand dune in Death Valley, California. Two 'diminutive bipeds' fled the craft.

This FBI internal memo has often been cited as 'proof' that UFOs crashed and dead aliens were found in the Southwestern USA in the late 1940s. In truth, the document reports one of hoaxer Silas Newton's public appearances as he spread his stories far and wide across the region.

The report inspired Newton to credit his phoney 'Doodlebug' (which supposedly detected oil and gold deposits) to alien technology retrieved from a crashed saucer. The eventual result was the Scully book, but not before the FBI and AFOSI had been alerted. For an understanding of the Roswell case, the most important passage in Moore's paper is this – and the emphasis is in the original text:

The key thing for crashed saucer researchers here is that Newton told his story, with variations to suit the particular ear he was bending, to large numbers of people all over the West. *And many of these people freely repeated it to others, either without naming the original source, or in painting Newton (and of course GeBauer) with labels of unquestionable respectability. The story, now third hand and embellished accordingly, went heaven knows where from that point.*

Moore cites a couple of examples of how the Newton-GeBauer yarn became a folk story about a UFO crash in New Mexico and spread all over the Southwest around 1950. It featured small dead humanoids with oversized heads; the wreckage was in the hands of the government; and there was even 'metallic cloth' involved, although it formed part of the aliens' clothing. The truly amazing thing is that Moore and his fellow researchers did not recognize these Newton-inspired elements in the Roswell stories that they assiduously collected and gladly believed three and four decades later.

By this time 'hieroglyphic writing' on saucer wreckage had also become embedded in the folklore. It was there in Scully's book (as was the lightweight and extra-strong material), and these were mentioned again by

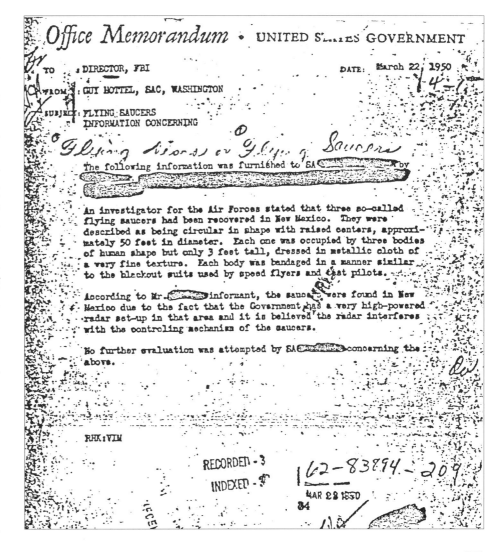

Robert Carr in 1974. The strange script cropped up too in a 1970s revival of a report of a 'Martian airship' that supposedly crashed in Aurora, Texas, in 1897, and in which 'hieroglyphs' were found.

Mysterious writing has consistently been associated with tales of crashed spaceships since 1878, and it is almost invariably described as 'like hieroglyphics'. In hypnotic regressions performed in the seminal Herb Schirmer contact/abduction case (see Chapter Three) the witness reported seeing 'symbols, like stuff you see in the movies about Egypt'. The wreckage that Mac Brazel found had 'letters on some of the parts… and some tape with flowers printed upon it had been used in the construction.' Legend and reality had almost coincided in the parched fields of New Mexico.

Memory games

There is, then, good reason to believe that in the minds of 'witnesses' quoted many years later, the legends and the reality did coincide over time – and that, no doubt with perfect sincerity, they recounted memories that conflated history, mental associations with more recent stories, and ancient rumors transmuted into 'fact'. Repeated retellings to the flock of interested researchers will, of course, have solidified and smoothed these memories. And some 'witnesses' were probably not sincere.

A marginal witness whose testimony has certainly been embroidered over time is Lydia Sleppy. Her story was first published in 1974. In that account the date is vague, and the other party was her own radio station manager (not a reporter in Roswell, which is not even mentioned). The famous teletype 'interrupt' appeared 'in the middle of her text, tapped in from somewhere, with the official order: "Do not continue this transmission!" ' The 'order' could have come

from the wire operator, but in later books about Roswell the FBI is credited with interjecting it, while the words of the 'interrupt' and some other details become more specific with each retelling.

Whether Sleppy herself is responsible for this slow burgeoning of her story is not clear. But on 14 September 1993, more than 46 years after the event, she signed an affidavit that quoted the 'interrupt' as saying: 'This is the FBI. You will immediately cease all communication.'

She did not remember the exact date when this occurred. When Friedman tried to interview John McBoyle, the station manager in question, about the incident in the late 1970s, he met with a 'wall of silence'. McBoyle told him: 'Forget about it. It never happened.' Friedman interpreted this as evidence of the cover-up that he believes is ubiquitous.

The FBI is the source of half of the guaranteed-genuine government records to have surfaced that mention the Roswell 'saucer'. The documents in question are the RAAF and 509th Bomb Group's Combined History, which contains two relevant sentences (the second reads: 'The object turned out to be a radar tracking balloon.'), and an FBI telex datelined Dallas, 8 July 1947 reporting telephone conversations with the Air Force.

This is a sum total of two pieces of paper. Advocates of the crashed-saucer and cover-up scenario appear to see the former as a deliberate lie and the latter as confirmation that a UFO crashed near Roswell.

How they reach the second conclusion challenges normal comprehension. The telex says (in part):

THE DISC IS HEXAGONAL IN SHAPE AND WAS SUSPENDED FROM A BALLOON BY CABLE, WHICH BALLOON WAS APPROXIMATELY TWENTY FEET [6M] IN DIAMETER. [CENSORED] FURTHER ADVISED THAT THE OBJECT FOUND RESEMBLES A HIGH ALTITUDE WEATHER BALLOON WITH A RADAR REFLEC-

TOR, BUT THAT TELEPHONIC CONVERSATION BETWEEN THEIR OFFICE AND WRIGHT FIELD HAD NOT BORNE OUT THIS BELIEF. DISC AND BALLOON BEING TRANSPORTED TO WRIGHT FIELD BY SPECIAL PLANE FOR EXAMINATION … NO FURTHER INVESTIGATION BEING CONDUCTED.

The cover-up proponents seize on the penultimate sentence quoted as 'proof' that the wreckage was something otherworldly. Its plain meaning is that Wright Field was unsure that the object was as innocent as it seemed, which was hardly remarkable in the context of the Cold War, and the fact that the 509th was then the only nuclear-armed combat unit in the world. Wright Field was not questioning the facts of the balloon or the cable or the hexagonal disk, but their purpose.

How many UFOs or flying saucers, hexagonal or otherwise, have ever been described as 'suspended from a balloon by cable'? Christopher D. Allan's comments on this document bear repetition:

To a rational person [the telex] *should suffice to both identify the object and to confirm the explanation given to the press. The USAF were at that time not obliged to inform the FBI and there is thus not the slightest reason to think either side was party to a cover-up. The teletype is unclassified; it refers to 'national interest', a very different concept from 'national security', which* [Friedman and Moore] *say was such an integral part of the Roswell affair. The final sentence shows how little interest the FBI showed in the Roswell disc.*

The cover-up, continued

On 14 January 1994, in response to continuous queries from his constituents, US Congressman Steven H. Schiff of New Mexico announced he was to ask the government's General Accounting Office (GAO) to search for any documents that would throw light on the Roswell incident. On 23 February the GAO told the USAF that it intended to review 'crash incidents involving weather balloons and unknown aircraft, such as UFOs and foreign aircraft, and... the facts involving the reported crash of an UFO in 1949 [*sic*] at Roswell, New Mexico' and an 'alleged DoD cover-up'. The GAO, as part of its brief to track government spending, has powers to burrow into the most highly classified files and projects. On 28 July 1995, Schiff released the GAO's report to him. The USAF had already issued a summary of the results of its research; in 1995 it published a vast tome, titled *The Roswell Report: Fact vs Fiction in the New Mexico Desert*, which contained all the documents it believed were germane to the case.

Having searched all the relevant records, GAO had found no evidence of a cover-up and no documents referring to the Roswell UFO apart from the two quoted above. It did note that the outgoing messages from the RAAF between October 1946 and December 1949 had been destroyed on no known authority. Ufologists seized on this as sure proof of a cover-up. However, the GAO made clear that many Air Force organizational records from about the same time had similarly been destroyed. So there was no great significance in the loss of the Roswell records. The believers might have said that the true records had – obviously – been buried in the vaults of some agency that the GAO did not approach, such as the super-secret National Reconnaissance Organization. But, as far as I know, none has yet

Cover of the official – and once classified – history of the nuclear-armed 509th Bomb Group at Roswell AAF. The document's only reference to the local UFO says simply that the Public Information Office was kept busy with enquiries on the subject, which turned out to be a radar-tracking balloon.

expressed so lateral a thought.

And in any case the records from RAAF were far from incomplete. In its report, the USAF made a more telling point than the GAO:

The history and morning reports [from RAAF]... showed that the subsequent activities during the month were... not indicative of any unusual high level activity, expenditure of manpower, resources or security.

Likewise, [USAF] researchers found no indication of heightened activity anywhere else in the military hierarchy in the July 1947 message traffic or order (to include classified traffic). There were no indications and warnings, notice of alerts, or a higher tempo of operational activity reported that

would logically be generated if an alien craft, whose intentions were unknown, entered US territory. To believe that such operational and high-level security could be conducted solely by relying on unsecured telecommunications or personal contact without creating any records of such activity certainly stretches the imagination of those who have served in the military who know that paperwork of some kind is necessary to accomplish even emergency, highly classified, or sensitive tasks.

The USAF also pointed out in its 1995 report that, in addition to an astounding talent for keeping secrets, those involved would also have needed powers of precognition:

COMBINED HISTORY
509TH BOMB GROUP
AND
ROSWELL ARMY AIR FIELD
1 JULY 1947 THROUGH 31 JULY 1947

Document 8-01

Four Theories and a Strange Coincidence

EXTRACT FROM A REVIEW BY PETER ROGERSON

Magonia 54, November 1995

There are I think a number of possible areas of explanation of Roswell. Here they are in decreasing order of likelihood and increasing order of interest:

● The object was just a balloon, either a weather balloon, Project Mogul or something even more experimental. What is being covered up is the egg on the faces of the military who were not able to tell a balloon from a saucer.

● The object was the top-secret, state-of-the-art device which was going to win the Cold War for the USA. Unfortunately it crashed on its first flight and any serious investigation would reveal that it was a hopeless non-starter and only went ahead because of a network of pork-barrel deals, corrupt government contracts, and back-handers.

● Maybe there really is a very dark and sinister Roswell secret such as a tethered balloon carrying a nuclear device set to explode at altitude. It broke free, depositing its lethal cargo near Roswell, the town avoiding incineration by a hairsbreadth. That is the kind of event some people would go to any lengths to hide, even by creating elaborate UFO contact stories as the investigators came sniffing around.

● Finally, assuming everyone is telling the truth at Roswell, we might have evidence not of an ET crash but of a charade to convince them that such a thing had occurred. A conspiracy not to suppress the ETH but to promote it.

There is a very curious piece of evidence which might be relevant. In the year following Roswell a British writer named Bernard Newman published a book called *Flying Saucer*, the plot of which concerned a group of scientists hoaxing a flying saucer crash as part of a plan to force world disarmament. Another book by Newman... was published in 1943 and gave detailed plans for the post-war reconstruction of Europe. It is clear from this book that Newman was someone close to those in power. In fact... it is virtually certain that he was an intelligence agent.

So we have a book written by a member of the intelligence community close to the political milieu, introducing the idea of a UFO crash being faked to further a political agenda – this within a year of Roswell. Was this the leak, ignored and unrecognized by ufologists, a warning from MI6 that they knew what their 'American friends' were up to and did not approve?

...if some event happened that was one of the 'watershed happenings' in human history, the US military certainly reacted in an unconcerned and cavalier manner. In an actual case, the military would have had to order thousands of soldiers and airman [sic], not only at Roswell but throughout the US, to act nonchalantly, pretend to conduct and report business as usual, and generate absolutely no paperwork of a suspicious nature, while simultaneously anticipating that twenty years or more in the future people would have available a comprehensive

Freedom of Information Act that would give them great leeway to review and explore government documents. The records indicate none of this happened (or if it did, it was controlled by a security system so efficient and tight that no one, US or otherwise, has been able to duplicate it since. If such a system had been in effect at the time, it would have also been used to protect our atomic secrets from the Soviets, which history has showed obviously was not the case). The records reviewed confirmed no such sophisticated and efficient security system existed.

Speaking of atomic secrets, it was a sudden dearth of academic papers being published by top Soviet scientists that alerted the West to the development of the Soviet nuclear bomb, as those researchers went 'underground' into the secret weapons program. No such symptom of a huge clandestine research effort was visible in the USA, as it surely would have been had the USA come into possession of an inscrutable alien craft and the corpses of its crew.

The USAF report makes it clear that so trivial was the actual Roswell incident that 47 years later the Air Force could make no more than an informed guess as to what 'instrument' did land (not crash) on Mac Brazel's property. Its best candidate was a balloon array belonging to the then top-secret Project Mogul.

The Mogul systems were intended to reach, and then stay in the atmospheric layer between the stratosphere and troposphere, which acts as a global 'whispering gallery'. Loud noises made on the ground, anywhere on earth, can be detected in this unique acoustic channel. Mogul balloons would listen for the sound of exploding Soviet nuclear devices.

If the Air Force lied about a 'weather balloon' in 1947, it was to 'cover up' the existence of Mogul – whose purposes, if not its balloons, were extremely sensitive. The USAF checked with survivors of the Mogul project and found that the reliable accounts of those who had actually handled the debris accorded with what was known about the material used in Mogul balloon arrays. The curious purplish flowers noted by Brazel, also known as 'alien hieroglyphics', turned out to be decorations by the toy manufacturer who had supplied the tape used to build the arrays.

Last thoughts

As the author of the USAF report anticipated, the crashed-UFO advocates took all this as evidence of yet more cover-up and conspiracy to

One of only two official documents ever found that refer to the Roswell UFO crash. It is not classified. Had the Air Force had a real UFO on their hands, it is unlikely – according to the believers' own slant on the affair – that they would have said a word to the FBI about it.

silence, and said so loudly. Kevin Randle published *Roswell UFO Crash Update* late in 1995 to voice his objections to the USAF's case and to parade more first-hand 'witnesses' to the 'real' events. This did not impress his fellow-believer Stanton Friedman who, while scoffing at the Air Force version of events, was now habitually referring to Randle as a 'fiction writer' (Randle has indeed published more than 70 novels, under a pseudonym).

And, maybe, just maybe, they are all wrong – from the USAF and civilian skeptics to the most fervent believers in crashed saucers, alien contact and a colossal government cover-up.

Reviewing Randle's latest book, British commentator Peter Rogerson offered yet another slant on the Roswell affair (see Document 8-01). The whole affair, he suggested tentatively, may have been part of an obscure battle of wits between British intelligence (MI6) and an American group of scientists intent on achieving world disarmament.

This seems to me a very long shot at an explanation, but it does serve to emphasize that no one can be entirely certain about what landed in New Mexico in the summer of 1947 – even if the smart money is mostly against an extra-terrestrial explanation.

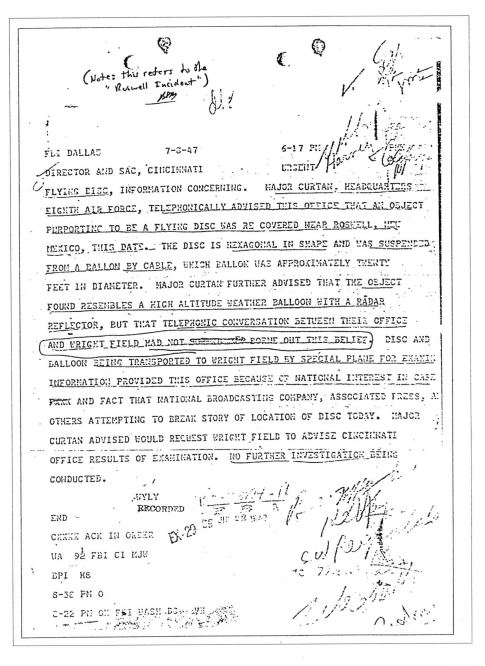

A LEGEND FOR OUR TIME

THE COVER-UP IN PERSPECTIVE

DO THE AVAILABLE official files betray any sign that a gigantic cover-up of the truth about UFOs is operating at the highest levels of government? Might some documents be hidden in the deepest recesses of the most clandestine agencies, within the most heavily guarded 'black' projects, that would confirm the suspicions of some highly vocal ufologists?

Here are two opposing views on the question. The first comes from nuclear physicist Stanton T. Friedman, who has had many years' experience of highly classified research programs:

No rational person can claim there is no government cover-up. To suggest... that because Nixon could not cover up the Political Watergate, the US could not cover up as vital a security matter as the intrusion of US air space by advanced alien space-craft, at least two of which crashed and were recovered in New Mexico, is absurd

This UFO allegedly appeared over San Jose de Valderas, a suburb of Madrid, Spain, on the evening of 1 June 1967. It came from the planet UMMO, according to a mass of papers circulated among ufologists at the time and that were produced for years afterward.

...Yes, Virginia, there is a Cosmic Watergate.[1]

The second comes from Major Dewey J. Fournet Jr, who in 1953 presented to the CIA-sponsored Robertson Panel the reasons for his considered opinion that UFOs were extra-terrestrial craft:

I have never seen any reliable evidence whatsoever that any US government agency ever participated in a 'cover-up' program. Quite frankly, I know of absolutely nothing that ever had to be covered up; it's only the myths and similar trash about the crashed saucer and little green men (circa late 1940s) that have, in my opinion, led to these accusations.[2]

It would be hard to find two people with a common interest so far apart in their assessment of the same phenomenon. Is one right, the other wrong? Or is the truth somewhere in between – and if it is, is it slap in the middle of these fundamentally opposed views, or nearer to one than to the other?

The government files released under FOIA show two things that surely no one on either side of this debate would contest.

First, the papers prove that the USAF, the CIA, the NSA, the FBI and other US security agencies were indeed intrigued by UFOs.

Second, they show that these agencies did not tell the truth when, in answer to queries from the public, they denied any interest in UFOs. The CIA said its involvement with UFOs ceased after the Robertson Panel reported in 1953. After 1969 the ritual response from the Air Force was that all UFO study had ended with the closure of Project Blue Book.

The FBI had a particularly devious way of lying to rubbernecking plebs – it told the truth. The standard FBI reply to requests for information it held on UFOs was: 'The investigation of unidentified flying objects is not within the jurisdiction of the Bureau.' That was beyond dispute. But there is plentiful evidence that the FBI has often done many things that were outside its jurisdiction, and it is also true that the Bureau disgorged some 1700 pages of UFO-related material in response to applications under the FOIA in the late 1970s.

Why were the military and intelligence worlds so interested in UFOs when they claimed there was no threat to national security, no evidence of extra-terrestrial origin, and so on?

Why did they pretend they were not interested? In other words – what were they trying to hide?

The secret culture

The answers to these questions may become a bit clearer if we address another one first: What did they do with the information they had?

The answer, judging from the reams of unevaluated sighting reports and the dearth of analysis in the released papers, seems to be: very little. No follow-up investigations were made, general theoretical discussions are few and far between, and none are very recent. On that evidence, there seems to have been no cover-up of cosmic secrets, or of any specifically UFO-related research project.

What was being hidden was the existence of the interest itself. Even this wasn't deemed to be so important that it remained hidden after access to official records in the USA was extended by the 1974 FOIA. So what was – or is – going on?

On the face of it, of all the security agencies' interest in UFOs, the FBI's seems to be the least explicable. The FBI is supposed to be concerned with domestic interstate crime and subversion, not with what may or may not

be visiting alien spacecraft. But the initial FBI concern was that malcontents might be creating UFO sightings or reports to stir up discontent – a hypothesis no more paranoid than the times in which it was conceived, even if it seems far-fetched now.

Inertia, habit, and curiosity could explain why the Bureau continued to seek out and receive UFO reports long after any hint of sedition had been rinsed out of the subject. But there was more to it than that.

The perennial problem faced by any intelligence agency is lack of reliable information. Any information about any activity is potential grist to the intelligence mill. The FBI notoriously wanted to know as much as possible about as many people as possible (and probably still does), and obsessively sought it out. The FBI files on George Adamski reveal that even those loyal citizens who complained when Adamski took the Bureau's name in vain were themselves routinely checked out, 'just in case'. J. Edgar Hoover may or may not have been a cross-dresser, but he was certainly possessed by a passion for power and

James Allen photographed this UFO from Pitlochry, Scotland, in October 1980. Scottish researchers described the picture as a hoax; others have suggested that it may show a balloon. It is just one of a number of UFOs that have 'appeared' in remote parts of the world. Lack of an explanation for such sightings does not automatically imbue them with credibility.

influence. For the FBI, power came through knowledge. Knowing what the Air Force or the CIA knew about UFOs, knowing how to manipulate that information might one day be handy in bureaucratic in-fighting or institutional blackmail.

Naturally, the FBI did not want the public to know about its UFO files. Apart from defusing their potential political usefulness, public awareness of the files would bring in its wake all the problems that the Air Force in the end wanted desperately to be rid of – kooks claiming to come from Saturn, accusations of cover-up, the endless questions of persistent ufologists, and the futile drain on precious manpower.

Of course, to begin with, the Air Force didn't see it that way at all. There was a real problem to be solved, one intensified by the imminent birth of the USAF as an independent armed service. There was internal as well as external pressure to show that the Air Force really could defend the nation's skies; prestige was at stake. But it may seem strange that after 1969, when it was official policy that UFOs did not represent a security threat, the USAF should continue to log UFO reports. The same goes for the CIA and other intelligence agencies, even if they hadn't 'got the UFO teeshirt' quite as comprehensively as the Air Force. Some ufologists read something distinctly sinister into this.

Here again, we have to remember that in intelligence, knowledge is power. UFO reports might, for instance, be useful in gauging whether a U-2, SR-71 or satellite overflight or re-entry had been reported as a 'flying saucer' – which would reveal something about the vehicles' visibility and still more about how hostile governments were dealing with the fact.

Short of having deep throats posted everywhere, the only way in which to unearth useful information in the secret world is to dredge up everything you can (even rather dull foreign press reports dealing with UFO sightings), and then sieve it for the few nuggets it might contain. And even deep throats are notoriously fickle: intelligence from general sources is always needed to cross-check and corroborate specific news from an individual agent.

An innocent enquirer after the FBI's knowledge of UFOs in 1973 receives the Bureau's standard brush-off, which is true to the letter of the law but not truthful about FBI practice. Note too the Bureau then checked the citizen's background for any sign of unorthodoxy.

The lack of analyses of UFOs, as such, in the previously classified files after 1969 would indicate that the information being sought from UFO reports was not ufological, but something less vaporous and altogether more serviceable. The useful data would in all likelihood not identifiably concern UFOs at all. It would probably be analyzed under a codeworded project that also had nothing to do with UFOs as such.

This brings us to the agitation that the famously censored NSA affidavit of 1980 still creates in some ufologists' breasts (see Chapter Four). What there is to see of this document gives few clues as to what lies beneath the broad expanses of the censor's ink. The blacked-out paragraphs may be about UFOs, or full of secrets about intelligence gathering. Few know, and none of them are ufologists crying 'Cover-up!'. Perhaps if one takes UFOs out of the equation for a moment it may be possible to see why an impartial viewer could fairly conclude that the NSA is simply telling the truth about the withheld documents.

Suppose the material was all about railroad locomotives. A railroad fanatic who collects minutiae of the iron way thinks the CIA holds world-wide information on a range of long-lost

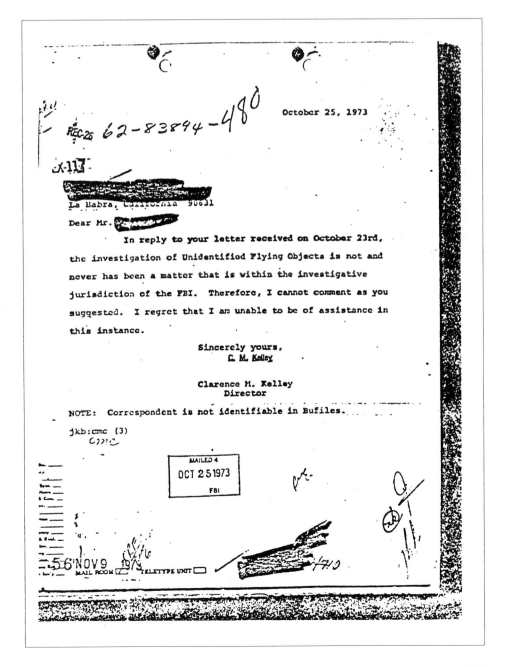

October 25, 1973

REC-26 62-83894-480

X-117

La Habra, California 90631

Dear Mr.

In reply to your letter received on October 23rd, the investigation of Unidentified Flying Objects is not and never has been a matter that is within the investigative jurisdiction of the FBI. Therefore, I cannot comment as you suggested. I regret that I am unable to be of assistance in this instance.

Sincerely yours,
C. M. Kelley

Clarence M. Kelley
Director

NOTE: Correspondent is not identifiable in Bufiles.

jkb:cmc (3)

MAILED 4
OCT 25 1973
FBI

56 NOV 9
MAIL ROOM   TELETYPE UNIT

and little-known steam engines. (As it undoubtedly does.) The CIA admits it has 57 documents mentioning steam trains but, backed by a federal judge and the Supreme Court, denies the fan access to the papers.

It looks weird – weirder than a UFO cover-up, indeed. What possible security interest could be compromised by releasing files on a few obsolete choo-choos? And the trainspotter insists he is a patriot. All he wants is the data on the trains. But even admitting it knows that a narrow-gauge 4-6-4 is rusting in a shed in the Pandemonian mountains could blow several CIA covers.

It reveals that the CIA can see inside train sheds in Pandemonia. From that snippet of information foreign counter-intelligence agents might be able, eventually, to deduce that the Pandemonian minister of transport, ostensibly a revolutionary zealot, is a CIA agent; or that a key railroad signals manager is; or that US spy satellites have X-ray vision; or that the CIA has hacked into the ministry of transport's encrypted UHF communications system – the only place where that particular antique train has received a mention in 30 years. Much investment by the CIA goes straight down the tubes – all without a mention of how the original, seemingly innocuous fact was acquired.

Translate this small fiction back into real-life ufological terms, which very likely encompass extremely sensitive military frames of reference, and the NSA's mysterious stubbornness in 1980 becomes altogether more comprehensible. And there's not an alien or a 'cover-up' in sight. Just common sense, for a spy.

The FBI papers contained no such sensitive material that was still 'live', and nor did the Air Force files. An intuition that the USAF really was not hiding anything vital may account for the inordinate interest ufologists took in the CIA, the NSA, DIA and other

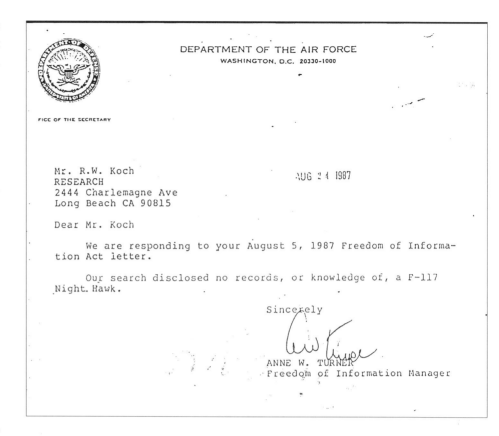

more secret agencies in the 1980s. So why did they all maintain that they had no UFO files until obliged to disclose them by the courts?

The answer, I suggest, lies in the overblown habit of secrecy, and a culture of arrogance, mentioned in the introduction to this book. And there was a practical problem: until FOIA made it a necessity, these agencies did not want to spare the manpower to sift through millions of pieces of paper just to satisfy a few inquisitve members of the public.

Seek and ye shall find

I doubt, however, that those for whom the NSA affidavit and many other documents represent 'proof' of a cover-up will be much impressed by these arguments. For years now, Stanton Friedman, for example, has responded to Philip Klass's denial that UFO secrets exist by 'challenging' Klass to 'prove' his case by producing the withheld NSA papers – uncensored, of course. Friedman sees Klass's unsurprising inability to do this as

The USAF denies all knowledge of the F-117A Nighthawk 'stealth' fighter. Today, the world knows the aircraft at a glance. The Air Force could make the denial truthfully by restricting information about the name to those with a 'need to know'. FOI managers knew only of a project called Senior Trend.

continuing proof of a ufological cover-up of vast proportions. I fail to see the reasoning here. Why would the NSA vouchsafe to Klass (and hence the rest of the world) what it will not divulge to a federal judge with top security clearance – whatever the documents say?

To believe that the NSA's demure refusal to expose its secret parts to public gaze is proof of a ufological conspiracy of silence requires believers first to credit a large number of other claims about UFOs and aliens, for which the evidence is frail at best. They also need to read their own meanings into government documents and UFO case histories. Two British ufologists are adept at presenting only evidence that suits their argument: Timothy Good and Jenny Randles.

Total suspicion

Good's monumental *Above Top Secret* was enormously influential in the late 1980s in reviving the notion of a cover-up and re-establishing it as an integral part of contemporary ufology. It is marred by treating every government document it discusses as written with an ulterior motive, and a startling reliance on the most fantastic assertions by persons whose credibility is not always obvious. An especially glaring example is the section solemn-ly devoted to one Mel Noel. He claimed to have filmed a score or so of UFOs in 1953 and 1954. He had been an Air Force pilot at the time and a member of a secret unit whose mission was to film UFOs from specially equipped F-86 Sabre jets. The Sabres carried no less than six cameras each, one in place of each of the .50-caliber M3 guns normally fitted.

'Suffice to say there is no doubt in my mind that Mel was describing genuine encounters with UFOs, and his knowledge of aircraft and flying is beyond dispute,' wrote Good.[3] A less impressionable ufologist might have done a little more research, and discovered that Mel Noel had been exposed as a hoaxer long before, in 1971, and had already admitted that he had never been either in the USAF, or a pilot.[4] There are many other instances of Good's gullibility, including taking Frank Scully's Aztec, New Mexico, 'crashed saucer' fiction as fact and tangling it up in an elaborate charade involving members of MJ-12.

Randles is a good deal less susceptible to fanciful tales than Good, but has developed a tendency to insist her readers 'make up their own minds' about matters like crashed saucers, while omitting to tell them all the facts and findings about individual cases. In her book *UFO Retrievals*, for example, Randles refuses to reject the 1952 crash of a flying saucer at Spitzbergen, Norway, as a myth, although it was long ago shown to be the invention of a German magazine about a Soviet secret weapon, not an off-world UFO.[5]

She describes local radar picking up 'a UFO emitting unknown radio frequencies' and says the downed UFO itself contained 'a radioactive unit… emitting energy at the frequency of 934 Hertz' which 'had probably been the cause of the radio and radar malfunctions'.[6] These are implicitly offered as what she quaintly calls 'unauthenticated facts'.

Randles had a scientific education; she must know that what is not scientific nonsense here is impossible. But she does not say so. Her equivocations (the book is full of them), and the credulousness of Timothy Good, together suggest minds looking for evidence that fits a pre-existing wish to believe, not arriving at an hypothesis from the available evidence.

All advocates of a UFO cover-up who delve into the government files sooner or later cite the 'top Canadian scientist' Wilbert B. Smith, who maintained in a 1950 TOP SECRET memorandum that UFOs were 'the most highly classified subject in the United States Government, rating

DEPARTMENT OF THE AIR FORCE
WASHINGTON DC 20330-1000

OFFICE OF THE ASSISTANT SECRETARY

MEMORANDUM FOR DISTRIBUTION   1 7 APR 1990

SUBJECT: Declassification of Association between F-117A and
          the SENIOR TREND Nickname

     This memorandum constitutes a "letter change" to the SENIOR
TREND Security Guide, 1 October 1989. Effective immediately, the
association of the nickname "SENIOR TREND" and the F-117A
aircraft is declassified. Each holder of the SENIOR TREND
Security Guide should post this memorandum to their copy of the
Guide. Documents classified solely because of the former
classification of this association are now unclassified; and may
be handled and stored accordingly. Each document should be
reviewed to assure that there is no classified information other
than the association.

     Documents declassified under the provisions of this change
should have their classification marked through, show the
initials of the individual reviewing the document; and reference
this memorandum as authority for the declassification. On bulky
documents, it will only be necessary to re-mark the cover and
title page, first two pages, and the back of the document. Post
a copy of this memorandum inside the cover of the document.

     The Air Force will continue a review of the classification
of SENIOR TREND information, and will notify program participants
of changes. I enjoin each organization and participant to
remember that much information remains classified and to redouble
efforts to protect this vital program.

                         JOHN B. HENNESSEY, Colonel, USAF
                         Special Projects Security Director
                         Assistant Secretary
                         of the Air Force (Acquisition)

                         JESSE T. MCMAHAN, Colonel, USAF
                         Deputy Director of Special Programs
                         Assistant Secretary
                         of the Air Force (Acquisition)

Dr Bruce Maccabee shows what can be done with a Polaroid camera. Maccabee, an optical physicist who works for the US Navy, has supported the extra-terrestrial hypothesis for decades, yet was accused of being involved in 'disinformation' because of a casual connection with the CIA.

higher even than the H-bomb.' What they do not tend to repeat for the benefit of their readers are the following facts, discovered by Christopher D. Allan in 1989 from Dr O.M. Solandt, head of the Canadian Defense Research Board (DRB) in the 1950s. Solandt knew Smith well and is mentioned in his famous memo.

In the opinion of those who worked with him at the Department of Transport in Ottowa, Smith was not a good scientist. The attempts he made to prove that UFOs had a magnetic propulsion system were later repeated by Frank Davies, the DRB's head of telecommunications research, and shown to be based on 'sloppy measurements with uncalibrated equipment. There was nothing in the theory.' Perhaps most significantly, Dr Solandt revealed that Smith's papers were never classified. He had no authority to classify documents; he

'just put TOP SECRET on his personal papers'.[7] Smith was eventually reduced to receiving communications from extra-terrestrials through telepathic channeling. Timothy Good describes him as 'one of the most intelligent and original minds in the field of UFO research'.

One other document that is unfailingly cited by believers in the ETH is Lt General Nathan Twining's letter of 23 September 1947 to Brigadier General Schulgen (see Chapter One). In this, Twining reported that his command believed UFOs were 'something real and not visionary or fictitious'. Skeptics like to quote this letter too, for it also remarks on the 'lack of physical evidence in the shape of crash recovered exhibits which would undeniably prove the existence of these objects'.

The letter at no point suggests that 'the objects' are extra-terrestrial, and the conclusion that UFOs were exactly as people described them is unsurprising given the state of UFO investigation at the time. Attempts have been made to get around Twining's categorical statement that no crash debris existed, to bolster the case for a crash-retrieval near Roswell, or the authenticity of the MJ-12 papers, or both. Kevin Randle believes

that Twining knew about the Roswell crash, wanted it kept secret, but wanted to gather more information about UFOs from observational data.[8] This would have been extraordinarily wasteful: rather like bird-watching when a perfectly good specimen lay waiting in the laboratory for dissection.

Stanton Friedman points out that the letter was 'only' classified SECRET, and infers that in more highly classified documents – still allegedly under wraps – Twining would not have had to maintain this fiction. If that were so, there would be no point in perpetrating it in the first place: the most economic way with the truth would have been to say nothing one way or the other.

The prudent option

On reflection, the last thing any government would sensibly do on finding a crashed saucer would be to keep it secret. The most prudent course would be to announce it speedily, and go for a massive damage limitation exercise. For what guarantee could there be that the next aliens to arrive would not land on the White House lawn, in full dress order, and demand their compatriots back for a decent funeral? Worse yet, they might land in Red Square. Once this point is grasped, it is easy to see how the supposed secrecy about Roswell had to be internationalized in principle by the conspiracy buffs. And this led inexorably to the Darkside Hypothesis – that the US and Russian governments are in league together, and with the aliens, against the rest of humanity.

Among many ufologists, the wish to believe in extra-terrestrial contact and secret official knowledge of it can, I think, quite fairly be said to displace the historian's or detective's or investigative journalist's usual wish to discover and consider all the available evidence before drawing a conclusion.

In ufology the evidence is often filtered to answer a wish to believe, not evaluated as a whole in the hope of uncovering its intrinsic, if not always unambiguous, meaning.

Realms of enchantment

By 1996 Stanton T. Friedman's belief that there was a government cover-up of 'cosmic Watergate' proportions had become pretty much the norm in American ufology, and a common assumption elsewhere. The Roswell case was generally regarded as fair 'proof' of this conspiratorial pudding. Budd Hopkins, through the Linda Cortile case, had brought the other major branch of modern ufology, alien abductions, into line with the belief in cover-up and official, super-secret awareness of the 'truth'. This doesn't mean that most of the well-known, published names in UFO research around the world endorsed Friedman's slogan or Hopkins's beliefs about alien-human breeding programs.

But it's apparent, from what many respected commentators take seriously, from readers' letters in British and American mainstream UFO journals, and from exchanges on the Internet, that almost any discussion of UFOs is now shot through by the concept of 'the cover-up' and speculation about the aliens' malign intentions.

It's contrary to common sense to say that everyone who suspects an institutional cover-up on UFOs is paranoid. Yet it is difficult to avoid the feeling that ufology displays a paranoid cast of mind. In an individual, this can exist quite comfortably alongside a generally sunny and confident mien. Consider, as an illustration of ufology's paranoid tendencies, the way the term 'disinformation' has come to be so useful, and so abused, in this field.

Suppose there is, locked away in vaults, a body of knowledge about UFOs and aliens, and that government is determined that no mere citizen shall have sight of it. Suppose too that the citizenry is constantly clamoring for access to those secrets and believes it has accurate clues as to what they might be. Government then has a choice of strategies. Among other things, it can deny the data exist, deny that the nation's arms and agencies are even interested in the matter.

Or it can lay a trail of half-truths, hoaxes, lies, and rumors, heavily laced with self-contradictions and inconsistencies. The disinformed will then spend more time and energy chasing their tails and arguing among themselves than they do burrowing into places where they are not wanted.

As with blanket denials, such ruses eventually wear thin and become partly transparent to the victims. But once the concept of disinformation got loose in UFO research, everyone became potentially suspect. As a result, elements of farce have occasionally disrupted ufologists' sober discourses.

For example, the Fund for UFO Research suffered a brief paroxysm in summer 1993 when it transpired that one of its luminaries, Dr Bruce Maccabee, had 'briefed' the CIA on ufology since 1979. He had actually given a few innocuous, informal lunch-hour lectures to CIA workers. Nevertheless, dark insinuations that 'disinformation' had occurred still flapped around briefly like startled chickens. But it never quite became clear who was supposed to have disinformed whom, or about what.

The supreme exponent of deploying the term 'disinformation' to mean everything and nothing was the arch conspiracy theorist William Cooper, who in the early 1990s greeted all requests to substantiate his many bogus claims (see Chapter Six) by proclaiming that his questioners were in the pay of the CIA. Several ufologists who had long been inflexible adversaries were thus amazed to find themselves supposedly arm-in-arm in the same preposterous bed.

Despite such revealing episodes, as the idea of the 'cover-up' has ripened into a barely questioned assumption in mainstream ufology, so the word 'disinformation' has become an indispensable item of ufological furniture. The trouble is that any evidence, speculation, debunking exercise or tall story, and any objection to the same, can be dismissed or embraced as 'disinformation', according to the prejudices or passions of the commentator. Such a pattern of charge and counter-charge is indeed characteristic of paranoia. Espousing the notion of disinformation is indeed to enter a hall of mirrors, every one of them potentially distorting.

A black and white issue

Modern ufology sees the world and the cosmos in harsh, unshaded tones of black and white: as if they were split, like ufology itself, between skeptic and believer, forces of light and powers of darkness, benign ufonauts and predatory, diabolic aliens, truth-tellers and disinformers. Any space that is left over for moderates is both cramped and sparsely populated.

The scheme of beliefs and legends that make up ufology has prompted many commentators to call the 'flying saucer story' a modern myth. This is not the place to explore in any depth its wellsprings or its nature, but official documents have been conscripted into that mythology, and like many mythic subjects they are remarkably ambiguous. Like a mirror, their interpretation reflects nothing so much as the interpreter, and tells us more about ufologists and their mythology than it does about UFOs.

The secrets that are revealed by the government files are not those of extra-terrestrials, their craft, their technology or their inscrutable purposes, but those of the human soul and its predicament. But that, Virginia, is another story.

REFERENCES

Introduction:
A Cosmic Watergate?

[1] Edward U. Condon, 'UFOs: 1947–1968' in Daniel S. Gillmor (ed.) *Scientific Study of Unidentified Flying Objects*, Bantam 1969 (pp520–522). This is the text popularly known as 'The Condon Report'.

[2] John Marks, *The Search for the "Manchurian Candidate"*, W.W. Norton 1991 (passim).

Chapter One:
Need to Know

[1] Quoted in Timothy Good, *Above Top Secret*, Grafton 1989 (p16).

[2] See Michael Wertheimer, 'Perceptual Problems' in Gillmor, *op. cit.* ('The Condon Report') (pp559–567).

[3] Paul T. Collins, 'The UFOs of 1942', *Exploring the Unknown* No 48. Cited by Good, *op. cit.* (pp16–17), and Jerome Clark, *The UFO Encyclopedia Vol 2 – The Emergence of a Phenomenon*, Omnigraphics 1992 (p379).

[4] Clark, *op. cit.* (p153).

[5] F.C. Durant, *Report on Meetings of Scientific Advisory Panel on Unidentified Flying Objects*, CIA 1953. Also cited by Clark, *op. cit.* (p156).

[6] Donald H. Menzel, *Flying Saucers*, Harvard University Press 1953 (pp97–100); Donald H. Menzel and Ernest H. Taves, *The UFO Enigma*, Doubleday 1977 (pp54–58).

[7] Edward J. Ruppelt, *The Report on Unidentified Flying Objects*, Ace 1956 (pp21–22).

[8] Project Sign investigators' report in CUFOS case files.

[9] Curtis Peebles, *Watch the Skies!*, Berkley 1995 (p14).

[10] Ruppelt, *op. cit.* (pp46–56); David R. Saunders and R. Roger Harkins, *UFOs? Yes!*, Signet 1968 (pp64–65).

[11] Clark, *op. cit.* (p82–84); Ruppelt, *op. cit.* (pp57–58).

[12] Peebles, *op. cit.* (pp35–40).

[13] William L. Moore, 'Crashed Saucers: Evidence in Search of Proof', *MUFON Symposium Proceedings 1985*, MUFON 1985 (pp131–153).

[14] Peebles, *op. cit.* (p55).

Copies of the official government documents quoted throughout this book are available under Freedom of Information Act requests to the relevant US Government agencies and departments. Selections are also available from the Fund for UFO Research, PO Box 277, Mt Rainier, Maryland 20712, USA, and from Quest International, 66 Boroughgate, Otley, near Leeds, LS21 1AE, United Kingdom. The J. Allen Hynek Center for UFO Studies (CUFOS), 2457 W. Peterson Avenue, Chicago, Illinois 60659, USA, has a smaller selection available, particularly of foreign sighting reports in the government archives, and the complete texts of both the Durant Report (minutes) of the Robertson Panel meeting in 1953 and *Project Blue Book Special Report #14*.

Chapter Two:
Men in Blue and Gray

[1] Keyhoe's three key books expounding his belief in interplanetary saucers, the imaginary politics of ATIC and the cover-up are: *The Flying Saucers Are Real*, Fawcett 1950; *Flying Saucers from Outer Space*, Henry Holt 1953; and *The Flying Saucer Conspiracy*, Henry Holt 1955. Typical of Keyhoe's perverse way with facts is the opening of *Flying Saucers from Outer Space*, in which he

claims that the de Havilland Comet airliner crash at Calcutta on 2 May 1953 was caused by a UFO. The initial investigation actually surmised that a bird had struck the aircraft, and by the time Keyhoe penned his chapter it was known in aviation circles that metal stress around the rectangular windows of the Comet had caused the pressurized fuselage to explode. There was no UFO report in conjunction with the disaster.

[2] Peebles, *op. cit.* (pp68–71); Ruppelt, *op. cit.* (p176).

[3] Just Cause, 'The 1952 Saucer Wave: A Story Behind the Story', *Magonia* 48, Jan. 1994; reprinted from Just Cause 36 (1993).

[4] Keyhoe, *op. cit.* Chapters I, III and V.

[5] Peebles, *op. cit.* (pp151–152).

[6] Information on the Socorro case has been compiled from the CUFOS case file, which includes the Blue Book investigators' reports and contemporary newspaper reports; Charles Bowen, 'Strange Encounters of Many Kinds' in Peter Brookesmith (ed.) *The Age of the UFO*, Orbis 1984 (pp181–182); J. Allen Hynek, *The Hynek UFO Report*, Sphere 1978 (pp223–229); Philip J. Klass, *UFOs Explained*, Random House 1974, Chapter 12.

Chapter Three:
Men in White

[1] J. Allen Hynek, *The UFO Experience*, [Henry Regnery 1972] Corgi 1974 (pp221–222).

[2] Hynek, *ibidem* (pp245–246).

[3] The complete text of the O'Brien committee's report is in Gillmor, *op. cit.*, ('The Condon Report') (pp542–544).

[4] Time-Life Books, *The UFO Phenomenon*, 1987 (pp106–109).

[5] Peebles, *op. cit.* (p207). Those wishing to judge this opinion for themselves may compare the contributions by McDonald and Donald Menzel to Carl Sagan and Thornton Page (eds), *UFOs – A Scientific Debate*, [Cornell University Press 1972] W.W. Norton 1974 (pp52–182).

[6] Peebles, *op. cit.* (pp209–212); Saunders and Harkins, *op. cit.* Chapters 12 and 18–20.

[7] The complete text of the submissions to the 'Roush Symposium' is available from NTIS, Springfield, Virginia 22161, USA.

[8] Hynek, *UFO Report* (pp274–2278). It is also worth noting that William Hartman in 'The Condon Report' (Section VI, Chapter 2) and Allen Hendry (*The UFO Handbook*, Doubleday 1979) both found that, paradoxically, the more detailed a UFO report the less likely it is to be consistent with the actual events observed.

[9] M. Polanyi, *Knowing and Being*, Routledge & Kegan Paul 1969 (pp49–72).

[10] Menzel and Taves, *op. cit.* (p89).

Dr Leo Sprinkle's report to the Condon team (Case #14) and his further comments on Herb Schirmer's first hypnotic regression are to be found in Coral and Jim Lorenzen, *Encounters with UFO Occupants*, Berkley Medallion Books 1976 (pp268–288). Dr Sprinkle also elaborated on this episode when in conversation with the author. A full account of the second Herb Schirmer hypnotic regression is given in Eric Norman [pseudonym for Warren Smith], *Gods, Demons and UFOs*, Lancer Books 1970 (pp169–193). There is also a useful summary in Ralph Blum, *Beyond Earth: Man's Contact with UFOs*, Corgi 1974 (pp109–123). Most other accounts wrongly conflate the Sprinkle and Williams hypnotic sessions.

Chapter Four:
Mutilating the Evidence

[1] Thomas Powers, introduction to Marks, *op. cit.* (p.xvi). Marks's book makes clear that the CIA's concern over UFOs' potential use as a weapon of psychological warfare in the 1950s was a natural consequence of the Agency's comprehensive obsession to learn how to manipulate and control human mental processes, whether of individuals or entire societies.

[2] Philip J. Klass, *UFO Abductions: A Dangerous Game*, Prometheus 1989 (pp18–20). Useful basic details of the Pascagoula pair's claims are in Ralph Blum, *op. cit.* Chapters 2 and 3. A good summary of both sides of the case is in Margaret Sachs, *The UFO Encyclopedia*, Corgi 1981 (pp241–242).

[3] Philip J. Klass, *UFOs: The Public Deceived*, Prometheus 1983, Chapters 16 and 17.

[4] Jerome Clark, 'Animal Mutilations and UFOs', *UFO Encyclopedia* Vol. 3: *High Strangeness*, Omnigraphics 1996 (pre-publication manuscript kindly supplied by author); Timothy Good, *Alien Liaison*, Arrow 1991, Chapters 2 and 3; Linda Moulton Howe: *An Alien Harvest*, LMH Productions 1989; 'Moving Lights, Disks and Animal Mutilations', lecture at Hallam University, Sheffield, August 1993; Peebles, *op. cit.* Chapter 14.

[5] Howe, *op. cit.* (p22).

[6] Daniel Kagan and Ian Summers, *Mute Evidence*, Bantam 1984.

[7] Lawrence Fawcett and Barry Greenwood, *Clear Intent*, Prentice-Hall 1984 (pp187–190). Republished with identical pagination as *The UFO Cover-Up*, Fireside 1992.

[8] Jenny Randles, *The UFO Conspiracy*, Javelin 1988 (p203); Good, *Above Top Secret* (pp430–431).

[9] Philip J. Klass, 'The "Top Secret" Papers NSA Won't Release', *Skeptical Inquirer*, Fall 1989 (pp65–68).

[10] Philip J. Klass, *UFOs: The Public Deceived*, Chapter 12. The story retailed by Linda Moulton Howe, op. cit. (pp23–24), and in Fawcett and Green, op. cit. (pp28–29), that at Malmstrom AFB a Minuteman missile's computerized target information was changed by a UFO is third-order hearsay and has only one source – Ms Howe's brother.

[11] Jan Harold Brunvand, *The Choking Doberman*, Penguin 1987 (pp197–198); Nigel Watson, 'Down to Earth', *Magonia* 43, (1992).

[12] George C. Andrews, *Extra-Terrestrials Among Us*, Llewellyn 1986 (pp188–191); Leonard Stringfield, 'The Chase for Proof in a Squirrel's Cage' in Hilary Evans and John Spencer (eds), *UFOs 1947–87*, Fortean Times 1987 (pp150–151).

[13] Peter Brookesmith, 'The Grudge 13 Affair', Parts 1&2, *Fortean Times* 75 and 76 (July and September 1994). Additional information from Don Ecker (private communications). English has also posted some of his claims on the Internet, notably in an 'Update' in 1988. Attentive readers will observe that he first claimed to see *Grudge #13* in 1977; to me he insisted the year was 1976.

Chapter Five:
Fear, Fraud & Loathing

[1] William H. Spaulding: 'UFOs: the Case for a Cover-up'; 'Agents of Confusion'; Peter Brookesmith, 'UFOs: a Federal Case'; all in

Brookesmith (ed.), *op. cit.* (pp32–43).

[2] Christopher D. Allan, personal communications; Howard Blum, *Out There*, Pocket Books 1991 (p275); Jerome Clark, *The UFO Encyclopedia* Vol 1: *UFOs in the 1980s*, Apogee 1990 (pp158–162); Stanton T. Friedman, *The Final Report on Operation Majestic 12*, Fund for UFO Research 1990; *Crashed Saucers, Majestic-12 and Debunkers*, UFORI 1992; *Operation Majestic 12? Yes!!*, UFORI 1994 (includes the quotations from Geisler in *UFO Magazine* (UK, n.d.); Stanton T. Friedman and Don Berliner, *Crash at Corona*, Marlowe 1992, Chapter 6; Good, *Above Top Secret* (pp403–4); *Alien Liaison* (pp112–121); Robert Hastings, *The MJ-12 Affair: Facts, Questions, Comments*, the author 1989; Howe, *An Alien Harvest* (pp143–155); Philip J. Klass: 'The MJ-12 Crashed-Saucer Documents' Parts 1&2, *Skeptical Inquirer* Winter 1987–8 and Spring 1988; 'MJ-12 Papers "Authenticated"?', *Skeptical Inquirer* Spring 1989; 'New Evidence of MJ-12 Hoax', *Skeptical Inquirer* Winter 1990, and personal communications; Joe Nickell and John F. Fischer, 'The Crashed-Saucer Forgeries' in George M. Eberhart (ed.), *The Roswell Report*, CUFOS 1991 (pp119–129); Peebles, *op. cit.*, pp317–326; Kevin D. Randle, *A History of UFO Crashes*, Avon 1995 (pp121–146); William H. Spaulding, 'Anonymity Guaranteed' in Brookesmith (ed.), *op. cit.* (p39).

[3] Jenny Randles, *UFO Retrievals*, Blandford 1995 (pp155–161); Tom Theophanous, Errol Bruce-Knapp and Graham Lightfoot, 'Guardian Case Gets Sacked by Canadian Researchers', *UFO Magazine* (USA), Vol.10 No2 (1995) (pp35–38); Bruce Maccabee, 'Canadian Hoax Accusations Mask Full "Guardian" Tale', and Tom Theophanous, '"Carp Case" Defender Skirts Main Issues', *UFO Magazine* (USA), Vol10 No4 (1995) (pp36–37); MUFON Ontario, 'The Carp Case', *The Canadian Ufologist*, March 1996; Errol Bruce-Knapp and Tom Theophanous, personal communications.

[4] Kevin D. Randles, in *A History of UFO Crashes* (pp157–169), gets into an even more convoluted argument to justify Moon Dust and Blue Fly as UFO-retrieval units. It is clear that a space-debris-retrieval unit would be the obvious choice to pick up apparently ET wreckage. But nothing in the released government files suggests that any such unit has ever been deployed on any such mission.

[5] Budd Hopkins: lecture at Hallam University, Sheffield, UK, August 1993; 'An Independently-Witnessed Abduction', in A. Pritchard, D.E. Pritchard, J.E. Mack, C. Kasey, C.Yapp (eds), *Alien Discussions*, North Cambridge Press, 1994 (pp254–261); Joseph J. Stefula, Richard D. Butler and George P. Hansen, *A Critique of Budd Hopkins' Case of the Abduction of Linda Napolitano*, the authors, 1993; Joe Stefula, personal communication.

Michael D. Swords' interpretation of the Bender case is in *International UFO Reporter* Nov./Dec. 1992; also summarized by Jerome Clark, Fate April 1993.

Chapter Six:
Beyond Dreamland

[1] William L. Moore, 'UFOs and the US Government', *MUFON Symposium Proceedings*, MUFON 1989. A complete transcript of Dr Sprinkle's hypnotic regression of Myrna Hansen is in Howe, *op. cit.* (pp341–373).

[2] The various documents by Bennewitz, Lear and Cooper, and the interviews with Bob Lazar cited in this chapter may all be found downloaded from the Internet on the CD-ROM *2000 Greater & Lesser Mysteries*, PDSL, 1994. See also Howe, *op. cit.*, and William M. Cooper, *Behold a Pale Horse*, Light Technology 1991.

[3] Sir John Hackett, *The Third World War*, Sidgwick & Jackson, 1978, and *The Untold Story*, Sidgwick & Jackson, 1982; the *Journal* of the Royal United Services Institute, London, UK, over this period and beyond contains many comments on the limitations of the Warsaw Pact's rigid chain of command and discouragement of junior ranks' initiative. It was standard doctrine among NATO forces that to destroy a Warsaw Pact unit HQ or command vehicle would render the unit ineffective.

[4] Moore, *op. cit.*

[5] Leo Sprinkle, personal communication to the author.

[6] The Jason Group is a US scientific consultancy established in the late 1950s, specializing in defense problems; see Vicki Cooper Ecker, 'DOD's Secretive, Scientific Elite', *UFO Magazine* (USA) Vol7 No6 (1992) (pp7–8). The Trilateral Commission is an international forum and pressure group of bankers, politicians and industrialists from the UK, USA, Europe and Japan; see Holly Sklar, *Trilateralism*, Southend 1980. The Bilder-burgers, another arm of the secret government according to Cooper, were founded in 1954 as a US–European discussion group on economic issues; see Robin Evinger, *Bilderburger*, Pentacle 1960. The Trilateralists and the Bilderburgers were demonized by the far left in the 1980s, and by the far right in the 1990s.

[7] Lt Col James Gritz, letter in *UFO Magazine* (USA), Vol6 No1 (1991) (pp3, 46).

[8] William F. Hamilton III, *Cosmic Top Secret*, Inner Light 1991 (pp106–113).

[9] 'Nightmare Hall', *Revelations of Awareness* No 363 – transcript of a CAC General Reading on 12 May 1990. CD-ROM 2000 Greater & Lesser Mysteries, PDSL, 1994.

[10] Hyam Maccabee, *Judas Iscariot and the Myth of Jewish Evil*, Free Press 1992 (passim and pp136–137).

[11] Jerome Clark, 'Friends and Enemies in High Places', paper given at the *Fortean Times* UnConvention, London, UK, 22 April 1995; Jacques Vallée, *Dimensions*, [Contemporary 1988, USA] Sphere 1990 (pp247–253).

[12] Clark, *ibidem*.

[13] Leon Davidson: 'Why I Believe Adamski', *Flying Saucer Review* Vol6 No1 (1960); *Flying Saucers: An Analysis of the Air Force Project Blue Book Special Report No. 14*, Blue Book 1976.

[14] Peter Brookesmith, 'The People of Atlantis' in Jennifer Westwood (ed.), *Mysteries of the Ancients*, *Reader's Digest* 1994 (p27).

Chapter Seven:
A Worldwide Web

[1] Philip J. Klass, 'Boylan's Views on UFOs and their Possible Relationship to Jesus', *Skeptics' UFO Newsletter* #38, March 1996 (p7).

[2] Vincente-Juan Ballester-Olmos, 'Spanish Air Force UFO Files: The Secret's End', *MUFON 1993 International Symposium Proceedings*, MUFON 1993 (pp126–168).

[3] Bill Chalker, 'The UFO Connection: Startling Implications for Australia's North West Cape, and for Australia's Security', *Flying Saucer Review* Vol31 No5 (1986) (pp13–21), and personal communication.

[4] Donald H. Menzel, letter to Richard Hall at NICAP, 27 November 1959 (CUFOS case file). Those who denigrate Menzel for his skepticism or characterize his work as 'pathological science' might do well to read this correspondence. Menzel's tone throughout is friendly, patient and courteous, and the scientific principles he enunciates are philosophically impeccable.

[5] D.H. Menzel and Lyle C. Boyd, *The World of Flying Saucers*, Doubleday 1963 (pp206–216); D.H. Menzel and Ernest H. Taves, *The UFO Enigma*, Doubleday 1977 (pp193–194). Other sources consulted include: 'IGY Team Snaps UFO', *APRO Bulletin* March 1958; Olavo T. Fontes, 'The UAO Sightings at the Island of Trindade' Parts I, II and III, *APRO Bulletin* January, March and May 1960; 'Exclusive IGY Photo Analysis', *APRO Bulletin* May 1960; 'New Evidence on IGY Photos', *APRO Bulletin* January 1965; APRO, 'Trindade Island Photos', in Ronald D. Story (ed.), *The Encyclopedia of UFOs*, Doubleday 1980 (pp366–370); Sachs, *op. cit.* (pp324–326); Jerome Clark, 'Trindade Island Photographs', *The UFO Encyclopedia* Vol. 2 (pp326–330); CUFOS case file.

[6] Steuart Campbell, *The UFO Mystery Solved*, Explicit 1994, Chapter 6.

[7] Robert Shaeffer, letter to *Magonia* 29 (1988) (p14).

[8] Letter from Wadsworth to Barauna, 18 January 1968, and memo from Wadsworth to Robert J. Low, 26 March 1968 (CUFOS case file).

[9] Chaim Herzog, *The War of Atonement*, Little, Brown 1975 (pp231–250). Herzog (p250) confirms the belief that the USSR was ready to intervene directly in the war by 24 October 1973.

[10] Vincente-Juan Ballester-Olmos, 'UFO Declassification in Spain', in M. Wootten (ed.) *UFOs: Examining the Evidence*, BUFORA 1995 (p56).

[11] Auguste Meessen, 'The Belgian Sightings', *International UFO Reporter* Vol16 No3, (1991).

[12] Wim van Utrecht, *Triangles Over Belgium*, Caelestia 1992.

[13] Wim van Utrecht, personal communication to the author, January 1996.

[14] Jenny Randles, *From Out of the Blue*, Berkley 1993. Other sources consulted include Jenny Randles: 'Impact and After', *The Unexplained* 106 (pp2101–2105), Orbis 1982; (with Dot Street and Brenda Butler) *Sky Crash*, Spearman 1984; *The UFO Conspiracy* (pp76–83, 142–6, 195–202); *UFO Retrievals* (pp131–148); Dot Street, 'The Rendlesham Forest Mystery', BUFORA Bulletin 004 (1982); Fawcett & Greenwood, *op. cit.* (pp214–219); Good, *Above Top Secret* (pp78–95); the Halt memo, tape and transcripts, and sundry press cuttings, Quest International (n.d.); Campbell, *op. cit.* Chapter 10; Roger Sandell, 'Down in the Forest Something Stirred', *Magonia* 18 (1985) (pp18–20); Terry Ecker, 'UFOs Still Cavorting Around Bentwaters AFB' *UFO Magazine* (USA) Vol6 No2 (1991). In personal communications, Jon Lake, Ian V. Hogg and Chris Bishop confirmed my suspicions that the standard accounts (including Halt's) are uniformly inaccurate on matters of military equipment.

[15] Jacques Vallée, *Revelations*, [Ballantyne 1991] Souvenir 1992 (pp153–65).

The Tsyklon re-entry and related sightings were summarized by Doug Cooper in Case 933: The Wales and Westcountry Sightings, Devon UFO Research Organization 1993.

Chapter Eight:
Bursting the Roswell Balloon

[1] The literature on the Roswell Incident is voluminous. Some of the key texts are cited in note [2] to Chapter Five, dealing with the related MJ-12 papers. Among those consulted in addition for this chapter are: Christopher D. Allen: 'The Roswell Non-incident: How to Make a Spaceship out of Sticks, Tinfoil and Rumor', (unpublished) 1990; 'Stretching Credibility', *Magonia* 45 (1993) (pp4–6); 'The Search for the Roswell Archaeologists', (unpublished) 1994; Review, *Magonia* 50 (1994) (p16), and personal communications; Charles Berlitz and William L. Moore, *The Roswell Incident*, [G.P. Putnam's Sons 1980] Berkley 1988; Jerome Clark, 'Crashes of UFOs, 1947–1959', *The UFO Encyclopedia* Vol. 2 (pp113–126); George Eberhart (ed.), *The Plains of An Agustin Controversy, July 1947*, CUFOS and

FUFOR, 1992; Hilary Evans, 'What Happened at Roswell?' in Brookesmith (ed.), *op. cit.* (pp48–51); Stanton T. Friedman, *The Roswell Incident, the USAF and the New York Times*, UFORI 1994; *Roswell Revisited*, UFORI 1995 and MUFON 1995; Stanton T. Friedman and Don Berliner, *Crash at Corona*, Marlowe 1992; Stanton T. Friedman and B. Ann Slate, 'UFO Battles the Air Force Couldn't Cover up', *Saga* Winter 1974 (p60); General Accounting Office, *Report on the Roswell Incident*, US Government Printing Office 1994; Good, *Above Top Secret* (pp246–50); W.A. Harbinson, *Projekt UFO*, Boxtree 1995 (pp133–143); John Harney, 'Roswell: the Search for the "Real" UFO', *Magonia* 41 (1991) (pp10–11); Philip J. Klass, *Skeptics' UFO Newsletter*, 1987–1996 *(passim)*; William L. Moore, 'Crashed Saucers: Evidence in Search of Proof' Part 2, *MUFON Symposium Proceedings 1985*, MUFON 1985 (pp154–179); *OMNI* Vol17 No8 (1995) contains: Dava Sobell, 'The Truth About Roswell'; Karl T. Pflock, 'Star Witness'; Paul McCarthy, 'The Case of the Vanishing Nurses'; Quest International reprint of the GAO report (includes affidavits of Lydia Sleppy and numerous other Roswell 'witnesses'); Peebles, *op. cit.* (pp295–302); Kevin D. Randle and Donald R. Schmitt, *UFO Crash at Roswell*, Avon 1991; *The Truth About the UFO Crash at Roswell*, Avon 1994; Kevin D. Randle, *A History of UFO Crashes*, Avon 1995; *Roswell UFO Crash Update*, Global Communications 1995; 'Ragsdale Romances Roswell', *Roswell Reporter* Vol1 No2 (1995); Jenny Randles, *The UFO Conspiracy*, Chapter 2; *UFO Retrievals*, Chapter 2; 'Alien Carve-Up', *Fortean Times* 81 (1995) (pp41–43); John Rimmer, 'Facts, Frauds and Fairytales', MUFOB New Series 9, Winter 1977/8; Peter Rogerson, Review, *Magonia* 54 (1995) (p17), and personal communications; Leonard H. Stringfield, *Search for Proof in a Hall of Mirrors*, Status Report VII, the author 1994; Keith Thompson, *Angels and Aliens*, Fawcett Columbine 1993, Chapter 13; Robert G. Todd, 'Major Jesse Marcel: Folk Hero or Mythomaniac?', *The KowPflop Quarterly* Vol1 No3 (1995); Martin Walker, 'Space Oddity', *The Guardian* 26 July 1995; Richard L. Weaver and James McAndrew, *The Roswell Report: Fact versus Fiction in the New Mexico Desert*, Headquarters US Air Force 1995 (includes photographs, interviews, affidavits, and a comprehensive collection of relevant government documents and contemporary press clippings).

Epilogue:
A Legend for Our Time

[1] Stanton T. Friedman, 'The Cosmic Watergate', UFORI 1991.

[2] Dewey J. Fournet Jr, letter to Jim Melesciuc (then MUFON Massachusetts State Director), 1 August 1989 (copy in CUFOS files).

[3] Good, *Above Top Secret* (p269).

[4] Ann B. Slate, 'The Great UFO "Ride"', *Fate* 1971; cited in Peebles, *op. cit.* (pp192–3).

[5] Kevin D. Randle, 'Spitzbergen Island Hoax' in Story, *op. cit.* (p348).

[6] Randles, *UFO Retrievals* (pp67–70).

[7] Christopher D. Allan, 'Wilbert Smith and MJ-12', *UFO Brigantia* Summer 1990 (pp32–38); letter from Omond Solandt to C.D. Allan, 3 August 1989.

[8] Kevin D. Randle, *A History of UFO Crashes* (pp147–156).

ACKNOWLEDGEMENTS

Everyone who tries to deal with the question of UFOs and government documents owes much to the labours of Timothy Good, Barry Greenwood and Lawrence Fawcett, Stanton Friedman and Jenny Randles, however much one may differ from them in interpreting the data they've unearthed. Years ago, Bill Spaulding first made me think critically about the notion of a 'UFO cover-up', while the dissident commentaries of Philip J. Klass, Donald Menzel, Curtis Peebles, Robert Sheaffer and Keith Thompson have brought illumination and entertainment to writing this book. I'm also grateful to Jerome Clark for hours of discussion on this and many other facets of ufology.

For aid and succor while in the USA, I owe special thanks to Ken Firestone and Bill Spaulding in Arizona; Prof. Ronald & Mrs Peggy Pendleton, and Don & Vicki Ecker in California; Mark Rhodigier, and George Eberhart & Jennifer Henderson at CUFOS, and the girls at Graziano's, in Chicago; and Paul & Charla Devereux in New York.

For books, documents, information, and advice, assistance and support of all kinds, I'm indebted to Jimmy Adams, Vicente-Juan Ballester Olmos, Keith Basterfield, Chris Bishop, Zoë Blackler, Janet & Colin Bord, Errol Bruce-Knapp, Bill Chalker, Doug Cooper, Fred Cooper, Claire Evans, Hilary Evans, Stan Friedman, Bob Giraud, Stasz Gnych, Vicky Hanson, John Harney, Ian V. Hogg, Mike Hutchinson, Pierre Lagrange, Jon Lake, Fiona Livermore, Jay Olstad, Quest International, Robin Ramsay, Jonathan & Dobbs Reed, Bob Rickard, John Rimmer, Peter Rogerson, Dr Leo Sprinkle, Joe Stefula, Tom Theophanous, John Timmerman, and Wim van Utrecht.

In particular I should like to thank Christopher D. Allan, Jerome Clark and Philip J. Klass for their comments on drafts of parts of this book.

However, any errors, ommissions, and boners in general that remain – and they happen – are my very own.

Finally, two very old and very dear friends, L. Small Riley and Barbara Skew, did more than perhaps they realize to help me grapple with this project. Both seem fundamentally bemused by my fascination with ufology, and so to them, with a big smile, this book is dedicated.

Index